La Paz's Colonial Specters

La Paz's Colonial Specters

Urbanization, Migration, and Indigenous Political Participation, 1900–52

Luis M. Sierra

BLOOMSBURY ACADEMIC
LONDON • NEW YORK • OXFORD • NEW DELHI • SYDNEY

BLOOMSBURY ACADEMIC
Bloomsbury Publishing Plc
50 Bedford Square, London, WC1B 3DP, UK
1385 Broadway, New York, NY 10018, USA
29 Earlsfort Terrace, Dublin 2, Ireland

BLOOMSBURY, BLOOMSBURY ACADEMIC and the Diana logo are trademarks of Bloomsbury Publishing Plc

First published in Great Britain 2021
Paperback edition published 2022

Copyright © Luis M. Sierra, 2021

Luis M. Sierra has asserted his right under the Copyright, Designs and Patents Act, 1988, to be identified as Author of this work.

Cover design: Terry Woodley
Cover image © Lucas Rachinski/Getty

All rights reserved. No part of this publication may be reproduced or transmitted in any form or by any means, electronic or mechanical, including photocopying, recording, or any information storage or retrieval system, without prior permission in writing from the publishers.

Bloomsbury Publishing Plc does not have any control over, or responsibility for, any third-party websites referred to or in this book. All internet addresses given in this book were correct at the time of going to press. The author and publisher regret any inconvenience caused if addresses have changed or sites have ceased to exist, but can accept no responsibility for any such changes.

Every effort has been made to trace copyright holders and to obtain their permissions for the use of copyright material. The publisher apologizes for any errors or omissions and would be grateful if notified of any corrections that should be incorporated in future reprints or editions of this book.

A catalogue record for this book is available from the British Library.

Library of Congress Cataloging-in-Publication Data
Names: Sierra, Luis M., author.
Title: La Paz's colonial specters: urbanization, migration and indigenous political participation, 1900-1952 / Luis M. Sierra.
Description: London; New York: Bloomsbury Academic, 2021. | Includes bibliographical references and index.
Identifiers: LCCN 2020035898 (print) | LCCN 2020035899 (ebook) | ISBN 9781350099166 (hb) | ISBN 9781350204225 (paperback) | ISBN 9781350099173 (epub) | ISBN 9781350099180 (ebook)
Subjects: LCSH: La Paz (Bolivia)–Race relations–History–20th century. | Indians of South America–Urban residence–Bolivia–La Paz–History–20th century. | Indians of South America–Political activity–Bolivia–La Paz–History–20th century. | La Paz (Bolivia)–Politics and government–20th century. | La Paz (Bolivia)–Social conditions–20th century. | Working class–Bolivia–La Paz–History–20th century.
Classification: LCC F3351.L29 A285 2021 (print) | LCC F3351.L29 (ebook) | DDC 981/.1205–dc23
LC record available at https://lccn.loc.gov/2020035898
LC ebook record available at https://lccn.loc.gov/2020035899

ISBN: HB: 978-1-3500-9916-6
PB: 978-1-3502-0422-5
ePDF: 978-1-3500-9917-3
eBook: 978-1-3500-9918-0

Typeset by Deanta Global Publishing Services, Chennai, India

To find out more about our authors and books visit www.bloomsbury.com and sign up for our newsletters.

For Jimena, Georgia, and Greta

Contents

List of Maps	viii
Acknowledgments	ix
Introduction: Indígenas, Vecinos, and Residents: Bolivian Urban History in the Twentieth Century	1
1 The *Extramuro*, History, Memory, and Urbanization in La Paz, Bolivia, 1900–52	11
2 The Racial Thinking of Bolivian Government Officials and Intellectuals in the 1920s	33
3 Alternative Identities: Labor and Race in La Paz, Bolivia, in the 1920s and 1930s	59
4 Alternative Identities: Negotiated Modernity and the Building of the Indigenous Neighborhoods, 1900–52	79
5 "Social Worries, Not Legal Theory": Race, Class, Gender, and Space in the Indigenous Neighborhoods, 1935–6	97
6 Race, Class, and Political Power: Urban La Paz before and after the Chaco War, 1900–52	117
7 Urban Revolution: Indigenous Neighborhoods, the MNR, and Those Three Days in April 1952	131
Conclusion: The Mobilization of Indigeneity in Bolivia, 1900–52	151
Notes	159
Bibliography	215
Index	227

Maps

1.1	La Paz, Bolivia. Circa 1900	21
1.2	La Paz, Bolivia. Circa 1930	22

Acknowledgments

It was Jimena Roses-Sierra who taught me how to write this book. Jimena supported this book long before it was conceived, and her critical eye has improved everything about it. Her unfailing faith, encouragement, love, and support in my pursuit of this project is inspiring. I would like to thank Pilar, Juan Ignacio, and Eduardo for their tremendous friendship, love, and support. I owe a debt of gratitude to my mother and father and brothers who showed me the value of hard work and education.

I would like to thank my colleagues and friends Edward G. Agran, Charlotte Fairlie, Elizabeth Haynes, Bonnie J. Erwin, Lisa Ottum, Daniel Kelly II, John Deignan, and Tammy Fraser who helped me settle in Wilmington. At Thomas More, Cari Garriga was the best office neighbor one could hope for and is an inspirational colleague and a wonderful friend. Jonathan Ablard has inspired me to become a better teacher, scholar, and a competent long-distance runner. I would like to thank Nancy Appelbaum, my advisor, for pushing me to think with my fingers and for supporting this project from its inception. I thank Dale Tomich, whose support and positivity helped motivate me to complete this project. Dale's wide-ranging interests, from football to food systems, capitalism, and teaching, were inspirational and intellectually stimulating. Heather DeHaan always brought thought-provoking deconstructions to my material, and her efforts improved this book in innumerable ways. Gabi Kuenzli, whom I met in the Archivo de La Paz, has shared her insights and expertise. Gabi's company and probing questions enhanced many of the ideas in this book. Ed Agran and Charlotte Fairlie welcomed me to Wilmington with open arms and provided a platform for me to succeed. Their dedication went beyond their duty.

I am especially grateful to the Provost's Office at Thomas More University, especially Cari Garriga, Elizabeth Hoh, and Kathleen Jagger for their generous support of this book throughout its development. This book would not be what it is were it not for my colleagues in the History and Political Science Department at Thomas More University, Patrick Egan, Ray Hebert, Jodie Mader, Jim McNutt, and J. T. Spence. I would like to thank the Binghamton University History Department, The Graduate School, and the Clifford D. Clark Diversity Fellowship, and the Tinker Foundation for supporting much of the research on which this book is based. Thomas More University Faculty Research Grants supported research for the manuscript in the final stages of writing. Kate Babbitt's expert copyediting improved the book immensely. Maddie Holder and Abigail Lane at Bloomsbury Academic Press were generous and supportive and helped guide this book to publication. I would also like to thank the Anonymous Reviewers at Bloomsbury Academic Press. Their insights and suggestions have improved this book tremendously. The ATLAS writing group reminded me why I fell in love with history and it has allowed me to grow as writer, researcher, and scholar. Bonnie Erwin's critical eye, enthusiasm, and deft touch were crucial to making this work what it is, and her ability to help me see the forest for the trees is much appreciated.

Many, many Bolivians and scholars of Bolivia also helped bring this book to fruition, including Pablo Choque, Claudia Riveros, Ivica Tadic, Rossana Barragán, Javier Marion, Juan de Dios Yapita, and Pilar Mendieta. The students and staff at the Archivo de La Paz were helpful, dedicated, and kind. The archivists at the Alcaldía Municipal were always available to answer questions and offer advice when the research took me to unexpected places. The staff of the Cementerio Municipal de La Paz gave me space in which to work and access to the incredible materials in their archive. Scholars in the United States were also fantastic in their support: Brooke Larson, Laura Gotkowitz, Marisabel Villagomez, Tasha Kimball, Liz Shesko, and Matt Gildner were wonderful resources and generous scholars.

Introduction: Indígenas, Vecinos, and Residents
Bolivian Urban History in the Twentieth Century

This book looks at the history of the city of La Paz, Bolivia, in the first half of the twentieth century from the perspective of its indigenous and working-class residents. These decades were a time of political upheaval for Bolivia. In the twentieth century, Bolivian society transitioned from a republic committed to nineteenth-century liberal values that tried to deprive the indigenous majority of political power and segregate them in the countryside to a republic that used the Bolivian identity as a unifying element. The transformations Bolivia underwent were fraught with conflict and instability. Sixteen presidents served from 1900 to 1952, most for very brief periods. The country underwent a military coup and a revolution; for a time the military was in power. The Great Depression of the 1930s hit Bolivia especially hard and made elites realize that an economy based solely on exports was no longer sustainable. Bolivia needed to modernize and its capital, La Paz, needed to look like other modern capitals. Bolivian elites were very sensitive about perceptions that their country was backward. They were especially concerned to avoid ridicule from people from the industrialized North.

For the elites who were on a mission to achieve modernity, indigenous people were undesirable. They dressed differently, they spoke different languages, and they brought rural ways and values into a city that elites hoped to make into a showplace. In the 1920s and 1930s, academics and politicians put forward racial theories that sought to justify policies that discriminated against indigenous people. In the 1920s, they succeeded in convincing the La Paz City council to pass regulations that sought to segregate indigenous people, even to make them invisible to the middle and upper classes. There was just one problem with these policies: elite Bolivians needed indigenous workers to cook their food, construct the new buildings of the beautiful city they envisioned, and produce their newspapers, among many other things. Thus began a subterranean dialogue between indigenous residents of La Paz and the elite and middle-class employers and politicians of the city. The overarching theme of this book is that the indigenous people won that debate. Throughout these decades, they made steady progress toward integration into the fabric of the nation, insisting consistently that as Bolivians they had rights to decent wages, electricity and water, schools in their neighborhoods, personhood through honorable behavior, and the right to build their neighborhoods as they wished.

The book touches on the economic, political, and social history of Bolivia in many places. Because the focus is on indigenous and working-class residents of the city, there is not always space to provide context for the broader historical themes in the individual chapters. At the same time, the book offers a corrective to the scholarship that has turned the Chaco War into *the* turning point in Bolivian twentieth-century history. Instead, I suggest that the Chaco War in some ways represented changes and, in others, continuity. What follows is a broad-brush sketch of some main themes in Bolivian history for the period from 1825 to 1952.

Bolivia's Indigenous People in the Colonial Era

La Paz's indigenous neighborhoods began as *ayllus*, units that organized indigenous people's payments of tribute to the colonial state. Each indigenous parish was the combination of several *ayllus*.[1] In the nineteenth century, the *ayllus* were the focus of new land tenure laws that sought to make land a commodity and take away the corporate social identity of indigenous peoples in order to groom them for future citizenship in the liberal nation-state.[2] The breakup of communal lands led to a pattern of dozens of small plots and a few very large haciendas in the areas north and west of La Paz's city center. In the east, several haciendas dominated the Miraflores valley. Several large properties were located in the south, in Obrajes, and in the farthest parts of the valley, indigenous communities owned some plots.[3] This land tenure situation led to a pattern of neighborhoods made up mostly of indigenous peoples in the outer suburbs of the north and west and large haciendas beyond them. In contrast, the vast majority of Spaniards and Creoles remained in the heart of the colonial city. The indigenous parishes of San Sebastián and San Francisco to the north and west of the city center contained the majority of the indigenous populations that La Paz had incorporated by the early part of the twentieth century. The Catholic Church played an important role in the organization of the *ayllus*, especially after the demographic collapse of the indigenous populations of the Americas. Directly to the south lay the indigenous parish of Santa Barbara. Residents of the city center began referring to the indigenous parishes to the north and west of the city center as "indigenous neighborhoods."

In the nineteenth century, both the city's expansion and developments in the countryside brought increasing numbers of the nation's indigenous population into La Paz.[4] The weakening of Bolivia's economic ties with Peru after independence and the decline of silver production in Potosí province created a new economic situation in which provincial trade between Bolivia's provinces and La Paz grew in importance. People arrived in La Paz searching for economic opportunities in this internal trade. Their arrival led to the dispossession of indigenous communal lands near the city and the inability of communities to remain separate from the expanding city. La Paz was second in importance to Sucre, the political and economic center of Bolivia from 1825 through the late nineteenth century. Historians of La Paz have chronicled the shift in the late nineteenth century from the silver-mining elite in Sucre to the tin-mining elite based in La Paz.[5] During the late nineteenth and early twentieth centuries, the elites of La Paz acquired investment capital through commerce and were in a better position to invest in the machinery and labor necessary for tin mining.[6] Liberal land laws, small-scale production, commerce, and land expropriation pushed rural migrants to the city permanently.[7] These transformations brought increased government investment in the region and in the infrastructure of La Paz. The city's need for labor gave new social and political opportunities to the residents of indigenous neighborhoods. La Paz became the national capital after the 1899 Civil War, and the incorporation of the indigenous parishes accelerated in the twentieth century.

After Bolivia gained independence from Spain in 1825, the rights and privileges of indigenous people came under assault.[8] In the republican era, the colonial category of *indio* lost its salience as a social and fiscal category. Elites began to use the term *indígena* to remove the connection between the obligations of *indios* and their rights and privileges under the Spanish colonial regime.[9] *Indios*' ownership of land and their right to cultivate it communally came under attack in areas of high productivity such as the Cochabamba Valleys during the colonial period.[10] In the highlands near La Paz, Aymara communities lost control of their lands in a piecemeal and uneven fashion, but the heaviest assault took place around La Paz and near railways in the late nineteenth and early twentieth centuries.[11] The Ex-Vinculación Laws of 1874 made it possible to sell communal lands and protected purchasers from legal repercussions related to their dubious acquisition of land. In the highlands, this process of alienation had been underway since the 1850s.[12] The fact that indigenous peoples constituted the lowest social caste aided the government's legal assault on their collective rights and the circumscription of indigenous legal personhood in the national period.

Yet indigenous peoples cultivated and maintained an indigenous identity that they used as a basis for organizing within their communities and for organizing for rebellion in the nineteenth century. Belonging to an *ayllu* continued to provide indigenous peoples with the right to land and sustenance. *Originarios*, for example, were full members of *ayllus*. Because of that membership, they had access to communal land and the right to full participation within the community and its leadership structures. *Forasteros*, in contrast, were migrants to the community or had ancestors who were migrants. While people in this category were not full *ayllu* members, they received reduced land and political rights.[13] Despite these rights to land, indigenous community members remained under assault throughout the nineteenth century as Bolivian elite politicians worked to curb colonial privileges and reduce the collective power of indigenous peoples and the political power that the *ayllus* held over the Bolivian government.

Despite the assault on communal landholding, the Bolivian national government continued to rely on income from indigenous tribute until the early twentieth century. This gave indigenous communities power in their efforts to organize and resist encroachments on their communal lands. Communities organized to negotiate with local and national authorities on such issues as paying taxes in exchange for the continued right to own land communally.[14]

The dispossession of indigenous communal lands in the period from 1880 to 1920 coincided with broader transnational debates about the effects and ostensible immutability of race and the obstacle that indigenous peoples posed to the nations of Latin America.[15] In Bolivia, the period of the heaviest attacks on communal lands coincided with the legitimation of racial science, social Darwinism, and eugenics in the 1870s through the 1890s.[16] This was also the time when liberal economic thought pervaded Bolivia's national politics. The liberals sought to turn communal lands into individually held plots, turn indigenous people into smallholders, and reduce the power of collective indigenous identities. Racial discourses and liberal economics hardened the social division between whites, mestizos, and indígenas and made including indigenous people as full members of the nation difficult.[17] In the early twentieth century, the label "indigenous" placed rural and urban Bolivians on the lowest rung of the social ladder.[18]

Urban Growth, Urban Planning, and Municipal Government Expansion

From 1900 to 1930, migration to the neighborhoods of La Paz west of Plaza Murillo expanded the geographical area elites defined as indigenous neighborhoods. The areas of most growth were Challapampa near the rail station and Sopocachi in the southwest.[19] Challapampa, Pura Pura, and Achachicala were the sites of the city's industrial zones. San Francisco, Santa Barbara, and San Sebastián came to house many workshops, markets, *tambos*, and warehouses of the city.[20] In San Pedro and San Francisco, residents built workshops, small stores, and larger commercial enterprises. They worked in several light industries such as a bottling plant and factories that produced matches, cigarettes, condiments, and textiles. Some operated artisan workshops. Elites lived in Sopocachi, on the Alameda (El Prado), in San Jorge south and west of the city center and, later, farther south, and in Miraflores. The Plaza Murillo and central La Paz housed the city's most important departmental stores, government buildings, convents, churches, and elite housing.[21] San Francisco, the main indigenous *reduccion*, had a large church and a plaza. It was located close to the Plaza Alonso de Mendoza, the first Spanish settlement in the valley, and was home to a monastery, a convent, markets, and artisans.[22] During this period, migrants settled in parts of Gran Poder, Sopocachi (southwest), north of Plaza Murillo, and in the south San Jorge and Obrajes. The Alto de San Francisco north and west of the cathedral (later called Gran Poder) was the location of several *tambos*.[23] The Garita de Lima was an important geographic and social nexus in the heart of the indigenous neighborhoods; it contained several *tambos*, small shops, artisans' workshops, and housing. It was also a central location for all the major rail lines in the area.

Some *tambos* collected and sold such products as cane alcohol, tobacco, quinoa, flour, shoe soles, and charcoal. Others sold potatoes, wheat, *chuño* (a freeze-dried potato product), and fruits and vegetables from the temperate valleys. Santa Barbara, south of the Plaza Murillo, included a market and the Santa Barbara Church. San Sebastián, north of the Plaza Murillo, had a large Aymara population and several *tambos* that specialized in lowland products. San Pedro, west of the Plaza Murillo, another large Aymara settlement, also had a large mestizo and artisan population and served as a warehousing area for many products.

The Choqueyapu River divided the Spanish central district of the city from the Santa Barbara, San Pedro, San Francisco, and San Sebastián neighborhoods and this geography established real and imaginary borders between La Paz and *extramuro* ("outside the walls") areas. The twenty bridges that crossed this river connected the Spanish old town and the indigenous parts of the city. Throughout the first half of the twentieth century, La Paz attracted migrants from provincial cities and Aymara indigenous communities. These migrants tended to be from highland provincial towns, highland indigenous communities, and other cities. After the Chaco War, the pace of migration increased, attracting even more people from the rural Aymara communities of La Paz province.

From 1900 to 1925, the government of La Paz and the national government invested in the infrastructure of the city. As the city and national governments prepared for the centennial celebration of the nation's independence, they invested in the infrastructure of the central district. The city government used contract labor gangs, prison labor, and forced labor to complete buildings, statues, sidewalks, electrical lines, and tramlines. The railway station that connected La Paz and Guaqui was completed in 1920. The Soligno, Forno, and Said textile factories were built in Challapampa and the city and national governments paved roads and extended electricity to the area.[24] In Miraflores, the national government completed two civilian hospitals in 1925. The municipality, the prefecture, and the national government improved water and sewage lines and built floodwalls along rivers.[25] The city also built a small workers' neighborhood in Challapampa near the rail terminals.[26] In 1930, the city government connected the indigenous neighborhoods, the Garita de Lima, and the railway stations by completing Buenos Aires Avenue, which crossed all of the indigenous neighborhoods and connected Sopocachi to Challapampa without crossing the center of the town.[27]

In the 1920s, labor unions began to recruit workers in La Paz's principal industries, government ministries, and artisanal crafts. At the time, there was no national labor federation, but regional and local federations were popping up in the principal cities. Efforts to organize miners also occurred at this time.[28] In the 1920s, President Juan Bautista Saavedra (1920–5) employed a vague proworker discourse and tepid support for workers' rights in an effort to strengthen his nascent Republican Party.[29] Workers used Saavedra's vague discourse as a basis for expanding their unions. After the Chaco War, the military socialists and the Gualberto Villarroel regime openly supported efforts to unionize and sought to use the unions to gain influence in the city's indigenous neighborhoods.[30]

Progressive social welfare laws, labor reforms, changes in the political base of the national and city governments, and the growth of the city's population provided new avenues of social inclusion for mestizo and indigenous city residents. It was still the case that when indigenous residents entered the city center, creoles and elites marked them as indigenous, but residents of indigenous neighborhoods often used the changes in the political and class discourses in Bolivia to blur the differences between rural, urban, mestizo, and indigenous identities.

Before the Chaco War of 1932–5, mutual aid societies and early craft unions faced government repression and persecution. Many scholars have conveyed that the Chaco War represented progressive changes. However, in the first half of the 1920s, the new political alignments that developed during Bautista Saavedra's administration made unionization safer. In this more open climate, both the city government and the national government faced challenges from urban unions.[31] Saavedra also faced challenges from miners and rural workers.[32] Urban labor activists challenged Saavedra's government to fulfill the promises of his pro-worker discourse and worked to build strong regional labor federations.[33]

When supporting workers suited his political needs, Saavedra encouraged labor activism. When the alliance no longer served him, he abandoned or repressed unions. In theory, Saavedra supported the workers of Bolivia, but in practice, his government withdrew that support any time workers challenged it or private industry to meet workers' demands about wages, work hours, or other issues.[34] Labor movements and indigenous organizing in the countryside suffered similar fates: as long as they were under Saavedra's control, he used them. However, when unions became liabilities, he repressed their activism.

During Saavedra's presidency and "revolution," whenever workers threatened to move beyond the confines of Saavedra's "revolutionary" programs or posit independent actions, the government repressed movements, jailed leaders, and controlled the course of union activism. However, the changes Saavedra made to the labor code (instituting the eight-hour workday and the six-day workweek and providing a legal framework for union recognition) and his courting of worker leaders inadvertently helped union organization grow. Evidence suggests that unions developed both independently of and in conjunction with a more permissive post-Saavedra political climate. Workers continued to organize during the pre–Chaco War period despite the difficult political climate, and after the war ended unionization continued.

Unions continued to grow after Saavedra was overthrown in late 1925. A printers' union gained members and strength and a construction workers' union grew stronger and allied with the Federación Obrera de La Paz (FOL, the La Paz Workers' Federation founded in 1926), an anarchist labor federation. The FOL supported the emergence of the Federación Obrera Femenina (FOF, the women workers' federation founded in 1927) and the Sindicato de Culinarias (cooks' union) in 1927. Hernando Siles Reyes created the Nationalist Party and ascended to the presidency in 1926 after Saavedra's attempt to manipulate the 1925 elections and topple the government of his successor whom he himself had handpicked. Siles's administration did not cultivate alliances with workers or enforce the labor codes passed during Saavedra's tenure.

Indigenous Rebellions in the Early Twentieth Century

Indigenous peoples in the countryside and members of labor unions regularly participated in protest movements in the early twentieth century. Some of these rebellions were related to local power struggles. Others began at that level but escalated to include more generalized grievances and encompass much larger regions. Both rural rebellions and strikes became much more common in the first quarter of the century. Specifically, a rebellion in La Paz province in 1917, the Jesús de Machaca rebellion in 1921, and the Chayanta rebellion in 1927 alert us to some significant transformations in Bolivian society at this time.

The year 1917 was transformative for Bolivian politics. President Ismael Montes handed power to his chosen successor, José Gutiérrez Guerra, in June of that year. That same month, former president Jose Manuel Pando (1899–1904), a founder of the Liberal Party and a general in the 1899 Civil War, was found dead at the bottom of a gorge on the outskirts of La Paz. These events contributed to increasing elite dissatisfaction with Liberal rule. In addition, Pando's death fueled suspicions of foul play. In this climate of heightened tension, news of an indigenous protest in La Paz province caused panic and spread fear of a larger conspiracy and rebellion. The elites of La Paz feared widespread revolution, especially a rebellion on the outskirts of the city. A 1917 rebellion in La Paz province demonstrates how local grievances and indigenous protests could generate widespread fear.[35]

The Jesús de Machaca rebellion of 1921 was a response to the encroachment of large haciendas on Aymara communal lands and also to the national government's efforts to parcel out and privatize communal landholding.[36] Evidence suggests that Jesús de Machaca rebellion was partially coordinated from La Paz. The police arrested twenty-one caciques from several *altiplano* communities who were planning a second "general uprising for Holy Week . . . were found in the outskirts of Chijini with money, arms, and documents relating to their collaboration."[37] The Aymara leaders of the rebellion also opposed the expansion of the railroads and the collusion of local authorities with elite interests. The national government, under Bautista Saavedra, sent in the Bolivian Army to quell the rebellion. The army massacred several hundred Aymara people. This violent repression also slowed the activism of the Cacique Apoderado movement, which sought the return of land to indigenous people.

The Chayanta rebellion of 1927 was one of the largest indigenous rebellions of the twentieth century. It involved 10,000 indigenous people who attacked haciendas and towns and protested the dispossession of lands, and the loss of lands to hacienda expansion. Some of the aims of the rebellion included the establishment of schools in indigenous communities and the redistribution of hacienda lands to Indians, whether landless peasants or community members. After the rebellion began in July 1927, rebels took control of haciendas in the Chayanta region (northern Potosí). Although they killed a landowner, few others died at the hands of the rebels. Other indigenous communities tried to join the rebellion but were quickly suppressed when the government mobilized the army. The uprising lasted about a month.

In La Paz, the elite response to these rebellions was paranoia. The rebellions of rural indigenous peoples threatened elites' hold on power and the stability of the nation. City officials who were worried about the consequences of indigenous rebellions used a variety of mechanisms intended to control Bolivia's indigenous population. Government officials proposed internal passports, prohibited tailors from making indigenous clothing in La Paz, and at times engaged in outright repression.

The Economy of Bolivia in the First Half of the Twentieth Century

Throughout the twentieth century, Bolivia relied on mining and the extraction of precious metals as its main economic engine. The Simon I. Patiño and the Aramayo and Hochschild companies controlled the majority of Bolivia's tin extraction operations. As a result, the owners of these companies retained a significant influence on Bolivian politics. During the Second World War, Patiño was thought to be one the five richest men on the planet and his support or lack of support for domestic and international policies in Bolivia was often enough to derail any initiative. Tin extraction required railways to connect Bolivia to the outside world. After Bolivia lost access to its only ports as a consequence of losing the department of Litoral in the War of the Pacific (1879), it relied on its neighbors' ports to send its tin to European and North American processing facilities. Mining continued to be Bolivia's main economic activity throughout the twentieth century. Although some light industry developed in La Paz in the 1910s, 1920s, and 1930s, the industrial capacity of Bolivia and La Paz was minimal before the revolution.

Land was another major resource in the Bolivian economy. Control of it had steadily shifted as owners consolidated huge tracts of land throughout the nineteenth century and the first half of the twentieth century. After the Chaco War (1932–5), the government continued to rely on tin and the extractive economy for much of its revenue and a small number of elites continued to control much of Bolivia's arable lands. Bolivia's economy was very vulnerable to the vagaries of the international economy—it could not protect itself from severe economic downturns or from a collapse in the tin markets. For some reformist politicians, the Great Depression and the Chaco War demonstrated that Bolivia needed to diversify the economy. Many were convinced that the nation needed to distribute its wealth in a way that would raise the living standards of Bolivia's poorest people.

La Paz's Colonial Specters: Urbanization, Migration, and Indigenous Political Participation, 1900-1952 makes several contributions to the historiography of this period. I argue that through their participation in the labor movement and the neighborhood associations they formed, indigenous people journeyed toward full integration into the nation's economic, social, and political life in the first half of the twentieth century. They did this by pushing back against the rigid racial categories elites had constructed with their actions, although they also skillfully wielded the discourse of race when it suited their purposes to do so. Some of their most significant actions consisted in the labor they supplied: they helped build both the city center and their own neighborhoods at a time when the elites were determined to create a beautiful, modern city.

The book also contributes to the historiography of Bolivian politics. The historiography of the Chaco War tends to privilege middle-class and elite perspectives regarding its importance to Bolivia's political evolution. The Chaco War has been seen as the foundation upon which the Movimiento Nacionalista Revolucionario (MNR) built its reformist and nationalist political discourse. However, for residents of the indigenous neighborhoods of La Paz, the war wasn't a sharp turning point. Their daily lives were much the same before and after that war. The book ends with some speculations about the historiography of the revolution of 1952. I argue that the history of that revolution won't be complete until we understand the contributions of the residents of La Paz's indigenous neighborhoods in April of that year.

1

The *Extramuro*, History, Memory, and Urbanization in La Paz, Bolivia, 1900–52

In 1918, an editorial in the *El Figaro* newspaper of La Paz argued that the city council and municipal government needed to outlaw prostitution within the city's walls.[1] After all, in the "civilized countries of the world the houses of prostitution are in the *extramuro*."[2] In actuality, the strict segregation of spaces was an ideal seldom reached, whether in Bolivia or in the "civilized countries of the world." Despite the reality of porous urban borders, the city's officials continued to discuss the *extramuro* as if it were the origin point for disease, crime, and prostitution. In 1933, a city health inspector reported hundreds of cases of typhus and varicella, noting that "a majority of the ill have their homes in the *extramuro* of the city."[3] The notion that all the negative elements present in the urban environment emerged in the *extramuro* continued to be pervasive. A La Paz municipal inspector reported to the city council in 1935 that the "large amounts of garbage [strewn about] in the *extramuro*, especially in [Chijini,] must be collected."[4] These fantasies about the emergence of disease, the location of prostitution, and the origin of urban filth remained part of the discussion about the *extramuro* and by extension about its indigenous and mixed-race population.[5] And yet by 1943, four *extramuro* neighborhoods housed the highest population densities in the urban core.[6] The new center of urbanization was no longer the political center of the Bolivian capital. By that time, both city and national governments had spent significant amounts of money on improving *extramuro* neighborhoods in order to improve the overall "health of the city."[7] This investment is one illustration of a significant reorientation of the discourse surrounding the *extramuro* and urbanization in La Paz in the period from 1900 to 1952. Despite the fact that the walls that divided La Paz no longer existed and had not existed since the Túpac Katari Rebellion of 1780–1, the memory of the walls and the attendant fantasies regarding the population living in these neighborhoods continued to structure and shape both municipal and national actions.

However, even though a significant social transformation had taken place by the mid-twentieth century, the walls that had been built and destroyed in the eighteenth century continued to be important in the imagination of Bolivians. This points to a collective memory that combined notions of race and space and echoed the social organization of a colonial era. Despite the fact that historians have shown that a nuanced spectrum existed that ran from strict inclusion to exclusion, historical actors such as politicians, academics, and urban professionals suggest a "flat" understanding of racial identity through much of the period under examination. I aim to expose the disconnect between a nuanced and complex lived reality and the ways those simplistic and dichotomous social and political discourses attempted to exert a "flattening" force on reality. While most of the *extramuro* neighborhoods were socially and economically mixed, socially and politically elite actors and the historical records they left behind continued to insist upon a clear-cut connection between race and space. Much had changed between the eighteenth century and the middle of the twentieth, and yet much remained the same; the *extramuro* served as a convenient shorthand to justify continuing discrimination against and political marginalization of indigenous people and their descendants.

The political marginalization indigenous Bolivians experienced was reflected in the attempts of La Paz elites to exclude them from urban life. These attempts never completely barred indigenous peoples from the cultural landscape of the city, but they did significantly affect the ability of indigenous peoples to craft an identity that would effectively straddle the categories of "Bolivian" and "indigenous." During the centennial celebrations of Bolivia's independence in 1925, indigenous people felt this exclusion keenly. Members of the anarchist labor organization Federación Obrera de La Paz (FOL; La Paz Workers' Federation) later recalled how President Juan Bautista Saavedra used the National Police to harass them when they entered the Plaza Murillo wearing "the *vicuña* poncho and the *calzón rajado*."[8] Elites considered the Aymaras and Quechuas who lived in rural communities to be savages who lacked culture and denied them citizenship rights. During the 1920s and 1930s, Bolivians used the word *cholo* to describe a mixed-race person, an identity that was somewhere between Indian and creole (white) Bolivian. This category could be empowering in certain contexts, and some politicians mobilized it to advance their careers in the nineteenth century. However, in La Paz in the twentieth century, *cholo* was an ambiguous racial category at best. Complicating racial notions and identities in the city, recent indigenous migrants, urban workers, and others who were marked as mixed race might also be classified as Indians. Thus, the categories of mixed-race and indigenous identities lacked clear definitions. For example, workers in the city and the mines were considered to be *cholaje* or urban *indiada* and were "humiliated daily for this condition."[9] Ximena Soruco notes that a mixed-race *cholo* was a threat to the established order of creole elites and describes how cultural and social elites symbolically marked *cholos* as the embodiment of disease and national decline as a way of minimizing their political power. Soruco also demonstrates that in the changing political context after the Chaco War (1932–35), *cholos* become the embodiment of the nation. This shift mirrors the broad transformations that took place in the period after that war.[10]

Rossana Barragán also notes the importance of the mestizo and *cholo* categories in Bolivian history.[11] She argues that elites used these categories based on the dress, occupation, and racialized markers of mixed-race persons. Thus, for elites, certain attire and the "look" of individuals marked them as targets. During the centennial celebrations, Saavedra's police harassed construction workers based on their attire, targeting those they believed to be indigenous by using the butts of their rifles to rip the ponchos and clothes off members of the Federación Obrera de La Paz. Such discrimination stemmed from people's identities as both workers and members of indigenous groups.[12] Indigenous people's experiences of harassment in the city center of La Paz included explicit targeting.[13] However, when I examined the decrees, laws, and resolutions, I did not find a specific prohibition that barred indigenous peoples from entering the Plaza Murillo for the centennial celebration. The silence in the sources suggested a different story about how indigenous peoples were excluded from the city center of La Paz. If the Bolivian government had enacted such a clear prohibition, the racism of the state would have been evident in its legal framework. Instead, national and municipal authorities prohibited interactions among indigenous and non-indigenous urban residents using indirect methods. These attempts were a constant theme in the pre-1952 era.

The story everyday people and scholars subsequently told of that prohibition is intriguing.[14] People remembered and then historians reproduced a narrative that alleged that indigenous peoples were prohibited by a *specific law* from entering the Plaza Murillo in the center of La Paz. In some ways, the myth that a legal prohibition existed begins with the myth that it ended in the post-Chaco period, as several La Paz newspapers reported in 1935.[15] The answers to the question of how the state prohibited indigenous peoples from joining in the centennial celebrations yield a complex and fascinating picture of indigenous peoples' participation in city life in the first half of the twentieth century. While there was no absolute de jure segregation of La Paz, the presence of a spectral wall had real effects on indigenous peoples that continued to hold them back from full participation in civic life despite their increasing participation in and contribution to shaping of many aspects of Bolivian society.

How unique was La Paz and how similar was it to other urban centers around the world in the first part of the twentieth century? The comparative frame is fruitful for understanding the significance of actions authorities around the world took in this period to gain control over urban populations perceived to be unruly. Similar juxtapositions of traditional and urban existed in a variety of circumstances and similar sorts of "othering" occurred even in the capitals of the modern era. Parisian officials sought to confine sex workers to the Latin Quarter.[16] London's officials struggled with the visibility of women in public in the Victorian era and after the First World War.[17] The United States, especially New York City, grappled with the effects of southern and eastern European migration and the outbreak of diseases throughout the nineteenth century.[18] In the twentieth century, the Great Migration of African Americans out of southern United States had a similar effect on urban centers in the north and west.[19]

The Latin American context also serves as an enlightening comparative frame for understanding how these countries chose to deal with suspect populations in the nation-states increasingly defined by race. For example, Sarah Chambers describes the construction of the Peruvian national identity in the context of changing sociopolitical dynamics. She examines how indigenous and working-class people claimed the identities of citizens and honorable individuals during the advent of the republic. Although elites believed that honor was a discursive category reserved only for themselves, it became a primary means for lower-class residents to assert their belonging in the republic.[20] The questions of honor and political rights continued to structure national belonging in Peru in the twentieth century, but those attributes became components of racial identity. Marisol de la Cadena demonstrates that indigenous peoples in Peru faced a racialization that rejected them as indigenous in the present while simultaneously valorizing the Indians of the past. One key component of that valorization was an association between honor and the "noble savage." In this context, honor and belonging were wrapped up in questions of racial identity and worth.[21] The nation-building process in Mexico also valorized the indigenous past, enabling the creation of a fabled mestizo nation. In contrast, in Bolivia, indigenous identity was a nearly insurmountable obstacle to building the nation.[22]

Ernesto Capello demonstrates the fraught process of the transition to modernity. His work demonstrates the importance of city spaces as textual and physical products of discourses of modernity: conflicts over space and discourse illustrate how race, space, and political discourse functioned as tools that enabled some people to achieve social and political dominance and empowered others to challenge social and political hegemony in Quito, Ecuador. He shows how the battles over modernity and modernization shaped both the image and reality of Quito. Capello develops a narrative schema for understanding a city as a series of juxtaposed ideals. He uses the idea of a chronotype to represent time and space through language and discourse. Thus, a chronotype is a discursive practice that captures discrete images of the city: for instance, ideas about what modern and traditional meant over time. The chronotype helps Capello trace the development of the idea of modernity through texts as he demonstrates how battles over the political and economic meanings of modernity shape the chronotype. Capello shows how ideas about modernity are at the center of ideas about Quito and the ideals that represent modernity. Capello's methodology and sources are instructive for the Bolivian case because he demonstrates how spaces such as the imaginary wall are both products and consequences of the collective imaginary. While the *extramuro* is imaginary and textual, it is also real and had real consequences for the urban population of La Paz.[23]

Historian Guadalupe Garcia shows the importance of the joint processes of colonization and the regulation of urban spaces and populations beginning in the late sixteenth century. She demonstrates how colonial Havana served as a model for the urban form in Latin America. Because of this, walls similar to the ones that surrounded colonial Havana can be found throughout Latin America. Garcia analyzes how imperial governments produced urban space that was explicitly built upon the politics of racial exclusion and social control. Havana and its elites always thought of themselves as white, and yet the reality and practice of slavery and exploitation created a mixed-race progeny who also ascended the social, political, and economic ladder and clearly demonstrate that such a stark separation between black and white was false. In addition, the city's walls reinforced the myth of whiteness and social control because it purported to protect the city from the nonwhite population by keeping them from sullying the white spaces. Garcia demonstrates how the colonial project included debates among elites over urbanization, the policing of public spaces, and the racial segregation of urban populations. Although in the Bolivian context the walls were imaginary and ephemeral after 1781, they segregated and racialized the people living outside them.[24]

Theorist Michel Foucault's concept of biopolitics is instructive for analyzing imaginary walls that function as real barriers. He argues that "there was also the emergence, in the field of political practices and economic observation, of the problem[s] of birthrate, longevity, public health, housing, and migration. Hence there was an explosion of techniques for achieving the subjugation of bodies and the control of populations, marking the beginning of the era of 'biopower.'"[25] The ultimate importance of biopower, according to Foucault, was the control of bodies: "The mastery [biopower] would be able to exercise over them would have to be applied at the level of life itself; it was the taking charge of life, more than the threat of death, that gave power its access even to the body." Biopower, then, deploys techniques of "mastery" and control and seeks to ensure that individuals regulate themselves.[26]

The imaginary wall around La Paz separated indigenous peoples from Bolivians who lived within the wall who justified discriminatory housing practices. Mastery over indigenous bodies in this context meant locating pathologies within those bodies. According to elite residents of La Paz, the definition of these pathologies included sex work and unhygienic bodies. Although race is a social construct that has no objective reality, it has social, economic, and political consequences. One need only examine segregation laws or community covenants in the United States that banned the sale of homes to racial minorities to see how real the effect of race is on human lives.[27] In Bolivia, people referred to a wall that had not existed for 144 years, yet the discourse about its existence differentiated urban spaces and marked people as outsiders.

The wall also had the function of substituting for a secondary and more "real" geographical boundary, the Choqueyapu River, which until the 1930s divided the Spanish half of La Paz from the indigenous half. However, by 1935, most of the rivers within the city limits had been channeled underground. After that happened, the discourse about the invisible wall demonstrated that people had internalized discourses of difference and racial otherness and geographic boundaries associated with indigenous spaces.

These political discourses and geosocial practices influenced the urbanization of La Paz and linked particular races to specific spaces. The legacies of colonialism, the nineteenth-century battles over citizenship and rights and conflicts over land reform, and the urbanization of La Paz provide context for the relationships between race and space and the ways Paceños linked indigeneity with the *extramuro* in the first half of the twentieth century. In this book, I will explore the discourses and practices that linked infrastructure, hygiene, and the *extramuro*. I analyze how elites marked the *extramuro* as the place for undesirable but necessary residents of the city and as the place where filth and disease originated. The relationship between La Paz as an inhabited space (its reality) and the discourses about *indígenas* in public space in the early twentieth century is a fruitful avenue for exploring what it meant to be indigenous and how that changed over time as more and more indigenous and mixed-race peoples began to inhabit the city. These debates take center stage as I explore the discourses that marked *indígenas* as undesirable social actors. I follow this exploration of discourses with an analysis of the close connection between the construction of race and the urbanization of the *extramuro*. I conclude by reassessing the links between race, space, and memory in twentieth-century Bolivia and laying out how indigenous people influenced the political transformations of Bolivia in the period from 1900 to 1952.

In her works on European colonization in East Asia, Ann Stoler examines the importance of biopolitics and race to the construction of the other and the imposition of European colonial structures on the people who lived in East Asia. She demonstrates that racial dynamics there were the product of the intimate sphere: that is, the disciplining of sexual desire and the marking of racial boundaries via the children of European men and East Asian women.[28] These by-products of racial education are instructive for the Bolivian case because they demonstrate the close connection between mastery over the body and the disciplining of sexual desire. In La Paz, marking indigenous bodies as other and using space to mark sexual boundaries served the purpose of assigning deviant bodies and deviant practices to the spaces beyond the imaginary wall. Stoler also demonstrates that Europeans attempted to use the techniques they had used to control colonial spaces to control deviant bodies in the metropole. In a similar manner, La Paz officials attempted to mark indigenous spaces as outside the city before working on improving the city in the period from 1920 to 1952. This transformation in the city's shape, composition, and politics is the subject of *Colonial Specters*. The Chaco War between Paraguay and Bolivia (1932–35) transformed the discourses about the city itself and the connection between the city and the *extramuro*. During this period, political elites began to conceive of La Paz as a living and integral organism. In this chapter, I focus on the importance of a long-destroyed wall for the construction of race and the public space in the context of the centennial celebrations of 1925. In the post–Chaco War period, military socialist dictators oversaw the professionalization of the urban bureaucracy. Some city officials had long tenures that spanned the military dictatorships and extended into several subsequent governments. This longevity enabled these men to transform urban planning and implement structural changes to the urban form. At the national level, the transformation in politics reached into the neighborhoods of La Paz as residents demanded more from both national and city officials. This was a period of intense political and social activism in the neighborhoods: neighborhood organization via lay Catholic brotherhoods, craft guilds and unions, and neighborhood associations helped generate tremendous transformation in indigenous neighborhoods.[29] In the period between 1935 and 1952, the municipal government made heavy investments in the infrastructure of the *extramuro* neighborhoods. One reason was that several military socialist mayors believed that disease in the *extramuro* affected the rest of the city and were thus motivated to improve public health in areas where indigenous people lived. This change coincided with the transformation of government apparatuses and discourses that sought to overcome racial differences by emphasizing class and nationalist identities and a common identity from which they could build the citizen of the Bolivian nation.

In this time of transition, powerful political and social forces fought back: as Bolivians began to see a more complex relationship between race and national identity, some tried to reassert clear-cut divisions between races and assert control of urban spaces in an effort to homogenize and neutralize the threat the rather extensive transformations posed.

Geography and Human Settlement

The long and complex history of La Paz begins with Spanish colonial settlement in the La Paz Valley in 1548. Spaniards established provisional housing near Quirquincho, an Aymara indigenous *tambo* (market). This was the city's first "Spanish" plaza; today it is called Plaza Alonso de Mendoza.[30] Later during this initial settlement period, Spaniards created the San Francisco indigenous parish and a permanent settlement at Plaza de Armas (now called Plaza Murillo), located farther south and across the Choqueyapu River. The indigenous parishes of San Sebastián, Santa Barbara, San Pedro, and San Francisco shaped the settlement of La Paz throughout the colonial period and the nineteenth century. These parishes and the Spanish settlement on the Plaza Armas put the Spanish town at the center of a group of indigenous settlements. The Choqueyapu River divided the city between the Spanish central district, on one side, and Santa Barbara, San Pedro, San Francisco, and San Sebastián, on the other. This geography helped establish real and imaginary borders between La Paz and *extramuro* areas. While the people of La Paz were not definitively separated by race, the separate parishes the Catholic Church established for creoles and Indians played a fundamental role in creating the divisions between the *extramuro* and central La Paz. Before the late 1930s, twenty bridges crossed the five major tributaries of the Choqueyapu, connecting the Spanish town to the indigenous parts of the city.

After independence in 1825, Bolivian elites used the term *indígena* to remove the mutual obligation and special status that *indio* denoted. The Bolivian state's attempts to abolish tribute and commodify land were largely unsuccessful because the indigenous peoples strongly resisted them and because the state relied on tribute payments from those groups.[31] The history of the social categories of *indio* and *indígena* is complicated. Both terms have been used as markers of race and social difference and extend to ideas about inhabiting rural or urban space. In Bolivia, these labels have justified exploitation and discrimination: they marked rural spaces as indigenous and urban spaces as Spanish and (more problematically) as mixed race.[32]

The Katari Rebellions

The Túpac Katari Rebellion of 1780–1 strengthened the imagined borders between the Spanish city and the indigenous populations of La Paz. This was a pan-Andean rebellion that sought to overthrow the Spanish colonial system and return to a more just and equitable society. In the La Paz region, Julián Apasa, an Aymara person, took the name Túpac Katari from the leaders of rebellions to the north (Túpac Amaru II) and the south (Tomás Katari). He rebelled against local Spanish authorities and assembled a large army in an attempt to overthrow the Spanish.[33] When La Paz's military leaders established defensive positions and built a wall around the city to defend it, Katari's Aymara troops laid siege to the city for 184 days. During that time, they destroyed several dams upstream, flooded the central district around the Plaza Murillo, and destroyed most of the northern and western sections of the wall. Because of these events, the wall has endured in Bolivia's collective memory. Although the wall ceased to exist, the population living beyond where it had once stood became part of the *extramuro*. Colonial troops from Lima and Buenos Aires ultimately captured and executed Katari. The wall the Spaniards built to protect the city and the memory of the Katari Rebellion demarcated the areas that were "Spanish" (the central city, protected within the walls) and those that were "indigenous" (the areas north and west of the city center, beyond the walls).

In the nineteenth century, the arrival of new people in the city led urban elites to dispossess indigenous communities of land.[34] In addition, political and social transformations in the period from 1840 to 1870 shaped Bolivian political elites' efforts to ensure the cities, the nation-state, the population, and the economy were modern. The results of these efforts were mixed at best and in the twentieth century, La Paz's indigenous neighborhoods housed several *tambos* that sold a variety of products. They also housed nonindigenous workers, mixed-race people, and foreigners, in addition to indigenous residents.

At La Paz's *tambos*, merchants sold a variety of goods. People could buy cane alcohol, tobacco, quinoa, flour, shoes, charcoal, potatoes, wheat, *chuño*, and fruits and vegetables from the temperate valleys at these markets. The areas surrounding the Plaza Murillo in La Paz were home to the majority of the *tambos*, craft workshops, and indigenous and mixed-race settlements. *Tambos* were located in Santa Barbara (south of the plaza), San Sebastián (north of the plaza), and San Pedro (west of the plaza). Throughout the first half of the twentieth century, La Paz attracted migrants from provincial cities and Aymara indigenous communities. Many Aymaras settled in San Sebastián and San Pedro. These migrants tended to be from provincial towns or indigenous communities in the highlands and from other Bolivian cities. After the Chaco War, the migration of rural Aymaras to La Paz increased; many settled in the northern and western neighborhoods of the city. In the period from 1900 to 1935, the high-density neighborhoods were San Pedro, Gran Poder, Locería, and parts of Chijini. Neighborhoods further north and west of the city center that had been rural in 1900 also urbanized.[35]

Migration from provincial cities and rural areas shaped the expansion of the city in the first half of the twentieth century. Although the land beyond the neighborhood of San Francisco was becoming suburbanized, some of it was still used for farming. The areas of most growth were Challapampa, located near the rail station, and Sopocachi in the southwest.[36] The Garita de Lima was the starting point for trips to Lima from La Paz and was an important geographic and social nexus in the heart of the indigenous neighborhoods; it contained several *tambos*, small businesses, artisan workshops, and housing.[37] In 1930, the city government connected the indigenous neighborhoods, the Garita de Lima, and the city's railway stations by completing Buenos Aires Avenue, which crossed all of the indigenous neighborhoods and connected Sopocachi to Challapampa without crossing the center of the town (Maps 1.1, 1.2).[38]

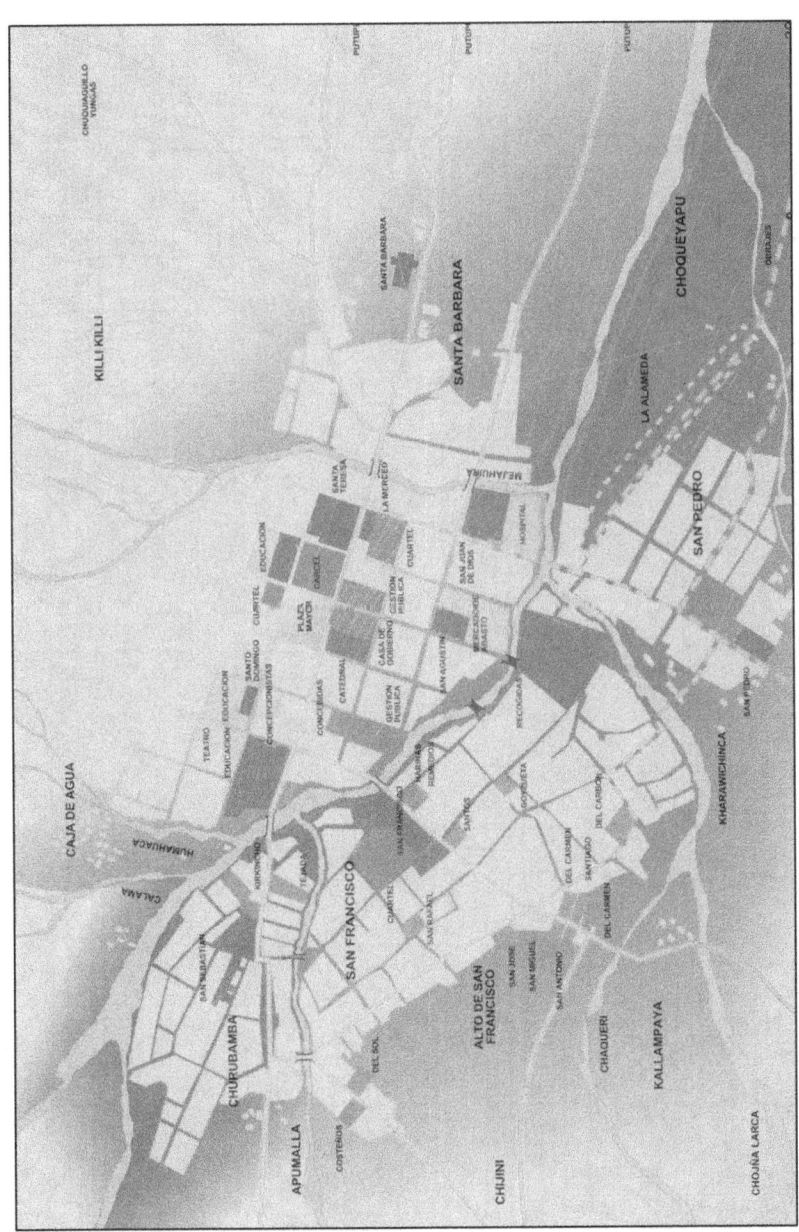

Map 1.1 La Paz, Bolivia. Circa 1900.

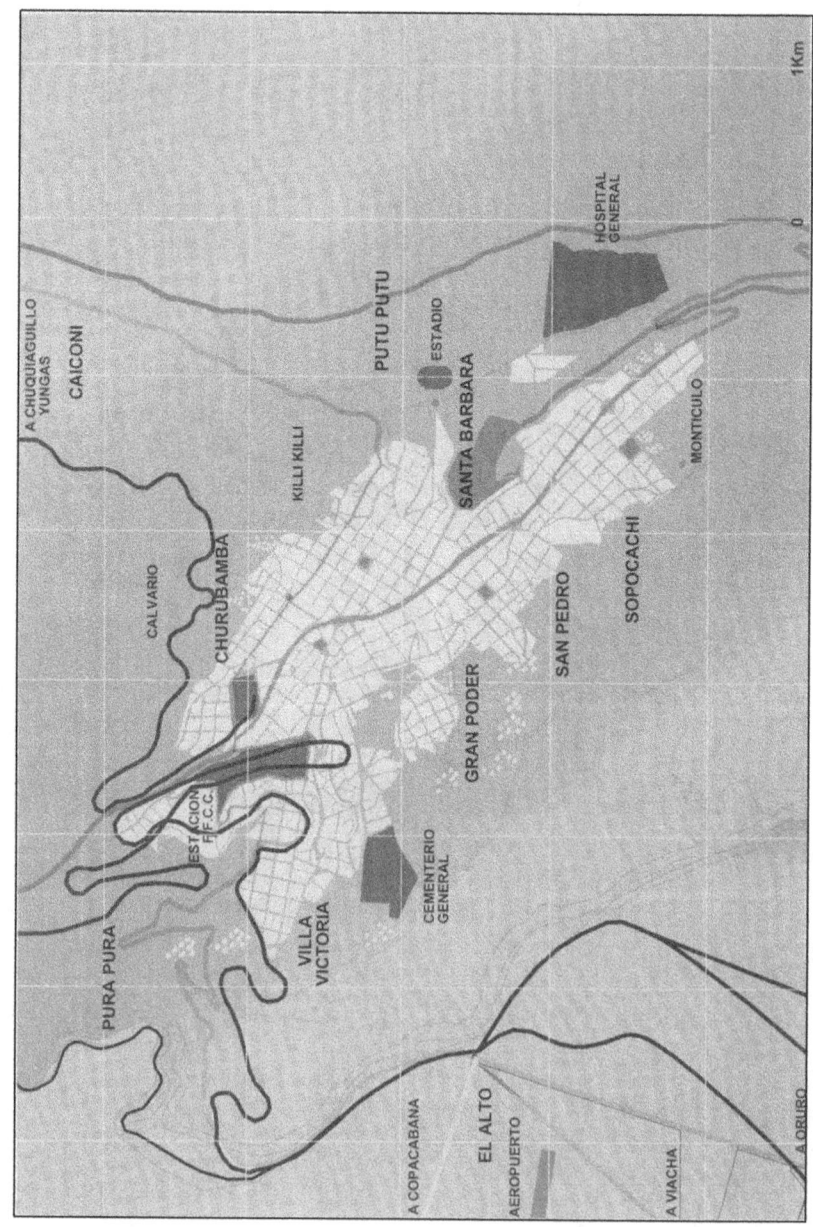

Map 1.2 La Paz, Bolivia. Circa 1930.

The Effects of the 1899 Civil War on La Paz

The geographic and social distinctions between the "city" and the "*extramuro*" were the products of colonization and the Katari Rebellion.[39] In part, the terminology used to describe the so-called indigenous neighborhoods reflected reality. While Aymara peoples settled in these neighborhoods, they were also home to people who would never have called themselves indigenous. It is possible that some residents who lived in the indigenous neighborhoods considered themselves mestizo or *cholo* (mixed race) or avoided labels altogether.[40] The use of the term *zona indígena* masked the ethnic and socioeconomic diversity of neighborhoods. One group these neighborhoods did not include was the elite class. Members of that group believed that living too close to these "commercial centers" would reflect poorly on them; they lived in the southern portion of the city and in the valley.[41]

In this period from 1900 to 1932, the 1899 Civil War, the persecution of Aymara peoples, and post–civil war dislocation shaped discourses among La Paz elites regarding the presence of indigenous peoples in the city.[42] The 1899 Civil War enabled elites to wrest control of Bolivia's political apparatus away from the traditional elite based in Sucre. The war pitted Sucre's silver-mining elites against tin-mining elites based in La Paz. In the search for allies, Paceño elites turned to Aymara communities in the highlands. Scholars Ramiro Condarco Morales, Pilar Mendieta, Brooke Larson, and E. Gabrielle Kuenzli have argued that the war demonstrated both the military capacity of the Aymara soldiers and leaders and their ability to articulate grievances and alternative visions of the nation.[43] Many Aymara community leaders saw this war as an opportunity to reverse the effects of the *Leyes de ex-vinculación* of 1874 and limit the government's concerted attacks on communal property.[44] However, the war enabled the victorious Liberal Party members to marginalize their Aymara allies and use them as scapegoats in their efforts to consolidate their hold on power and heal the fracture with the opposition Conservative Party elites. As soon as the Paceño elites gained the upper hand in the war and took control of the political apparatus, they blamed their Aymara allies for the "massacre" of Conservative enemies.[45] Even though the Aymara allies had been a formidable ally in the civil war, elites came to see them as a threat to the newly established political order. Both Liberal and Conservative politicians characterized them as barbaric after the war.

The dislocation caused by the war and its aftermath shaped much of the Aymara migration to the city. It also shaped Paceño elites' discourses regarding the presence of indigenous peoples in the city. In part, the regulations and ordinances that imposed spatial restrictions on the Aymara in the early twentieth century reflected the perception on the part of elites that they needed to contain their potential political power. Paceño elites also sought to distance their nation-building projects and the establishment of La Paz as a seat of government from what they perceived to be the problematic Aymara peoples. This history is important for understanding many of the early twentieth-century projects that alternately excluded or sought to reform Aymara peoples in the city and the countryside.

The social disruption of the Civil War shaped elites' perceptions of the Aymara migrants settling in La Paz in the early twentieth century. As historian E. Gabrielle Kuenzli argues, "the liberals' very victory drove the Indian question more pressingly to the forefront of national debates, demanding limits and explanations in the construction of Bolivian citizenship and identity. Yet before 1899 and after the war, many Aymaras continued to fashion themselves as supporters of the Liberal Party."[46] The Aymaras' participation in the war and the liberals' victory encouraged the Liberal and Conservative parties to marginalize Aymaras in Bolivian political discourse. La Paz government officials sought to demarcate the space indigenous peoples were supposed to occupy. Kuenzli argues that elites rejected the idea of working with the Aymara population and, instead, constructed idealized pasts for Incas and ancient Aymaras.[47] This helps explain why politicians in the early twentieth century sought to create such a stark contrast between the acceptable populations in the city and the populations they believed belonged outside it. The biopolitics of the Bolivian state classified indigenous bodies as outside the acceptable bounds of citizenship as both residents and political actors.

After the 1899 Civil War, many Paceño officials argued that controlling indigenous residents and regulating artisans and domestic workers more closely was extremely important.[48] A 1918 government decree relegated "*indígenas*' use of masks to the outskirts of [La Paz]" and set the tax on indigenous dances that used masks at "two bolivianos, one boliviano, and a half-boliviano [per person] for the three categories [first-, second-, and third-class] dances."[49] Another national decree against vagrancy suggested that as a result of constant rural migration, the city had experienced a "steep rise in theft and the organization of several bands of thieves. The security police need better tools to fight against these gangs of vagrants."[50] In addition, the city government proposed that a central registry be created of "domestic workers from the countryside" who worked in the city. Several councilors wanted to regulate the "contact domestic workers had with food" and establish an "ordinance for frequent health inspections."[51] The council put forward plans to "enroll artisans and other craftsmen [already engaged] in useful occupations" and to require workers to carry identity cards.[52] Councilors argued that implementing these plans would emulate the way the Western capitals of the world, particularly Paris, London, and New York, functioned in an orderly manner and minimized the presence of undesirable populations. Other council members and city administrators argued against placing restrictions on indigenous residents and sought less forceful avenues of control. These opinions were not exclusive to any political party or specific faction. Officials from the same party often disagreed about the best way to govern indigenous peoples within the city.[53]

The question of how to treat indigenous peoples has been a recurring theme of the Bolivian discourse since the nation was born in 1825. In the nation's cities, which Bolivian elites typically associated with the modern ideals of anonymity, social uniformity, and order, questions about race, the identity of indigenous peoples, and how to incorporate indigenous peoples took on particular salience. A Foucauldian analysis suggests that the urban ideal in Bolivia turns on a distinctive notion of identity. Disciplining the individual functioned to create the "out" group within urban spaces and subject the areas of residence for this group to double marginalization: indigenous neighborhoods are inhabited by indigenous peoples and function as the site of urban decay. In early twentieth-century Bolivia, it was inconceivable to many elite politicians that people could be both indigenous and civilized urban residents.[54]

The concept of *cholo* or mixed-race identity complicated matters, as did the fact that nonindigenous workers and artisans also lived in the *extramuro*. In part, these seemingly mutually exclusive categories of race and class were the product of scientific and social discourses and legislation that treated indigenous peoples as incapable of acting politically or using higher reasoning and logic.[55]

Transforming the Infrastructure and Public Health of La Paz

Before the Chaco War, city, prefecture, and national governments ignored indigenous neighborhoods. Instead, they invested heavily in the city center and in projects that linked the center to middle-class neighborhoods and wealthier suburbs. According to the census of 1929, the areas with the fastest growth in the 1910s and 1920s were San Pedro and parts of Gran Poder.[56] Yet San Pedro and Gran Poder did not receive much attention because these neighborhoods did not fit elites' discursive portrayal of a clean, modern, and orderly city.[57]

When the city and national governments did spend money on improvements in peripheral areas, they did so only as a function of what people in the city center needed.[58] The city government's general tendency was to prioritize an appearance of modernity over less visible infrastructure projects even when there was a pressing need for them.[59]

In the minds of city officials, ordered public spaces contributed to the ideal of a modern city. As part of their efforts to create an orderly façade, they worked hard to regulate interactions among passengers on the public tramway system by imposing de facto class and racial segregation in the city's public transportation system.[60] The city council discussed how to regulate bodily contact and separate groups on the tram, deciding that the electric company should separate first-class passengers from second-class passengers. This separation would have ideally included separate entrances for each class. On routes where such separation was not possible, the council wanted the tram operator to install barriers that completely separated the first- and second-class passengers within the same car. In Bolivia, the public transportation system was a site where racial and social groups mixed. In addition, its cars literally crossed boundaries between the *extramuro* and central La Paz. The council believed that preventing contact between passengers would prevent the spread of diseases.[61]

The city council also sought to govern interactions between tram workers and customers. It passed regulations that stated that "the [Bolivian Power Company] shall provide conductors with rolls of tickets encased in a metal box so that the conductors do not use saliva to separate tickets. They should also be provided leather satchels for keeping money because they currently carry coins in their pockets and this is one of the worst agents of contagion."[62] According to this logic, money was a literal carrier of disease: it was dirty and by implication the conductors were also dirty. The council's focus on tram regulations demonstrates its desire to remove "threats to hygiene" from the city and that officials saw the trams as carriers of suspect populations and diseases.[63]

In several other Latin American contexts, governments used a variety of tactics to assuage elites' anxieties about racial others and the working classes. Thomas Holloway shows that policing subject populations to garner control in Rio de Janeiro both led to an increase in the "problem" behaviors regulation was meant to police and provided mechanisms for direct rebellion and indirect resistance to these strategies.[64] Pablo Piccato shows that the social control police in Mexico City sought was both elusive and illusionary.[65] Setha Low demonstrates how people in San Jose, Costa Rica, used their ability to occupy and control public spaces to assert their rights to those urban spaces.[66] Mary Weismantel shows how market women in Peru suffered open racism and police harassment, but at the same time used their roles as cultural intermediaries and market mediators to assert their rights as women, to control their labor, and to demand respect in public spaces.[67] These studies illustrate that contestation over public spaces formed a dialectical dynamic in which space and identity were intertwined. In Bolivia, this dynamic made it unlikely that elites would allow people with mixed-race identities to participate in nation-building and created discourses that starkly contrasted indigenous and creole spaces. These discourses formed a powerful countercurrent to the attempts of indigenous people to achieve full inclusion in Bolivian society and exerted a real force in continuing to divide the spaces of La Paz by race.

In a similar vein, officials in the municipality's departments argued that its problematic populations originated in the *extramuro*. Employees in Bolivia's public health apparatus attempted to argue that disease originated beyond the imaginary walls. For instance, one public health officer argued that the problems with prostitution and "public women" originated in the *extramuro*.[68] The public health office reported that the city's police needed to monitor the movements of sex workers in the central city, which included the Plaza Murillo, the Alameda, Miraflores, San Jorge, and southern Sopocachi. In addition, central city neighbors regularly complained about the existence of clandestine *casas de tolerancia* (a euphemism for brothels) in their neighborhoods and near schools and government buildings.[69] During outbreaks of disease in the city, journalists and municipal and national government officials argued that epidemics originated in the *extramuro*.[70] Municipal government officials reported on their efforts to quarantine, fumigate, and disinfect the indigenous neighborhoods. Newspaper editors put pressure on city, prefecture, and national governments to address the problems of the *extramuro* when they emphasized that it caused problems for the rest of the city.[71]

The evidence suggests that national and municipal government discourses wove together strands of discourse about race, hygiene, indigenous neighborhoods, and the *extramuro*. Thus, the city's newspapers and municipal government officials linked the *extramuro* and indigenous neighborhoods to prostitution, disease, and indigenous peoples who did not belong in the city. In La Paz, these discourses linked race and physical space. In 1918, the police and the city council forced the Club Select, a "first-class club," to close its doors for five months while the council investigated whether "women from Chijini" were present in the club. The owner claimed that he had never invited these women into the club because he knew the regulations against having these types of women in his club and because his was a "high-class" establishment.⁷² After the council completed its investigation, the owner had to reapply for all of the permits and licenses to open the club again. The Club Select case illustrates how the municipal government officials and city residents associated "the residences of the *extramuro*" with epidemics and prostitution.⁷³ According to another city government report, Chijini was the "*extramuro* location of serious garbage heaps and an area that was perfect for the propagation of disease."⁷⁴ In a similar vein, a letter from a concerned citizen who lived in Challapampa, in the *extramuro*, stated that the police and city council had to regulate the *extramuro* because *indígenas* were only capable of drinking, fighting, and playing their "primitive and ridiculous instruments all night long for weeks after all the festivals [have ended]."⁷⁵ He stated that *indígenas* treated the *extramuro* like a garbage dump and that the city had to monitor these areas because disease could come from these areas and infect the city. The city's politicians focused on controlling, clearing out, and organizing the symbolically powerful areas of the urban landscape.

City government officials also invested heavily in beautification projects as part of their efforts to create public spaces that fit their vision of a modernity that excluded *indígenas*, prostitutes, vagrants, and beggars. These projects included building public fountains; retiling the sidewalks of Alameda; creating plazas; paving several major traffic arteries; erecting public buildings including the Palacio Consistorial, the main building of the Universidad Mayor de San Andrés, the Mining Bank, the Patiño Mines building; paying for the initial plan for Miraflores; constructing a plaza in Sopocachi; building the Montículo park in Sopocachi; expanding the electrical grid; and extending the transportation system to the wealthier suburbs. All of these were completed before the Chaco War.⁷⁶ City government officials' focus on the infrastructure of the central city and which people they wanted to allow in that space are examples of their emphasis on visible representations of Bolivian modernity.

Despite the efforts of city government officials to create policies for removing the ostensibly undesirable elements from the city, the reality was that those groups were a necessary part of urban social life. These efforts prohibited indigenous dress and costumes at indigenous dances and prohibited indigenous peoples from entering the city during carnivals. However, La Paz needed the people who lived in the *extramuro* areas as laborers, vendors, housekeepers, and small-scale farmers. The city government needed these residents as consumers and taxpayers to fund its infrastructure projects and the city needed them to serve as laborers on these projects.

The La Paz City Council and *Indígenas* in Public Space

For government officials and many political elites, indigenous people could not become fully integrated into the urban space and the nation until they could become part of the vague conceptions of "civilization" then in vogue. The La Paz City council, Paceño elites, and government officials used a variety of terms to describe "civilization," including *civilización, civilizado, moderno, modernidad, países civilizados, capitales modernas, capitales más ordenadas,* and *progreso*.[77] Elite Bolivians believed that education would "civilize" indigenous peoples. A 1917 national circular argued that a "rural normal school was founded with the hope of solving the problem of civilizing the Indian [*indio*], . . . inculcat[ing] the [Indian] children with the basic knowledge of writing, reading, mathematics, geography, and national history."[78] In 1921, a commentator writing anonymously in a La Paz daily argued that the "only way to civilize" the "Aimara [sic] and Quechua races" was to create "rural, normal, and technical schools."[79] For other elites, while providing education was commendable, "civilizing a race is more than education. . . . We must create a new system or suffer the lamentable consequences of a social revolution."[80]

City officials felt that improving public health was the cornerstone of all other reforms. According to city council members, "hygiene is among the problems cities must resolve in order to attain progress. In Bolivia, hygiene has been relegated to the background. The modern conveniences of schools, roads, and other signs of civilization are of little use to those who are sick."[81] In the aftermath of the rebellion in the Jesús de Machaca district in March of 1921, another Paceño social commentator argued that Aymara "*indígenas*" were "crafty, taking land by force" and that they needed to be "forced into submission because they are a warrior people." He continued, "[Indígenas] take [from others] because they are envious, not because they need. They fear anyone who has more or does more with the land."[82] This discourse reveals a cultural dictum among certain elements of Paceño elites regarding plans for education and general uplift but also highlights their fear of an angry populace in La Paz.

Before and during the nation's centennial celebrations in 1925, the city council used ordinances it had passed in the late nineteenth and early twentieth centuries to monitor La Paz's indigenous population. The council prohibited *indígenas* from participating in the centennial celebration in the city center and from wearing costumes (*disfraz*) during civic processions. It fined dance halls for admitting *indígenas* who were dressed in traditional Aymara attire.[83] It used a 1904 ordinance that listed the components of the indigenous outfit and prohibited craftspeople from producing these garments.⁸⁴ It used an 1899 ordinance to prohibit *indígenas* from dancing within the city limits and established the radius the urban police would patrol.⁸⁵ The council's redeployment of that ordinance excluded indigenous neighborhoods for policing purposes, but considered them part of the city for administrative and taxation purposes.⁸⁶ City officials and police used these older ordinances to closely monitor the urban environment and present the city center as a space with no *indígenas*.⁸⁷

The imaginary walls officials used to segregate public spaces were not effective barriers. The major terminals where producers brought food products were located in indigenous neighborhoods. The most popular and best-attended markets were in those neighborhoods. People who lived in indigenous neighborhoods provided the labor that made the city function, that made it move. Residents of indigenous neighborhoods who worked in elite homes crossed the invisible boundary every day. They passed through that phantom wall to build the very city they did not belong to.

In La Paz, these racist prohibitions were embedded in other concerns. They were subtle and therefore more insidious: they did not state in plain Spanish that La Paz did not want any Indians on the Plaza. Instead, the ordinances cunningly prohibited indigenous dances in the city center and barred tailors from creating indigenous costumes. The council directed police to cordon off indigenous peoples' celebrations.⁸⁸ While the exclusion of indigenous peoples based on these prohibitions was not absolute—they continued to participate in many elements of civic life and were not entirely hidden from view—their identity as indigenous people was obscured. The policies prevented them from forging an identity that would be fully Bolivian and at the same time fully embrace their indigeneity.

In the period before 1935, the city government used its resources on projects that emphasized that La Paz was a civilized and methodically designed city. During this time, the presence of indigenous neighborhoods thwarted the desires of those who wanted to exclude their residents. In addition, the populations of those neighborhoods always included groups who were not indigenous; clearly, the concept of a separate indigenous space outside La Paz was difficult to maintain. The city government's constant redeployment of laws and ordinances suggests that the *extramuro* was simply a fiction. Indigenous space did not, in fact, remain outside the boundary: it permeated the fictional wall and bled into city life. Yet the fiction matters because it prevented indigenous people from completely integrating into city life and made it easy for elite residents of the city to reject complete acceptance of indigenous peoples into city life. The ways in which indigenous neighborhood residents used and adapted indigeneity, labor, gender, and national identity is the subject of Chapter 5, "'Social Worries, Not Legal Theory': Race, Class, Gender, and Space in the Indigenous Neighborhoods, 1935–56."

Throughout the period under examination, the geography of La Paz had racialized characteristics. For elites and government officials, indigenous neighborhoods were retrograde spaces: the sources of diseases that infected the rest of the city and the homes of all the city's undesirable elements. According to them, the city center was devoid of indigenous people, who were foreign to these spaces. The municipal and national governments went so far as to prohibit indigenous people from attending and participating in the centennial celebrations. The city government prohibited indigenous attire in central La Paz. It consistently redeployed late nineteenth- and early twentieth-century regulations. In all of these ways, race and space were reflections of elites' discriminatory practices and the city and national governments' idealized visions of the city and its people. In Mexico, the "mestizo nation" resolved the issue of incorporating indigenous people by enforcing an ideology of assimilation.[89] In Brazil, the discourse of "racial democracy" masked racial discrimination and upheld a notion of racial inclusion. In contrast to the discourses of other South American nations with large indigenous populations or large populations of color, in Bolivia's racial grammar, indigeneity was an obstacle to national belonging. As a result, efforts to police public spaces were designed to create a central city devoid of Bolivia's *indígenas*. Yet these efforts were always in conflict with the reality of city life. *Extramuro* residents were part of city life. They participated in religious processions and they worked in markets, on construction crews, in light industry, as artisans, as porters, and as domestic servants. It was impossible to exclude *indígenas* from the central city because many upper-class residents who owned rural properties required their indigenous servants to work in the city as part of their service to the hacienda.[90] In addition, given the layout of the city, the roads, and transportation network, *indígenas* could not move in the city without circulating in public spaces and entering the central city. Thus, while the laws that sought to prohibit *indígenas* from entering public spaces largely served to address elite people's fears of large indigenous gatherings, they were practically unenforceable.

2

The Racial Thinking of Bolivian Government Officials and Intellectuals in the 1920s

In order to understand the relationship between race, class, and elite conceptions of the nation, it is necessary to explore attitudes, policies, and discourses of local and national elites about *indígenas* during the period from 1900 to 1952. In the twentieth century, Bolivian politicians and elites struggled to build a cohesive national polity because most elites found that indigenous Bolivians did not fit their vision of a strong Bolivian nation. The political shifts in Bolivia from the time of the closed-shop party control of the Liberals and Conservatives (1870–1920) to Juan Bautista Saavedra's populist rule (1920–5) laid bare a series of questions that had plagued Bolivian elites since independence: how to build a cohesive nation when most elites believed that indigenous Bolivians were not ready to become full members of Bolivian society. Saavedra's political rhetoric sounded populist in many ways, but the discourse did not match government actions regarding workers and indigenous peoples. In the late 1920s and early 1930s, the old order of Liberal and Conservative politicians returned; they were in power until the end of the Chaco War of 1932–5.

How did the nationalist and class discourses that developed in the early decades of the century address indigenous identity? Racial discourses shaped the possibility that new arrivals to the city and residents of indigenous neighborhoods would be incorporated into mainstream Bolivian political and economic society. In Chapter 1, I explored how the government and some elites attempted to use race to limit *indígenas*' movement within the city in the period before the Chaco War. This chapter examines how elites struggled to justify why indigenous Bolivians could not be full participants in national politics. The mental gymnastics required to justify why indigenous peoples of the present should be excluded from meaningful political power even though indigenous peoples could be connected to a mythical and magnificent past present a paradox.

This chapter investigates the evolution of racial discourse in the writing of several elite Bolivian authors, intellectuals, and politicians. They often wrote about Aymara- and Quechua-speaking indigenous peoples, the two dominant indigenous populations in Bolivia.[1] Education was their overarching theme. Their goals ranged from seeking the most radical separation of indigenous peoples from mainstream urban society to partially including them in Bolivian society. None of these intellectuals adequately addressed mixed-race people, referred to at the time as mestizos or *cholos*; none of them believed that mixed-race people could be nation builders. In addition, all of these writers reduced *indígenas* to one male archetype. This discursive strategy reduced complex and diverse groups of people into one basic type that intellectuals could then deploy for their own ends. When they spoke of incorporation, they meant a limited inclusion of male *indígenas*. They did not mean giving *indígenas* citizenship and they did not address the political rights *indígenas* were denied. These intellectuals struggled to find a way to either incorporate *indígenas* and mestizos or to ensure that they were totally separated from the rest of Bolivian society.[2] These were not simply theories; these ideas affected practices and policies.

In 1925, Daniel Sanchez Bustamante, a liberal politician, a former minister of instruction and agriculture, and a member of the La Paz Geographical Society, posited that only after acquiring an education could *indígenas* acquire the capacity to participate fully in Bolivian society. Bustamante wrote in the context of a Liberal Bolivian state that was struggling to make sense of its indigenous populations. Bolivian elites were wary of an Aymara population whose members had participated in the 1899 Civil War and who posed a significant threat to the liberal order if they remained in a backward state, as some Liberals claimed they were. Reports of rural disturbances and uprisings in government documents suggest that officials were nervous about the prospect of violent rebellion. The Cacique Apoderado movement of 1920–50 also posed a significant threat, even though the indigenous activists who joined it fought primarily in the political realm rather than through violence.[3] For Bustamante and other elites, indigenous activism and violence substantiated their position that elites should control Bolivian society. Bustamante argued that the "natural state [of *indígenas*] is one of jealousy, lies, and theft,"[4] but he also felt that *indígenas* had the ability to digest knowledge and philosophy. After all, their ancestors had built Tiwanaku and Machu Pícchu. Bustamante believed that indígenas had the capacity to receive instruction but that the right type of education would be important if *indígenas* were to be incorporated into the Bolivian nation.

Importantly, Bustamante insisted that in order for the right type of education to take root, the government should keep *indígenas* in their natural, rural environment. *Indígenas* were indispensable for agricultural production and the countryside was where they should remain. In addition, Bustamante stated that the *indígena*'s capacity for "imitation made him the greatest possible student" and would lead to a better Bolivia. For Bustamante, the way forward was clear: to "govern [Bolivia, it is necessary] to educate the *indígena*," but at the same time, to "Hispanicize is to take him out of his element and [it does] the nation a disservice."[5] Moreover, immigration was not the answer to the challenge *indígenas* supposedly posed to Bolivia's progress toward becoming an economically and socially advanced nation because adding new immigrants to the nation's population would not remove the influence of *indígenas* so easily; their numbers were too great.[6] Bustamante also maintained that importing what he considered to be inferior "broken Chileans or Peruvian Blacks" would only add to Bolivia's problems.[7]

Bustamante and other Bolivian scholars argued that Aymara indigenous people were indomitable and rebellious and that giving them tools not suited to their place in society would lead to disorder. By this logic, they held that urban and European social identities and structures would corrupt Bolivia's indigenous peoples. They believed that Indians were not suited for political participation. They also believed that the Andean environment contributed to what they viewed as indigenous peoples' penchant for social disruption; in the discourse of some Bolivian intellectuals, the environment played a fundamental role in defining the Bolivian nation. In a January 1917 circular, Bustamante argued that the Bolivian government had founded rural schools to solve the "problem of civilizing the Indian [and] to inculcate him with the basic knowledge of reading, writing, mathematics, and geography."[8] However, the government needed to be careful because

> the education that serves the white and mestizo does not serve the Indian because it takes him out of his medium, out of his element, and brings about a semi-lettered person aspiring to be a *corregidor* (a local authority in a rural area); an extortionist of his own people [who] becomes the most base element of politics. [For the government] to continue in such a manner we would Hispanicize [*castellanizaríamos*] the *indio* and we would half-way instruct him and pull him out of his sphere; [that] is to say that we would make him useless in his medium, his environment, [we would make him] pernicious among his own people, in the towns, or in the city and no one would benefit.[9]

Corregidores were significant political and social actors who served as local representatives of the Bolivian state and as political and social mediators between the state and provincial towns, rural elites, and indigenous communities. Discussions of *corregidors* often focused on their assumed mestizo racial category. Bustamante's use of the *corregidor* trope referenced the idea that indigenous peoples were innately corrupt.

Social anthropologist Tristan Platt, who has studied the highland areas of Chayanta and Cochabamba during this period, found that one local *corregidor* became pro-indigenous in his policies and work. In the minds of officials, his alliances made him a danger to the Bolivian state. Local elites accused him of corruption and Bolivian national officials removed him. Platt found evidence that another local *corregidor* was too closely allied to *hacendado* interests; residents of indigenous communities argued that he was corrupt because he did not serve his indigenous constituency.[10] According to Bustamante, indigenous people who became close to powerful interests would become disconnected from their indigeneity and would eventually abuse their own people. This theory stemmed from the fear that *indígenas* would be able to move into positions of power in the countryside, in cities, and in the larger society. The corrupt local official trope accused any indigenous person in a position of power of being corrupt or easily corrupted.

Bustamante's theories also linked race, geography, and behavior. He subscribed to a common belief in Bolivian society that a harsh environment determined the nature of the people who lived in it. According to this belief, the climate and landscape of the altiplano, a cold, high desert environment, explained why Aymara indigenous people were harsh, cold, and aggressive—a group of Aymara indigenous communities had fought as allies with Bustamante's Liberal Party to help it defeat the conservatives in the 1899 Civil War. Indigenous Aymaras expected to be taken seriously in their demands for the return of communal lands and to have a greater say in the governing of Bolivia. However, a similar logic shaped the thinking of Bolivian elites about indigenous peoples. Elites and intellectuals viewed Aymaras and Incas of the precolonial and ancient past as superb stock. The Aymara-speaking peoples were the descendants of the great mound builders of the Lake Titicaca Basin region who had built Tiwanaku, and the Quechua-speaking peoples were descended from the Incas. Thus, elites believed that if the indigenous peoples of the twentieth century drew on innate inherited qualities of intelligence and courage that lay dormant within them, they might have the capacity to become full members of Bolivian society.[11] Beliefs about language were an extension of this logic; Bolivian intellectuals believed that the structure and sound of the Aymara and Quechua languages were linked to racial characteristics. They argued that Quechua was a soft, sweet, melodic language that was linked to the culturally superior Incan tradition. In contrast, they claimed that Aymara was a harsh, throaty language. They constructed an ethnic hierarchy in which the Quechua were slightly above the Aymara.[12] Racial theorists and government officials saw Quechua peoples as more receptive and culturally superior to the Aymara but, nonetheless, degenerated. They claimed that neither group was capable of participating independently or fully in Bolivian political life.[13]

The 1925 centennial celebrations offered Bolivian elites an opportunity to assess the progress of the nation. They emphasized the commercial potential of the altiplano's agricultural products and the ways in which Bolivia was ready for industrialization and urban growth.[14] Some elites focused on the value of quinoa, wheat, and potatoes and the resources that were needed for industrial expansion, while others explored historical examples of flawed elite-popular alliances and the problems with the indigenous population that elites wanted to use in their project of industrializing the nation. Despite Bolivian elites' skepticism about the idea of indigenous people participating in governance and in Bolivian society, they saw some possibilities for the Aymara and Quechua peoples of the twentieth century if they drew upon the "good" qualities of their ancestors. Yet just as other Latin American elites struggled when exploring the possibility of including marginalized groups politically and socially, Bolivia's elite viewed the Aymara and Quechua of their own time as incapable of taking full advantage of all the benefits of modernity and the modern world.[15]

Bolivia's elite thinkers wanted to control the transition from a nation that included "backward" indigenous people to the modernity that would supposedly unify the country. They sought a unified sense of purpose that would create an industrial, modern, and sophisticated nation modeled on the UK, France, and North American nations they admired as ideals. These efforts were part of a broader endeavor to understand how Bolivia could become a "modern" nation.[16] E. Gabrielle Kuenzli points out that Bolivia's political and social elites did not simply parrot European definitions of progress. Rather, they defined Bolivia as a unique nation with a unique history. They based their ideas of progress on idealized notions of Bolivia's indigenous past. Elites portrayed the antecedents of indigenous people as highly intelligent, organized, sophisticated, and peoples to be admired. Elites put a lot of stock in the architectural sophistication of Tiwanaku and in the sophistication of the Incas' accomplishments, which included aqueducts, the rotating labor system, impressive architecture, and a system of roads.

Most of these theorists sought solutions to the problem of including indigenous people and used the terms "integration" and "incorporation" interchangeably. When Bolivia's intellectual and political elite, particularly Daniel Sanchez Bustamante, Manuel Rigoberto Paredes, Luis Terán Gómez, and Vicente Donoso Torres, used these terms, they meant including indigenous people as something less than full members of Bolivian society. This "inclusion" ran the gamut from keeping them in the countryside as agricultural workers to providing an education that was suited to their supposedly lower intellect and social position. None of these intellectuals saw indigenous peoples as prepared for the responsibilities that full membership in Bolivian society represented. Paredes, an Aymara intellectual and politician, was in some ways an outlier in this group of intellectuals by virtue of his ethnic origin.[17] In other ways, particularly with regard to his view of mixed-race peoples, he fit right into the intellectual discourse. Paredes argued for a process of incorporating indigenous people that centered on maintaining a separation between the Aymara and preventing racial mixing that would produce offspring.[18]

Racial discourses legitimated economic hierarchies and justified blatantly excluding ethnic groups from formal political participation such as voting and holding office. In urban settings, racial discourses were a response to the challenges rural and urban indigenous residents posed to the Bolivian social and political system in the period from 1910 to 1950.[19] Indigenous people did not fit into elites' ideas about who belonged in the city and what that city was supposed to look like. Some Aymara had fought against the liberal order by challenging land dispossessions in court, through protests, and in several rural uprisings throughout this period. The arrival of poor migrants to La Paz meant added pressure on the local and national government for improvements to the city's housing and infrastructure. Moreover, their presence hinted at a deeper form of exclusion. In a democratic system, the political exclusion of the indigenous Bolivians could not remain a legitimate practice in the twentieth century because these people could build the city, improve it, and participate in their neighborhoods, but this same group of people could not vote. The presence of indigenous peoples highlights the contradiction of a democratic form of government that excluded the vast majority of Bolivians. Importantly, as this chapter will show, in the intellectual discourses of the period, when elites used the term *indígenas*, they were not talking about urban residents. *Indígenas* were supposed to remain in rural areas, where they would acquire a separate education that would turn them into modernized agricultural producers. In the second half of the 1930s, after the Chaco War, class-based and nationalist discourses became prominent, yet race remained a considerable discursive barrier to fully integrating indigenous Bolivians into Bolivian society.

After the war, reformist politicians sought to use class and nationalist discourses to unify a polity that had historically been divided by race.[20] Class-based social movements that theoretically "erased" race transitioned smoothly from racial separation to class solidarity and cross-class alliances. Residents of indigenous neighborhoods could and did identify as neighbors, *indígenas*, and workers at the same time, which suggested that racial and class discourses and identities coexisted. In both the city and the countryside, race and class intermingled as political and social identities. Importantly, while class and racial status coexisted, class and race were not synonymous, even though people who identified as Indians were more likely to be poor.

Before the Chaco War, the activism, rebellions, and presence in cities of indigenous people influenced government policies and elites' ideas about how to limit and control indigenous peoples and their participation in Bolivian society. This was the context as Sanchez Bustamante examined the best way to incorporate *indígenas* through education. During the 1925 centennial celebrations, Bolivian intellectuals and politicians reflected on the evolution of the nation. Manuel Rigoberto Paredes argued that Spanish culture and religion had made little inroads in the altiplano and that this impeded the integration of *indígenas*. Paredes posited that there was a noticeable difference in behavior between whites and *mestizos*; he argued that the mestizos, the offspring of whites and indigenous persons, would "retain the negative traits of each race." Moreover, he argued that *cholos* and *mestizos* were not the same: the *cholo* was an *indígena* who lived in the city and took advantage of "his own kind."[21] Thus, for Paredes it made little sense to attempt any transformations without first addressing the lack of appropriate education. He argued that the *indígena* was surrounded by "barbarism and hate."[22] A separate and appropriate education would be necessary to help bring improvement among *indígenas*. And yet, after the Chaco War similar kinds of analysis emerged from Bolivia's political and intellectual class. After the Chaco War, Luis Terán Gómez, another politician and intellectual, argued that *indígena*s were obstacles to the progress of the nation. Despite the dominance of class discourses in the post-Chaco period and the triumph of an apparently cross-class nationalist revolution, elites argued that race was a central element of social hierarchies and that indigenous people were a roadblock to effective nation building.

Politics and Racial Discourse before the Chaco War

The 1899 Civil War influenced how elites viewed Aymara peoples. In addition, it shaped the Aymara migration to La Paz in the early twentieth century. Indigenous people from the countryside who settled in La Paz became cheap labor in the city. They filled skilled and unskilled positions and benefited from the investment the Bolivian government had made in modernizing La Paz. The Liberal repression of their Aymara allies included show trials for the leaders of the Aymara communities and reprisals against participants in the civil war. The Aymara had demonstrated their mettle on the battlefield, and elites continued to fret about the possibility of uprisings and violence. Attempts to educate indigenous people in a way that would make them moldable and useful was one way elites sought to diminish what they perceived to be a threat to the liberal order. Long-term activism such as the Cacique Apoderado movement and periodic uprisings in the countryside—a rebellion in La Paz Province in 1917, the Jesús de Machaca rebellion in 1921, and the Chayanta rebellion in 1927—placed significant pressure on elites and the Bolivian state to address the political position of indigenous peoples.[23] This activism through both legal political channels and violent uprisings gave rise to laws that prohibited indigenous people from wearing their traditional dress in La Paz and restricted where they could be present in that city and who could vote. In the first decades of the twentieth century, academics and politicians put forward racial theories that sought to justify limiting the degree to which indigenous peoples' presence would be tolerated in urban spaces and in Bolivian society. These theories sought to explain why indigenous peoples were "backward" and why they had participated in the various rebellions that rocked the nation before the Chaco War.

The number of laws that restricted what indigenous people could wear and do when they were in La Paz suggests that cities were never free of the indigenous peoples the national government sought to marginalize and erase. In Chapter 1, I discussed one mechanism of exclusion: the ordinances the city of La Paz used to limit the participation of indigenous people in the centennial celebrations of 1925. La Paz officials also passed ordinances that prohibited groups of indigenous Bolivians from congregating in the city center and from using carnival masks during the centennial celebrations. These efforts suggest that the elite sought to harass and intimidate indigenous peoples in the city, to mark them as foreign, and to drive out their influence. City councilor Abel Iturralde vehemently opposed a visible indigenous presence in central La Paz.[24] For example, in 1921, when the Sopocachi indigenous lay brotherhood requested permission to hold a mass and a procession, Iturralde argued that the city council needed to eliminate indigenous "social elements" from public space because their presence damaged the Bolivian nation. He said:

> Those ridiculous dances and the state of inebriation that takes place for days on end during the festivals constitute a social leprosy and a scandal for the civilized. Foreign visitors mock us and not only this, they dare to photograph and publish these *indígenas*' dances with the byline of "national army." . . . I believe there should be no place for such "celebration" since it only damages our prestige. Foreigners—I repeat—mock us when they see these dancers because in their eyes we are still a country of savages.[25]

A commentator in *La Reforma*, a La Paz newspaper, argued that "civilizing a race is more than education. . . . We must create a new system or suffer the lamentable consequences of a social revolution."[26] Another Paceño social commentator argued that Aymara "*indígenas*" were "crafty, taking land by force." They must be "forced into submission because they are a warrior people. [*Indígenas*] take [from others] because they are envious, not because they need. They fear anyone who has more or does more with the land."[27] City councilors apparently agreed with these views; in 1921, they passed regulations that fined the owners of bars, cafes, and theaters for serving *indígenas* and the owners of "first-class" establishments that allowed them in.[28] To complement these efforts in 1921, the council used a 1904 ordinance that spelled out the components of traditional indigenous attire and prohibited tailors from making those clothes.[29] In addition, the city council used an 1899 ordinance to prohibit *indígenas* from dancing within the city limits. The ordinance established the areas where city police would arrest anyone caught dancing and it excluded most of the indigenous neighborhoods from police protection during festivities.[30]

This discourse did not always fall neatly into discrete categories. No one party or theoretical approach became the exclusive domain of any specific elite group. Moreover, the discourses did not fit neatly in a progression over time from less to more enlightened discourses. For example, José Tamayo, a Liberal politician who wanted to allow *indígenas* to participate in their procession in Sopocachi, also believed that *indígenas* should have separate institutions.[31] Likewise, Paceño intellectual and politician Juan Bautista Saavedra argued that *indígenas* needed the judiciary branch of government to protect their rights, separate court systems for cases involving land disputes, and an informal system that separated *indígenas* from the rest of Bolivian society.[32] Like Sanchez Bustamante, Saavedra was a member of the Geographic Society of La Paz. When he became president of the nation, he instituted many of these reforms, but he later repressed indigenous people and workers who mobilized for various causes, including labor reforms.[33]

The La Paz Geographic Society is an example of the efforts of Bolivian elites to understand, incorporate, and control the indigenous population. Members of the Geographic Society researched and published in the *Boletín de la Sociedad Geográfica de La Paz*.[34] For example, Manuel Rigoberto Paredes published articles about Bolivian history and especially emphasized popular culture and folklore. His 1925 article "Altiplanicie: El Habitante y La Población" (The Andean Highland Plains: Their Inhabitants and Their Population) examined the foodways and habits of the population of the highlands and the economic potential of the region. He argued that culture and education were the origins of human transformation and racial characteristics and losing their customs and dress would change the racial classification of a people. It is unclear if his argument meant that whitening could occur through a process of losing one's "ethnographic" identity or if the change would always be incomplete, as Sanchez Bustamante had claimed.[35] What is clear is that Paredes did not like mestizos. He argued that mestizos and *indígenas* looked too much alike, basing his assessment in part on physical appearance and in part on the mestizos' "inherited" characteristics. He also argued that mestizos would lead *indígenas* to degeneration. Thus, he wrote, an *indígena* who dressed like a mestizo hated his own people. Paredes' supposed "biological" differentiation between mestizos and *indígenas* was unclear. He also argued that whites' influence had not done much to change the altiplano people, noting that Spanish culture and the Catholic religion had made little inroad in the highlands.[36] Paredes thought that Indians should emulate European attire, but the distinction he made between indigenous, mestizo, and European dress was ambiguous.[37] Paredes argued that indigenous people did not really believe in Catholicism because they still worshipped inanimate objects and idols.[38]

In one study the Geographic Society published, Paredes stated that *indígenas* had both redeeming qualities and qualities that needed correction by elites. For instance, *indígenas* were strong fighters. They were good bargainers in markets and fearless fighters for righteous causes, but they were surrounded by barbarism and hate. Paredes argued at the same time that *indígenas* barely met their physical and social needs through their own endeavors, yet despite this lack of drive, they seemed happy with the bare minimum.[39] He stated that *indígenas* were unable to manage their emotions or understand how to abstain from participating in conflicts, that they were vindictive, aggressive, prone to violence, and unable to think outside their own emotions.⁴⁰ According to Paredes, environmental factors added to these internal, biological problems and the issues of decline as a race.

Two significant nodes in the racial theories of elites during this period were the environment and language—in short, culture. Paredes argued that the environment *indígenas* lived in limited them and placed them in very difficult situations. He wrote that the *indígena* was miserly and refused to expand his own house and property. He concluded that this was the result of the combination of a poor environment, *indígenas*' low social status, and economic exploitation. Without access to proper education, the *indígena* did not aspire to more; he would rather live in a hovel. Paredes reported that the homes of rural indigenous people were usually three or four rooms that were surrounded by stables for their animals. They had what he considered to be unhygienic thatched roofs, narrow and short doors, and no windows.⁴¹ The main room also served as a bedroom. Raised platforms covered with straw and llama skin or sheepskin served as beds.⁴² He argued that poor air circulation created a state of filth and that unhygienic floors made the transmission of diseases and epidemics very common.⁴³ He believed that environmental factors circumscribed the social level of *indígenas*, even though they had the capacity for change and "imitation."⁴⁴ He argued that "In addition to the lack of material aspirations and hatred of his own kind, the indígena was unable to manage his emotions or understand how to remain outside conflict and aggression." He was "vindictive, aggressive, prone to violence," and unable to think outside "his own emotions."⁴⁵ However, Paredes would not go so far as to say that indigenous peoples' capacity for imitation would lead to improvement in the "racial stock" that would make them fit for inclusion in Bolivian society.

He also claimed that the mestizo was little or no better: "The mestizo looks just like the Indio but refined."⁴⁶ His social behavior was "rude," and he took advantage of "Indios and strangers in equal measure." He had "no conscience."⁴⁷ Unlike some other Bolivian intellectuals, he distinguished between mestizos and *cholos*, arguing that the former were of a higher social class and the latter worked more directly with *indígenas*.⁴⁸ Paredes argued that the *cholo* was so cruel that the *Indio* did not believe that a *cholo* could be just with regard to the issue of land rights.⁴⁹ He wrote that the *cholo*'s disrespect for the law led to the *Indio*'s distrust of the system and the election of corrupt sub-officials in the countryside and in cities. Paredes also claimed that *cholos* had inherited the worst of both races. They preferred to drink than see their families fed, they stole what *indígenas* earned, and learned nothing from whites. *Cholos* taught *indígenas* negative things, used the advantages they had gained to live in towns, and then took advantage of *indígenas*. They ran from the law and had no notion of contracts and of completing tasks.[50] For other Bolivian intellectuals, however, "*cholo*" and "*mestizo*" were synonymous.[51]

Some elites were unsure whether *cholos* and mestizos could become members of the Bolivian nation. For these individuals, mestizo identity could not remove the influence of indigeneity. Many elites' rejection of an explicitly Aymara or Quechua racial identity and distrust of mixed-race people left only one alternative: the construction of an idealized and whitened Inca identity. This development made indigenous identity in urban settings complex. E. Gabrielle Kuenzli demonstrates how intellectuals' construction of the idealized Inca of the ancient past enabled the Aymara peoples of the altiplano to create and deploy an identity that would allow them to assert their identity as Bolivians through theatrical productions that created an idealized and fictional connection to the Inca empire and thus legitimate them as part of Bolivia.[52] Living indigenous peoples could not belong in the city as Aymara- and Quechua-speaking peoples; they had to deploy multiple identities (*indígena*, "popular," occupational) in urban areas. Despite this balancing act, residents of indigenous neighborhoods demonstrated that they valued their indigenous identity.

The Jesús de Machaca rebellion of 1921, the massacre of miners at the Uncía mine in 1923, and the preparations for the centennial celebration in the period from 1920 to 1925 were the context for Paredes's arguments against *cholos* and in favor of keeping *indígenas* in the countryside.[53] The allegation that some of the individuals who had planned the Jesús de Machaca uprising lived on the outskirts of the city contributed to the fears of elites that they could easily lose control if mestizos and indigenous people formed an alliance.[54] The Paceño elite attempted to mark and define indigenous peoples as La Paz was transitioning during this period, as the city grew.[55] The mestizo population was also growing.[56] In order to represent Bolivia as a modern nation, intellectuals argued that the city's problematic elements had to be removed.

Municipal and national officials limited people's movements in public space. The city government imposed curfews and restricted public assemblies during times of political and social turmoil such as the Jesús de Machaca rebellion, the efforts of workers to unionize in the 1920s, strikes by taxi drivers and telegraph operators in 1922, the indigenous rebellion in Chayanta in 1927, and the Chaco War. Periods of heightened security included saints' days, urban festivals, and secular holidays, when large groups of indigenous peoples would gather.[57] The government used ordinances and decrees to regulate and control public spaces. Another national decree against vagrancy suggested that as a result of constant indigenous rural migration, the city had experienced a "steep rise in theft and the organization of several bands of thieves." It stated that "the security police need better tools to fight against these gangs of vagrants."[58] In addition, the city government proposed a central registry of "domestic workers from the countryside" whom elites had brought to the city. Similarly, several councilors wanted to regulate the "contact domestic workers had with food" and establish an "ordinance for frequent health inspections."[59] The council put forward plans for work and identity cards to "enroll artisans and other craftsmen [engaged] in useful occupations."[60] In fact, the legal discourse maintained that vagrants and *indígenas* were the same thing.

The racial discourses present in Bolivian politics before the Chaco War suggest that the racial theorizing of government officials in positions of power (Saavedra, Sanchez Bustamante, and Paredes) was directly related to the efforts to remove indigenous peoples from the city.[61] Although Saavedra ostensibly sought to protect indigenous peoples,[62] as president of Bolivia in 1920–25, he chose to use violence and repression in response to the Jesús de Machaca rebellion and several urban strikes and supported the initiatives of the La Paz council to limit the participation of indigenous people in the centennial celebrations. A fear of racial mixing shaped Paredes's theories on racial mixing. Although he argued that very little differentiated mestizos and *cholos*, somehow (and this point remains unclear) the *cholo* was "closer" to the *indígena* archetype than to whites and had the negative characteristics of both races. These theorists wrote in the context of a fracturing political apparatus. Saavedra's ascension to power began a fracturing of the Liberal and Conservative parties into various personalistic factions and enabled the rise of the Nationalist Party. Elites' fears about the indigenous and mixed-race elements of Bolivian society were a reflection of the tenuousness of their control over the political system.

The 1930s: The Effect of the Chaco War on Racial Discourse

During the Chaco War, the government relied on indigenous peoples to do the bulk of the fighting. The racial discourses in the pre-Chaco period justified this practice. The government's military failures affected most indigenous and non-indigenous Bolivians involved in the fighting and they grew frustrated with the conduct of the war. These men and women later became the main supporters of the reform-minded parties of the postwar period. Several leaders of the reformist parties spent time at the front and witnessed the great divide between elites and the indigenous and peasant masses who did most of the fighting and suffered most of the casualties in the war.[63]

Despite the impact of the Chaco War on Bolivian politics, it did not alter the basis of the economy or the fundamental social and economic inequality that most Bolivians faced. The political discourse of Bolivian elites aimed to transform the country's social and economic system. In part, the political changes of the postwar period expanded the opportunities residents of indigenous neighborhoods had to help shape La Paz and Bolivian society, in the process increasing their visibility in an evolving city. Because Bolivia lost the war, it lost part of the Chaco region. The war left many wounded veterans who were unable to work, created economic dislocation, and led many rural residents to migrate to the nation's cities. These outcomes shaped how Bolivian politicians addressed the social, economic, and political injustices workers and indigenous peoples faced. After the Chaco War, reformist politicians were willing to spend money in indigenous neighborhoods and offered a limited degree of support for the labor movements indigenous workers participated in, but they were not ready to think about giving indigenous Paceños full political rights. Although politicians tried to use the class trope to unite the disparate elements of Bolivia's population, racial discourses continued to argue that indigenous peoples were not ready to be full members of Bolivian society.

The elements of the political left who had been on the fringe of politics before the war became central to the reimagining of postwar society.[64] Middle-class urban residents, reformist military officers, and reformist elite politicians sought new forms of political organization that relied upon class-based discourses to build a cohesive nation. However, race continued to play an important role in social identification. It is clear that elites and government officials tried desperately to pin down the identities of the residents of indigenous neighborhoods. They also used race, class, and space to mark these residents as different.

The period of military socialist rule (1936–9) was one of political ferment and maturation for the political left. Military socialists studied the social and political problems of Bolivians living in cities and in the countryside. They helped create more bureaucratic institutions and standardized the roles of several state and local government officials. They built roads, markets, housing, and sewer lines that helped indigenous and mixed-race peoples and extended electric power lines into their neighborhoods. The military socialist governments put experts in positions of power in many of these institutions. While their policies seem to have left room for negotiation about who was part of the nation and in what ways, a corporatist, urban model predominated in military socialist political ideology and practice.

Leftist parties blossomed under the rule of the military socialists, and many of the politicians who had been involved in the exile movement and the Siles government of the late 1920s joined these parties and created new ones.[65] Military socialists moved the government's political positioning to the left. They instituted the eight-hour workday, the six-day workweek, pensions, and unemployment benefits and recognized unions' right to collective bargaining and the right to strike. While military socialist governments sought to address the social imbalances in society and to incorporate unions into their vision of society, they did relatively little to address the plight of rural indigenous peoples. Their main focus remained on urban populations and the "popular" or "laboring" classes.[66]

An article in the La Paz daily *La Calle* that profiled Adolfo Paco Cariaga, who was from Sicasica, an Aymara altiplano region, exemplifies the ambiguity and slipperiness of the notions of worker and *indígena*. Cariaga was a driver in La Paz who worked for the city government and had won the election to the national congress. He argued that the only way to improve his life and that of other workers was "to create a workers' cooperative for production, consumption, and transport." He maintained that Bolivian workers suffered because the nation's institutions and government functioned in the service of the capitalists. Education for the "proletarian children should follow the model school in Chijini where breakfast and lunch are served because a healthy mind and a healthy body are one."[67] The author of the article defined Cariaga as a "worker" who subscribed to the syndicalism of the post-Chaco period but his racial identity is ambiguous: it is unclear from the text whether Cariaga was an Aymara indigenous person, what languages he spoke, or what his connections to rural Aymara communities were. It is clear that *La Calle*'s editors wanted to present Cariaga as a generic worker. However, Cariaga lived in one of La Paz's indigenous neighborhoods (Chijini), and he represented his home region of Sicasica, which historically had been a hotbed of Aymara resistance to the Bolivian state. Unions, education, and self-help were key aspects of the nationalist programs designed to help Bolivia as a nation in the post-Chaco period; the proponents of these ideas hoped that their focus on occupation and class identity would unite Bolivia's diverse populations.

The end of military socialist rule in 1939 led to an elite-oriented coup and military dictatorship in the shape of the Concordancia, an alliance between La Paz's traditional elites and planter elites who were tied to the Liberal era of the 1920s. The Concordancia unsuccessfully sought to reverse many of the reforms the Chaco War brought about in the political life of Bolivia. In 1943, it was replaced by a more progressive dictatorship led by Col. Gualberto Villarroel in alliance with the formative Movimiento Nacionalista Revolucionario (MNR) leadership. However, indigenous peoples, unions, and mutual aid societies continued to have significant effects throughout the 1940s.[68] Rural and urban populations continued to challenge and pressure the government despite a swing to more conservative policies at the national level. For example, the *Sindicato de Culinarias* (culinary union) of La Paz mobilized to gain basic wage protections.[69] The pressure neighborhood associations brought to bear on the city government to provide infrastructure and development resulted in improvements to the infrastructure of and quality of life in indigenous neighborhoods.[70] Rural indigenous movements continued to pressure the government for rights.[71]

In the face of these challenges, the Peñaranda government sought to enforce an identity card requirement and mandatory registration for all porters and informal vendors in La Paz. In addition, the Concordancia refused to follow many of the decrees of the military socialists and worked to replace them. It reestablished the Constitution of 1880, which did not recognize labor unions or the right to strike. These efforts suggest that the members of the Concordancia feared radicalism just as much as the military socialists had.[72]

During the transition from elite-oriented political structures to populist dictatorship and back to the elite-controlled government, Bolivian racial theories changed very little. Yet, national politics continued to swing from left to right after the Chaco War and before the 1952 Revolution. In late 1942, the officers involved in RADEPA (Razón de Patria, a Chaco War–era military political lodge) decided to overthrow the elite-controlled government. La Paz's transit police and the MNR joined these officers and succeeded in overthrowing the government. Col. Gualberto Villarroel ruled Bolivia in the years from 1943 to 1946. Villarroel's reformist ideas included several projects to help indigenous Bolivians and workers attain further rights. He passed a union rights law, a Christmas Bonus law, a law that gave workers paid vacations, and a law that reduced rent in cities. He also established a public employees' cooperative.[73]

However, the alliance between Villarroel and the MNR was fraught with conflict; he was unable to control the MNR as the latter sought reform and greater independence. The MNR leadership began to support workers in La Paz and the growing labor movements in the mining sector.[74] In late 1943, under pressure from the United States, the Villarroel government expelled the MNR from its cabinet.

In late 1944, the government brought the MNR back into the fold and the latter set about developing a much more ambitious plan of reform. After that, Villarroel's regime legalized unions and delineated workers' rights. The miners' confederation formed the Federación Sindical de Trabajadores Mineros de Bolivia in 1945. It was also in this period that the Villarroel government made major advances in the area of indigenous legislation. Villarroel decreed the end of forced indigenous labor and unpaid labor, established schools in rural areas, and prepared a rural labor code.[75] He also helped sponsor the first National Indigenous Congress in Bolivia in 1945.

Racial and Class Discourses after the Chaco War

Despite the rise of class discourses and nationalist political reformers, intellectuals and government elites continued to use essentialist language to describe Bolivia's indigenous peoples. Luis Terán Gómez emphasized the failures of colonialism and the Bolivian republican period to resolve the question of how to manage the social and political rights of indigenous people given all the ways that Terán viewed efforts to do so as failures. The poverty and "backwardness" of contemporary indigenous peoples were Terán's evidence of those alleged failures. Terán was an intellectual who wrote several books about Bolivia, including one on the influence of Afro-Latin Americans, one on the influence of indigenous people, a biography of Simón Bolívar, and a history of the nation's political parties. He argued that elites and the government should control the education of indigenous people and that indigenous peoples should stay in rural areas. In a 1941 article, he reasoned that education for indigenous people was necessarily different from the education for the rest of the Bolivian population. He also maintained that the Bolivian state should invest in the modernization of agriculture. According to Terán, the most appropriate occupation for indigenous people was agriculture and the most appropriate environment for them was the countryside.

Terán's 1941 article "El Indio ante la realidad" (The Indian in Reality) reflected on some of the issues Bolivia had been facing in the post–Chaco War period. Terán argued that Indians had not benefited from what he called "republican democracy" (his term for the periods of semi-democratic rule that punctuated Bolivia's dictatorships), that they lived in "ignorance," and that the republican system that elites propagated kept them "in subservience to the dominant groups of society." He wrote that in the pre-Columbian past, Indians had had good housing and agriculture but in the present, they needed "civilization and social justice."⁷⁶ He argued that Indians lost their civilization when Spaniards destroyed their culture. In the national period, Indians had had little recourse but to sell their labor to the highest bidder and routinely suffered abuses as servants on haciendas. Terán argued that the abuse they suffered worsened after the Chaco War: they lacked good nutrition, suffered from poverty, had no access to cash, and little knowledge of hygiene, all of which contributed to the "degeneracy of the race."⁷⁷

He also claimed that the coca leaf and alcohol had contributed to the "deterioration of the Indian race."⁷⁸ The use of alcohol created a people who were a burden on public resources since they ended up in jail and in the hospitals. Terán wrote that the coca leaf had once "belonged to the Incas" and then became something that "every Indian used and abused." He argued that elites and Indians needed a basic strategy for managing the ill effects of alcohol and coca on indigenous communities so that advances in education could benefit indigenous peoples.⁷⁹ Whites and mestizos "venerate but do not ingest the coca plant," he claimed.⁸⁰

According to Terán, education was the primary solution. However, he said that the Indian needed education that was suited to his circumstances so that he would not abandon his best profession [in the fields] for the chance to learn rudimentary reading and writing skills so that he might become a *tinterillero* [two-bit lawyer]."⁸¹ Terán's solution was to educate the Indio in rural areas and to send better equipment and seeds to those areas. This would make Indians more productive for the nation. The problem was one of "biology and ethnic needs, not education."⁸² Preventing consumption of alcohol, controlling the type of education available, and bringing capitalism and modernity to rural areas were only part of the solution. Terán argued that the Bolivian elites needed to change the thinking that regarded indigenous people as obstacles to progress.

Terán's proposals reflect the idea that the city was the bastion of the elite. For Terán and other intellectuals, the Chaco War had failed to remove a fundamental "roadblock" that living indigenous peoples ostensibly posed to a homogenous national population. In this view, indigenous peoples should have been kept out of the cities and should have been trained as agricultural workers in the countryside. His clear disregard for the collective capacity and ability of indigenous people limited the extent to which government policies sought to include them in the transformation of the nation in the postwar years. The presence of Indians was a source of tension and friction within the nation-building ideas of reformist politicians in the period from 1935 to 42. Terán's theories were not much different from those of the intellectuals of the era before the Chaco War. His advocacy of specialized and separate rural education illustrates the disquiet that indigenous peoples caused among politicians as large numbers of indigenous, rural peoples settled in Bolivia's cities.

After the war, the reform government attempted to stem the mass exodus of indigenous people from the countryside. It tried to lease rural land back to *indígenas* so they would return to farming and therefore would not have a reason to move to the city.[83] The government also discussed the possibility of fines and the use of internal passports to prevent *indígenas* from moving to cities. These proposals did not come to pass but demonstrate that the realignment of society after the war was complicated and filled with uncertainty. It was still common for elites to blame *indígenas* for urban hygiene and other problems and it did not mean their position had changed simply because the political system and dominant discourse had changed. Luis Terán Gómez, Manuel Paredes, Baustista Saavedra, and José Tamayo were among those who sought to implement programs that would keep *indígenas* working in agriculture and living in rural areas.

In 1941, Terán argued that race was innate. Others such as Arturo Posnansky, Bolivia's most respected pre-revolutionary era archaeologist, argued that innate intellectual divergence was attributable to physical differences. In 1945, Posnansky, a migrant to Bolivia from Europe, continued to defend the intellectual capacity of the historical Aymara and Quechua races. Posnansky's theories connected race and landscape and associated the different levels of civilization with rural and urban distinctions. In the modern period, Posnansky argued, there continued to be a substantive difference between highland and lowland *indígenas*. He posited that the monumental architecture in Peru and Bolivia proved that indigenous people were highly intelligent and had a complex social organization. He categorized Quechua- and Aymara-speaking indigenous peoples who lived in settled agricultural societies as part of the same "civilized" group and those in the lowlands as "more savage" and different.[84] He based this argument on anthropometric studies he had done among the Bolivian people.[85] Other Bolivian scholars defended his theories and studies, even though the scientific community rejected the idea that race was a biological reality in the post–Second World War era.[86] Posnansky argued that anthropometric measurements proved an innate physical difference between indigenous and nonindigenous peoples and between the indigenous peoples of the highlands and lowlands.[87]

Essentialist discussions of race informed government policies and intellectual analysis in the 1940s. The intellectual Vicente Donoso Torres illustrated this continuity in his article "El Factor Humano en la Geografía Nacional" (The Human Factor in National Geography), which the *Boletín de la Sociedad Geográfica de La Paz* published in 1945. Torres was an important education expert in Bolivia. He was also a lawyer, a writer, and a historian. He was minister of education from 1939 to 1943 and he founded the Pedro Domingo Murillo Industrial School in northern La Paz. He was the author of three volumes on education and pedagogy in Bolivia.[88] In his 1945 article, he argued that the discussion of the *indígenas'* plight belonged in the practical realm rather than the realm of theory and that the government needed concrete strategies for incorporating indigenous people into mainstream Bolivian society. Torres argued that practical incorporation did not mean that indigenous peoples could be "de-Indianized and [that one could] remove the autochthonous culture from them."[89] For Torres, the real question was how the nation would accomplish *indígenas'* incorporation because they constituted "fifty-six percent of the population." Bolivia was

> nothing [without the *indígena*]; there would be no workers and there would be no one to inhabit the cold altiplano or the hot jungle. To maintain the *indígena* in such conditions is unjust, inhumane, anti-economical, and it is against the culture of Bolivia and the whole of the Americas. The *indígenas* [possess] both vitality and the adaptability to be in these harsh situations and all of this despite the fact that they rely on coca and alcohol and the fact that addiction [keeps] them undernourished.[90]

Torres admired the tenacity, chastity, and hardworking nature of *indígenas* despite their difficult circumstances. According to Torres, "Three races dominated Bolivia; the Aymara who were energetic, hard, and difficult, the second was the Ksejwa [*sic*] sweet, soft, and malleable, and the Guaraní . . . were warriors, indolent, inscrutable, and difficult to bring to civilization."[91] For Torres, indigenous Bolivians were capable and had the potential to contribute to Bolivia's economy and politics, but without the proper education and guidance they could not be good members of the nation and homeland. He argued that it was important that Bolivia's political leaders do the right things for indigenous Bolivians.

Torres's strategy for diluting the influence of indigenous Bolivians on the racial composition, politics, and economy of Bolivia was immigration. It is unclear how Torres proposed to implement this policy since, as he pointed out, Bolivia had no port. Torres argued that immigration should respect and incorporate *indígenas* by regarding them as "element[s] of society not to be changed but to be validated and incorporated." The "inclusion of the *indígena* should be accomplished through a process of *mestizaje*."[92] According to Torres's strategy, the new arrivals would mix with Bolivians, including indigenous people, and would dilute the proportion of indigenous peoples. After this weakening of the culture of indigenous people, they "must be incorporated and there must be no racial distinctions[;] the *indígena* must be incorporated into the broad nationalism of Bolivia."[93] This incorporation not only needed to be both biological and social but also needed to erase any influence of indigenous people on Bolivian society.

Torres laid out the various intellectuals' strategies for incorporating indigenous peoples into Bolivian society. Some stated that it was a matter of education. Others posited that *indígenas* should be "Castillianized [sic]."[94] Others wanted high rates of white immigration. Torres argued that none of these was an effective solution in isolation. He felt that acquiring education had not helped the *indígena* at all. "[Teaching the *indígena*] helped electoral politics but has kept the *indígena* in a low social position." The literate *indígena* "learned that the city is [a] better [place] for him to rent out his services to anyone that will hire him."[95]

Torres's solutions echoed those of other theorists: he advocated that the government keep *indígenas* separate, make them literate in their own language, and teach them Spanish only as a second language.[96] The separate education system he suggested would require an investment in the education infrastructure; 80 percent of the money that Bolivia invested in education remained in the cities and did not help *indígenas* in the countryside. According to Torres, the government should build an educational system in rural areas that would provide education about hygiene, seed selection, crop science, new methods of agricultural production, livestock breeding, and the latest fertilizers and tools. It should also teach indigenous people about cooperatives for production and consumption.[97] All of this investment in education would enable Bolivians to take advantage of *indígenas*' "aptitudes for social good."[98] Torres argued that indigenous peoples would learn their role in democracy through work. He posited that the problem *indígenas* faced was not just that the education available to them did not benefit most of them; they also faced problems of inadequate sanitation, lack of infrastructure, lack of access to credit for agricultural production, and obstacles to benefiting from a strong economy. He claimed that without improvement in these areas, improvements in education would not change the economic situation of indigenous people or make them acceptable to elite Bolivians.

According to Torres, indigenous people who wanted to enter more fully into Bolivian society needed to forego their traditional dress. When indigenous people were in the city, they should wear something other than the clothing that nonindigenous Bolivians interpreted as markers of race—the *lluchu* or knit hat; the *bayeta* shirt; short pants; and sandals. This was because Bolivians would not respect a person wearing indigenous attire. *Indígenas* would be "forced to do the bidding of those above him, the soldier who stops the *indígena* in the streets, and forces him to sweep up the barracks. Worst of all he will continue to be disrespectfully called 'Indio.'"[99] The government could prevent this discrimination by creating schools in rural areas that would enable indigenous peoples to acquire the education they needed to prevent more educated people from exploiting them.

Like the theorists who had preceded him, Torres argued that *indígenas* belonged in rural areas, but unlike those theorists, he made land reform a central point in his arguments. He advocated returning land to indigenous people, but on terms that benefited elites. According to Torres, *indígenas* had collective rights to land but elites needed to prepare them to exercise those rights. He saw the necessity of "bringing the *indígena* to the right place and not simply try[ing] to replace the feudal system with a new regime without first preparing the *indígena* for this great responsibility."[100] Torres advocated new laws that would regulate work, contracts, salaries, religious festivals, coca leaves, and alcohol. He wanted the Bolivian state to build roads, fund an agricultural bank, provide health clinics, and supply an irrigation system.[101] Torres looked to Mexicans and their revolution for inspiration. More than anything else, Torres feared the consequences of a communist revolution. He argued that these changes were necessary and "must be accomplished through a peaceful evolution rather than a social revolution that [would] take private property and turn it all into communist property with no regard for anyone's individual intelligence or ability."[102]

Torres's program sought to uplift and maintain *indígenas* in rural areas instead of offering true political inclusion. He proposed an evolutionary process the state would control. He was not interested in making every man or woman equal before the law.[103] His ideas had much in common with those of the intellectuals analyzed throughout this chapter. He claimed that his program was progressive, yet it had much in common with older notions of hierarchy and separation. The education that *indígenas* received "in the barracks" (through compulsory military service) was not the right type of education. Torres sought a program that ostensibly centered on the needs of indigenous people, tightly controlled land reform, and sought to ensure that the nomadic and semi-nomadic tribes of the lowlands would settle in permanent hamlets.[104] He thought that immigration would ensure that indigenous peoples would no longer constitute the majority of Bolivia's population and that it would eventually lead to *mestizaje* for all *indigenistas*.[105] This *indigenismo* argued for total and complete separation of indigenous people from the rest of society for their own protection, for indigenous people to shed markers of their identity when they were in cities, and for the lowland indigenous people to become "settled" and live in permanent housing (most lowland indigenous peoples were semi-nomadic hunter-gatherers). All of the legal protections related to land, contracts, and salaries he suggested were designed to keep *indígenas* in a separate legal and social position.

Torres published his theories in the period between 1950 and 1952, a time when the city and the nation were transforming. Miners were forming unions and striking for better working conditions. The government's response was always repression. In addition, continued migration from the countryside transformed La Paz. As a result, the city government invested in infrastructure, schools, and markets to improve the quality of life of the people settling in many of the indigenous neighborhoods. Torres sought controlled incorporation and tightly controlled land reform in this context of social and demographic change. Despite the social and political changes Bolivia experienced during and after the Chaco War, Torres's separatist proposals shared much with the proposals his pre-Chaco counterparts had made. And little had changed about how white Bolivians viewed indigenous people: Posnansky's theories of absolute racial differences continued to mark them as different.

Conclusion

The racial discourses in the texts of elite thinkers and government officials reveal that they saw the *indígena* as a problematic element of Bolivian society that was not prepared for full citizenship with all the rights and responsibilities this entailed, nor for complete incorporation as members of the nation. While all of these authors focused on how best to make indigenous peoples part of the nation, they disagreed on what incorporation meant. All of them focused on education as the primary means of incorporation, but they did not agree on the type of education indigenous people should have. For them, "incorporation" meant putting *indígenas* to work as modern, rural agriculturalists who lived in rural areas and had little or no involvement in the power structures of Bolivian politics. These projects focused exclusively on elite anxieties and on elite visions of the Bolivian nation. They reveal that elites did not believe in the abilities of indigenous peoples.

The idea of a separatist incorporation pervaded intellectual thought throughout the twentieth century. In the early twentieth century, Saavedra argued that indigenous people were rural people who were focused on agricultural production. In 1917, Daniel Sanchez Bustamante made a similar argument, adding that the government should teach Spanish only as a second language. Paredes, who wrote at the time of the Cacique Apoderado movement and the Jesús de Machaca rebellion, argued for separation and education and sought to remove the influence of mestizos and *cholos* because they were exploitative intermediaries in the social system.[106] Even after the Chaco War, when it seemed that class and nationalism might overcome racial divisions, intellectuals such as Vicente Donoso Torres and Luis Terán Gómez continued to write about racial difference and separate incorporation. Thus, while the Chaco War changed many things about the social and political context of Bolivia, racial discourses remained relatively stable. The underlying racial assumptions of both oligarchic and reformist elites were largely similar. To varying degrees in these texts, immigration and "breeding out" indigenous elements was another possible solution. Overall, intellectuals did not see indigenous peoples, mestizos, or *cholos* as productive members of the nation.

However, historical developments prevented the erasure of indigenous peoples from La Paz. The migration of indigenous peoples to the city throughout the first half of the twentieth century forced elites and the city government to contend with this population. The fracturing of the elite political system after the Chaco War forced realignments among the elite and the transformation of political discourses in the context of expansion in indigenous neighborhoods. In addition, periodic mobilizations of urban indigenous people made it impossible to overlook their presence in cities. Yet even the political mobilization of urban indigenous people throughout the twentieth century did not put an end to discourses that sought to make indigenous peoples both separate and irrelevant.

The discourses covered in this chapter saw *indígenas* as politically irrelevant because elites did not consider them to be cogent, coherent, cerebral political actors.[107] They argued that indigenous people were subject to base urges and vulnerable to manipulations of mestizos and *cholos*. In these writings, *indígenas* were always portrayed as rural people and were invariably disparaged.[108] Ultimately, these writings reveal that elites viewed indigenous peoples as problematic elements of Bolivian society. Intellectual elites insisted that incorporating *indígenas* was difficult because they could not shed their innate physical, social, and geographic characteristics. The pervasiveness of racial assumptions throughout the pre-revolutionary period helps explain the power and attraction of class discourses. For both indigenous neighborhood residents and elites, redefining indigenous people in class terms as workers or peasants could provide a mechanism for eliminating racial distinctions in favor of social, economic, and political cohesion. These discourses became more attractive in Bolivia in the 1920s through the 1940s. How indigenous neighborhood residents helped redefine what it meant to be a worker and citizen is the subject of the next chapter.

3

Alternative Identities

Labor and Race in La Paz, Bolivia, in the 1920s and 1930s

Introduction

In the twentieth century, workers in La Paz developed strong organizations *before and after* the Chaco War.[1] Mining unions, the heart of the Bolivian labor movement, were some of the most radical unions in Bolivia. The urban-based printers' union, the Sindicato de Graficos, was the first to emerge in the modern union movement. In the 1900s and 1910s, mutual aid societies and early craft unions faced government repression and persecution, but new political alignments during Juan Bautista Saavedra's administration (1920–25) made unionization safer. In this more open climate, urban union activism increased.[2]

In this context, most of the unions discussed in this chapter emerged in the mid to late 1920s. Most labor unions were divided by gender. The federations also tended to be divided by gender. The Sindicato de Constructores y Albañiles (construction workers' union) was formed in 1925. The Sindicato de Culinarias (cooks' union) was formed in 1926. In 1927, the Federacion Obrera Femenina (Women Workers' Federation; FOF) was an anarchist union and it unified under its federation cooks, market vendors, ambulant vendors, and flower sellers. The Federación Obrera de La Paz (La Paz Labor Federation; FOL) was a male-dominated anarchist union and it was also established in 1927. The Federación Obrera del Trabajo (The Workers' Labor Federation; FOT) was initially formed in 1908 as a mutual aid society and was influenced by liberalism. In 1918, the FOT reorganized as a social democratic federation. By the 1930s, the anarchist federations and the FOT were politically at odds, but tended to retain class solidarity. By late 1940s, the FOL, FOT, and the FOF represented a sizable portion of the working population in La Paz. The unions were powerful enough for the local and national government to fear mobilization by them. Bolivia also witnessed increased labor activism in the mines and in the countryside.[3] Unions continued to grow after Saavedra was overthrown in late 1925. Before the Chaco War, cohesive regional labor federations had already developed.[4]

The Chaco War curbed the political activities of unions. Liberal president Daniel Salamanca (1930–34) persecuted labor movement leaders and outlawed unions. However, unions quickly reformed after the war. The unions associated with the FOL supported the unionization efforts of other laborers. The FOL was founded in 1926 and was part of the burgeoning union movement in La Paz. Federación Obrera del Trabajo was founded in 1908, but transformed from a mutual aid society, it became a social democratic union in 1918 and continued to function until the 1950s. The two labor federations became relatively large and influential. The industrial capacity of Bolivia and La Paz was minimal before the revolution and consisted of mostly light industry. The predominant factories in La Paz manufactured matches, beer, condiments, shoes, and textiles. The labor regimes varied in these industries. The shoe factories, for example, used a putting-out system that included both large and home-based workshops. In the textile factories, specialized assembly lines predominated.[5] The FOL worked to organize the industrial workers as well as the craft laborers.

In the 1920s and 1930s, printers, telegraphers, taxi drivers, and construction workers in La Paz recruited their colleagues into unions, organized strikes, and participated in solidarity strikes with unions in La Paz and sometimes with unions in other parts of Bolivia.[6] They pressured the government and private employers for better wages, shorter hours, and basic labor protections. Their labor unions helped master artisans gain the right to vote in 1926.[7] The FOL and the construction workers' and printers' unions continued to recruit new members in this period. Although workers still could not participate in formal electoral politics, they served Saavedra's interests by becoming his "muscle" during local and national elections and political rallies.[8] The FOL leadership argued that they were the "base of [Saavedra's] Revolution" and they fully supported Saavedra's programs.[9] At the same time, Saavedra used discourse that distinguished workers from indigenous peoples and tried to manage them as distinct interest groups. As we will see, the aftermath of the Chaco War opened up new possibilities for the city's unions and for class-based organizing.

A 1922 strike illustrates both the growing strength of urban unions and the Saavadra government's ambivalent relationship with the labor movement. That year, a city ordinance restricted travel at night in La Paz in response to alleged conspiracies against the government on the part of a shadowy group of Liberal and Conservative politicians. The La Paz taxi drivers' union lobbied the city council to reconsider the curfew because it was damaging their business. When the city council denied the request, the taxi drivers' union asked the president, Juan Bautista Saavedra, to step in and lift the curfew. After all, Saavedra had said he supported workers. However, the president promptly rejected this seemingly straightforward petition. Seeing few options, the taxi drivers asked two independent labor federations—the FOL and the FOT—to mediate the dispute. Both the city and the national governments refused to negotiate, arguing that the curfew prevented anti-government plotting and maintained political stability. In response, the FOT leadership called for solidarity strikes. At this point, railroad workers, printers, and tram workers joined the taxi drivers, halting all traffic in the city. The Sindicato de Graficos joined the strike, shutting down all the La Paz newspapers. These actions forced the city council to rescind the nocturnal taxi ordinance.[10] In this case, the national government could have mediated the dispute and Saavedra could well have looked like the workers' president he had claimed to be by working to end the impasse between the taxi union and the city council. Instead, both city government and the national government faced intense pressure and had to submit to the strikers' demands after the strike spread to other unions.

While this strike successfully lifted the curfew, the Saavedra government met other strikes with swift repression. One example occurred in 1923, when La Paz–based telegraph workers sought to consolidate all their labor organizations into one union and ally it with the FOT and railroad workers' union. Telegraph workers asked for and received the support of several mutual aid societies and unions around Bolivia. Emboldened, the Sindicato de Telegrafistas sought the support of mining unions. The telegraph workers sought wage increases, improved working hours, and the option to form an independent union rather than being forced to belong to a "company union." When the Saavedra government refused to meet with union leaders to negotiate their demands, the Sindicato de Telegrafistas decided to strike. The Sindicato de Graficos supported the telegraph workers, just as it had supported the taxi drivers. When the Sindicato de Telegrafistas struck, the Saavedra government suppressed the strike and broke it. It severely damaged the unionization movement among telegraph workers and the Sindicato de Telegrafistas's efforts to create a regional confederation with other labor organizations, including the FOT.[11] The Saavedra government made it illegal for government workers to unionize and rejected the proposal that it mediate on behalf of private sector unions. For a "revolutionary" government and a "pro-worker" president, Saavedra's policies were surprisingly anti-labor.

Although Saavedra's actions demonstrate that he was not particularly interested in aiding unionization efforts, he enjoyed workers' support for his government when he could mobilize that support to intimidate the opposition. Saavedra's flirtation with labor and unions shifted the political ground upon which the traditional elite had built their political alliances. These politicians had come of age steeped in late nineteenth-century liberal ideology. Despite the efforts of some elites to counteract these shifts away from liberal politics, certain changes could not be undone. Saavedra's rise is what shaped the increased activism of unions and guilds, which became vehicles residents of the indigenous neighborhoods used to push for improvements in La Paz's infrastructure.

Union Activism before the Chaco War

In December 1920, after Saavedra and two associates led a coup against Liberal Party president José Gutiérrez Guerra, a constitutional convention declared Saavedra president. Letters to editors of newspapers emphasize that workers had helped Saavedra in his quest to become the new president because he supposedly represented them and their interests. The newspaper *La Reforma* published letters from workers throughout Bolivia, including La Paz, Beni, Oruro, Santa Cruz, and Potosí, that supported Saavedra's candidacy and ascension.[12] These letters argued that Saavedra's presidency was the most "correct course for Bolivia and for the working class." His presidency would "give voice" to those that would "bring Bolivia its glory."[13]

Saavedra courted labor leaders. He passed decrees that created a six-day workweek and an eight-hour workday and established a framework for official government recognition for unions.[14] Newspapers across the country reported that labor leaders supported Saavedra's candidacy and presidency.[15] Saavedra told workers that Bolivia needed them to continue producing for it and that he was the best man to represent them in government and to stabilize Bolivian politics.[16] Workers supported Saavedra because he was "genuinely interested in the workers' plight" and because the revolution was about creating "stability."[17] According to one labor leader, his revolution was a departure from the personalistic rule of the Liberal Party and a return to "constitutionalism."[18] The irony was that despite Saavedra's presentation of himself as the workers' president and his revolutionary stances, workers and unions in La Paz experienced repression during his administration.

For instance, in 1920, slaughterhouse workers in the city-owned slaughterhouse, who believed that they had an ally in Saavedra, struck against the city council and the "two or three capitalists" who owned most of the livestock and ran most of the butcher shops in La Paz. They demanded better wages and an eight-hour workday.[19] When the union could not settle the strike with the city council, the national government quickly and violently put down the strike. Saavedra declared martial law and outlawed labor organizing among slaughterhouse workers.[20] While the president supported the workers of Bolivia in theory, his government withdrew that support any time workers challenged the government or private industry regarding wages, hours, or other demands.[21] Most urban unions suffered similar fates: as long as they were under Saavedra's control, he would use them. However, whenever unions became liabilities, he repressed their activism.

While Saavedra and La Paz's workers negotiated the meaning and consequences of his "revolution," the city government instituted several laws in its efforts to control the city's population.[22] In 1925, both the city council and the national government prohibited indigenous peoples from participating in the nation's centennial celebrations, from entering the city center in large groups, and from participating in other civic celebrations. These laws relied on an 1886 municipal ordinance that the national government and the city council rewrote in 1913 and again in 1925. They made a distinction between vagrants (who did not have an acceptable job), mendicants, and those who were engaged in idle enterprise (*mal entretenidos*).[23] This last category was composed of people who spent their days in gambling houses or bars, people who engaged in "immoral or scandalous commerce,"[24] and people who survived by engaging in fraud, deception, and theft. The category included people who enticed others, especially dependents such as children and domestic servants, into criminality. The punishment for vagrants and *mal entretenidos*, according to the 1925 law, was imprisonment in the San Pedro Prison; for mendicants, it was removal to the San Ramón Asylum (a hospital for those with tuberculosis that later became a detention center for the mentally ill).[25] The ordinances used class-based criteria to limit the presence of undesirable populations in the city.

The life and work histories of several leaders of the FOF and the Sindicato de Culinarias (a union of cooks) demonstrate the impact of these laws on workers and how these laws contributed to a conflation of worker and indigenous identities. The experiences of Petronila Infantes, a union leader and cook, and a mixed-race woman, illustrate these points. In the early twentieth century, her father moved the whole family out of La Paz so he could find work in the

Colquiri tin mines near La Paz.[26] While her father was still working in the mines, Petronila married. She followed her husband back to La Paz, where they lived in the indigenous neighborhoods. When her husband died in the Chaco War, Infantes began selling vegetables in the streets as a way to help her immediate family and her mother and siblings. Feeling like an outsider in La Paz, she began wearing a *pollera* (a pleated petticoat skirt) to fit in with the other market women and to look less indigenous.[27] She was not successful as a market vendor, so she decided to learn how to cook.[28]

After the Chaco War, Infantes became active in the Sindicato de Culinarias because she wanted stable employment and better wages. She learned about anarchism in the workers' schools that anarchists and university students organized.[29] She worked for a variety of employers, including private households and several foreign legations. Infantes preferred working for foreigners because she felt that they were less likely to discriminate against members of the *sindicato* and paid better wages.[30] She and her children lived in several areas of La Paz's indigenous neighborhoods: in the cemetery district, in the Chijini district, and near the Rodríguez market. Infantes became one of the leading members of the Sindicato de Culinarias; she helped organize union meetings and coordinate activities and services for the *sindicato* and the FOF throughout the 1940s and early 1950s.

Infantes's migration pattern departed from the typical pattern of rural-to-urban migration, but it reflects larger trends in the economy and historical development of Bolivia. Her father searched for work in the tin mines, where she met and married her husband. She then migrated back to La Paz with him. Her life was reflective of her generation—the Chaco War made her a widow and forced her to become the sole provider for her family. In addition, her settlement in the indigenous neighborhoods, her chosen line of work, and her efforts to "fit in" by wearing *polleras* shaped her life circumstances.

Other members of the Sindicato de Culinarias were migrants to La Paz and had chosen to become cooks out of necessity. Tomasita Patón migrated to La Paz after her father, an Aymara trader, died during a trip. Patón's mother moved the family to La Paz to live with relatives. She learned the craft of cooking from her urban relatives. Patón lived on the outskirts of the city with her relatives and then when she married and had her own children, she left to live near the Garita de Lima in the indigenous neighborhoods. Graciela Barrios married young to escape the confines of her family life on the altiplano. She and her husband moved to La Paz to find a better life in the city. She learned to cook and found employment with several elite families on the Prado and then in

Sopocachi.³¹ Exaltación Miranda left her home in Chuma in rural La Paz at sixteen or seventeen to live in La Paz.³² Several women working as cooks decided to form a union when it became clear that employers could fire them at any time, that they had no recourse when they suffered mistreatment, and that employers could block their move to another employer or ensure they were unemployable by suggesting that they were thieves.³³ Patón recalled facing discrimination for speaking Aymara in her employers' homes and being accused of theft when she took leftover food home or ate at work.³⁴ These labor movement participants shared the experiences of settling in indigenous neighborhoods, choosing cooking as their craft, and becoming politically active residents of the city. This pattern reflects larger trends in the urbanization of Bolivia.

In addition to the discrimination they faced, members of the Sindicato de Culinarias earned low wages compared to other working-class women. Cooking was one of the lowest-paid occupations in La Paz.³⁵ In contrast to members of other unions, these women often worked in isolation or at most with one other woman. They distinguished themselves from the women and men employed as maids and household servants in elite households because those servants were usually brought to the city from the countryside through the *pongueaje* arrangement.³⁶ While *culinarias* and these servants faced similar abuses, it was extremely difficult to create cohesive alliances with other household staff because they rotated from the countryside to the city and back again.³⁷ The Sindicato de Culinarias helped female cooks protect themselves from arbitrary abuses, build a community, and create alliances with other working-class women and other craft unions.

The women involved in the Sindicato de Culinarias and the FOF analyzed their lives through the lenses of class exploitation and racial discrimination. Petronila Infantes's speech during one workers' congress explained how the capitalist system took more from women than it did from men.³⁸ Moreover, wealthy employers treated them as they did the "India and the chola."³⁹ Infantes's decision to wear the *pollera* to fit in with other market vendors suggests that Aymara culture was crucially important to the identity of female workers in La Paz. It demonstrates how important urban networks and markers of indigenous identity were to workers in a context where elite employers repressed and condemned indigenous people and passed laws to segregate them from the city's public spaces.⁴⁰ For their employers and many urban residents, these women never escaped or overcame the indigenous base of their identity and its implied rural contexts. *Culinarias* used how elites saw all workers to their advantage: they embraced the conflation elites made of "worker" and "indigenous person" and formed alliances across ethnic lines.

The experiences of members of the Sindicato de Culinarias reveal several patterns of residence in the city. The leadership of the union hailed from the La Paz area or the surrounding provinces. Some of them had migrated to the city as children and stayed there for the rest of their lives. Some had lived all their lives in La Paz. Some had lived in the countryside and moved to the city as adults due to economic circumstances and family migration. Circular migration between rural Aymara communities and the city was another pattern.[41] Whether *sindicato* members were lifelong residents of La Paz, recent migrants, or had migrated years earlier, they were all integral residents of indigenous neighborhoods and became active in the city's labor organizations.

The migration of Aymaras and Quechuas from rural communities to La Paz forced them to contend with stereotypes and discrimination in the city. Many urban residents of all classes drew upon ideas that these migrants were supposedly savages who lacked culture and did not deserve citizenship rights.[42] Elites painted these workers as *cholajes* (a term that assigned a negative connotation to mixed-race people) or as urban Indians.[43] These workers had little recourse and no one to complain to about the treatment they received at the hands of authorities. Mistreatment was one reason they were keen to organize into unions.

Elites failed to differentiate between residents of the indigenous neighborhoods; it was much more useful to see them as part of the masses, as workers, and as *indígenas*. They also labeled them as miscreants, mendicants, outside agitators, or criminals when it suited their purpose to do so. Seeing individual workers as part of "the masses" enabled elites to manipulate that category: they could depict them as dangerous or they could regard them as useful allies in their efforts to achieve political goals. However, indigenous neighborhoods were heterogenous spaces and some workers had complex identities: they were Aymara in the countryside and Indians and workers in the city.

Members of the Sindicato de Culinarias asserted their right to occupy public spaces, despite the fact that city ordinances sought to banish them from those spaces. Sometimes they faced discrimination as Aymara peoples. Theater owners used laws that prohibited *indígenas* from entering theaters of the "first class," which included all of the theaters on the Prado, La Paz's main avenue, to refuse them entry.[44] Owners and managers of ice cream shops on the Prado refused to sell *culinarias* ice cream because of how they spoke and dressed.[45] It is unclear if these businesspeople discriminated against them because they were working-class women or because they looked like indigenous women.

In 1937, the Sindicato de Culinarias became a member of the FOF, which had close ties to the FOL. Men and women workers' shared experience of discrimination helped them create alliances in La Paz. One of the unions the Sindicato de Culinarias formed a particularly strong alliance with was the Sindicato Central de Constructores y Albañiles de Bolivia (Central Union of Construction Workers and Bricklayers of Bolivia), whose members also suffered discrimination during this period.[46] They were targeted for their outfits and clothing, for their manner of speaking Spanish, and for their perceived "backwardness." Members later recalled that one reason they formed a union was to protect themselves.

In the early 1920s, the Sindicato Central de Constructores y Albañiles became more radical when the government began repressing indigenous political mobilizations in the countryside and union activism in the city. Although the Saavedra government presented itself as a supporter of workers, both it and the government of La Paz persecuted indigenous peoples and workers in the city. In oral histories collected in the 1980s, many construction workers recalled that the city's master artisans wore the *calzón rajado* (short pants worn in the countryside), crisply ironed white pants, a fine vicuña poncho, and a hat made of the best leather. Women wore Castile shawls and *polleras*.[47] They recalled how elites targeted both workers and indigenous peoples based on their clothing, which was often homemade using rough-spun cloth and was a visual marker of race and class. Many elites saw workers in the city and in the mines as *cholajes* or as urban *indiadas*. One worker later recalled that they were "humiliated daily for this condition."[48]

The members of the Sindicato Central de Constructores y Albañiles suffered a double oppression: they worked long hours for low wages and they were discriminated against for their "cultural traditions, languages, and their way of life which was not well seen by the dominant caste."[49] Construction workers remembered how the police who patrolled in the city during Saavedra's time as president harassed them when they entered the Plaza Murillo wearing vicuña ponchos and *calzónes rajado*. Some police ripped the clothing of these workers with the butts of their rifles.[50] Some of them recalled that by 1924, they avoided entering the Plaza Murillo wearing a *poncho* because they knew they would be harassed. Workers surmised that the "indigenous" dress conveyed to some the idea that they "were not well-civilized" and believed that "the change of clothes helped civilize us."[51] To the employers of La Paz, "worker" and "indigenous person" were not mutually exclusive categories. Workers believed that giving up indigenous dress made it less likely that they would be singled out and dismissed as indigenous. While abandoning their traditional clothing in public spaces must have been painful, unions gave indigenous workers another avenue for integrating into urban life and culture. The solidarity and power unions cultivated gave members the freedom to highlight their identities as workers. But choosing that identity came at the cost of suppressing their indigenous identity in public. In effect, these craft workers felt compelled to "pass" as nonindigenous when they entered the city center to work.

The Chaco War and Postwar Realignments

In 1932, ten years after Juan Bautista Saavedra crushed the efforts of telegraph workers to unionize in Bolivia, those workers organized a union and struck to demand better wages. When the Sindicato de Telegrafistas (Telegraphers' Union) asked the FOT to support the strike, the FOT began mobilizing its member organizations. However, before these workers could organize any actions, President Daniel Salamanca (1931–4) declared the strike illegal and ordered the military to occupy all of the nation's telegraph offices. He also refused to negotiate with the FOT. He persecuted the leadership of the Sindicato de Telegrafistas and successfully stifled the strike. Not surprisingly, Salamanca's administration faced challenges from Bolivia's unions and significant political opposition from elites. The president's inability to build a cohesive alliance among elites for his domestic programs led him to focus on international politics. To distract from his unpopularity, Salamanca focused on the Chaco territory to garner popular and elite political support and unify the nation against a manufactured threat of Paraguayan aggression and invasion of the Chaco region.

The Chaco War, which began in 1932, was by all accounts a failure. Salamanca gambled that the Bolivian economy and its political apparatus would withstand the double strain of war and economic depression. Inept political decisions caused thousands of deaths and foolhardy military decisions caused thousands more. Soldiers on the battlefront lacked basic provisions, yet another disaster in a long line of missteps that demonstrated the inadequacies and shortcomings of Bolivia's military hierarchy and institutions.[52] In 1934, Salamanca's obstinacy and meddling in military affairs led the military to remove him from power. It fell to Vice President José Luis Tejada Sorzano to finish Salamanca's term in office, which ended in August 1935. Tejada Sorzano sought a quick conclusion to the war and a peace treaty with Paraguay.

The war heavily influenced the generation of politicians who challenged the political system after the war. Augusto Céspedes, Víctor Paz Estenssoro, Carlos Montenegro, Hernán Siles Zuazo, and several others had experienced the failures of the Bolivian state while serving in the Chaco War. Before the war, many had served as junior ministers in the governments of the late 1920s. Some had served as soldiers on the front. Many of these politicians had witnessed the highly unequal class and race systems that engendered the needless death of many mestizos and *indígenas* and had experienced the ineptitude of many army officers and political elites.[53] These experiences radicalized these men. After the war, as journalists and politicians, these leftists helped bring about political realignments in Bolivia. The politicians in this group were involved in the military socialist experiment from 1936 to 1939 and in the Villarroel government from 1943 to 1946. In this way, the Chaco War represented continuity with the participation of prewar politicians in the reformist political groups and governments after the war, and with the resumption of working-class activism, and at the same time the Chaco War represented the demise of the Liberal order.

The period of military socialist rule was a time of political ferment for the left. The military socialists were receptive to policies and programs associated with political movements across the ideological spectrum. The Toro government (May 1936–July 1937) decreed that all government employees were to join unions and that union representation was the only valid way to interact with the government. For the military socialists, no aspect of social and political life was outside the corporatist model. Each sector of society would have unions to represent them, the unions would elect a percentage of the members of the Bolivian Congress, and the popular vote would elect another portion of the Congress.[54] Beyond these visions and frameworks, university students were instrumental in developing links between reform-minded politicians, radical parties, and unions. The university union was particularly radical.[55] Even though military socialist decrees in support of a corporatist model of government were never followed, the initial organizing efforts and openness from the Toro, Busch (July 1937–August 1939), and the early Quintanilla (August 1939–April 1940) labor ministry helped unions expand in the mines, in the light industry, among artisans in La Paz, and in several government ministries.[56] While the military socialists did not last long in power, their support of unionization and popular organizing had a tremendous impact on the growth of unions in La Paz's indigenous neighborhoods.

The military high command, wary of the calls of Chaco War veterans for justice, labored to control how responsibility for the failures of the war was doled out. In determining how the war would be seen, the military demonstrated how much control it had over the political process. The high command worked hard to prevent any kind of judicial trial to determine civilian or military responsibility for mismanagement, ineptitude, and negligence during the war. The military thwarted processes of legal redress and openly declared that in the service of "uniting the Bolivian Nation there would be no political trials." Instead, it granted amnesty to most officers for failure on the battlefield.[57]

Many rank-and-file Chaco War veterans, alienated and angry as a result of the hardships and devastation of the war, unsuccessfully pressured the government to punish military officers and politicians for their failures during the war.[58] Beyond this popular discontent on several occasions, the military socialist government declared states of siege in La Paz to curb politically motivated plots supposedly led by the members of opposition parties.[59] In addition to its policing of ideology and political dissidents, the military socialist government sought to control the political implications of defeat for the military corps and to manage the extent of social and political reforms. The military imposed its will on the political apparatus to ensure that the prewar political parties would never regain control of the government.

Worker Activism in La Paz after the Chaco War

In this period of social transformation for Bolivia, workers rebuilt or expanded their unions, strengthened their claims to public space, and insisted that they too belonged to the nation. Their use of trams in La Paz illustrates these developments. In 1935, trams became a major site of mobilization for the FOF and the Sindicato de Culinarias. In that year, the tram administrator, a city employee and a liaison to the privately owned Bolivian Power Company, prohibited women with baskets from boarding the city's trams. Several members of the Sindicato de Culinarias later recalled how upper-class women complained about "these cholas with their baskets" when they boarded trams.[60] In 1935, *El Diario* published an article that stated that keeping the bulky bags and baskets off trams would prevent the spread of disease because the baskets would no longer touch other passengers and "ladies of high society."[61] The prohibition meant that members of the Sindicato de Culinarias had to walk to and from the markets. At the time, their employers preferred La Paz's two principal markets—one in front of the Basilica de San Francisco and the other near the Club de La Paz—both of which were located in central La Paz. Most elite homes where *sindicato* members worked were located south of the city center in San Jorge and Sopocachi, although some were located in the center of the town along the Prado and others in Miraflores. The trek to the markets might be as long as an hour from Miraflores and twenty-five or thirty minutes uphill from Sopocachi and San Jorge. Carrying a load of fresh groceries, bread, cheese, and meat back down from San Francisco Plaza would be cumbersome, tiring, and time consuming. This hardship led members of the *sindicato* to protest the prohibition, which angered even women who "had never been active in the union before."[62]

The prohibition galvanized the women involved in the union and motivated them to recruit new members. The Sindicato de Culinarias wrote several petitions and presented them to the prefect, the mayor, and the Bolivian Power Company. The FOL supported the *sindicato*; its leaders worked with the union to increase the organizing capacities of its members, provided them with a place to hold meetings, helped draft petitions, and publicized the issues the *sindicato* was raising.[63] The FOL also mobilized other unions, including the construction workers', butchers', and printers' unions, in support of the Sindicato de Culinarias' protest. The petitions and protests of the *culinarias'* union earned its members the right to use the tram as long as they were carrying burlap sacks and not baskets. The Sindicato de Culinarias' success in opposing the tram prohibition helped attract more members to the *sindicato* and connected them to men and women in other unions.

In 1937, the city council passed laws requiring that all market women, all *culinarias*, and all food vendors purchase health ID cards. The council also required market women and food vendors to pay fees for operating licenses; in addition, market women had to pay fees to operate their stalls. Market women, food vendors, and *culinarias* belonged to separate unions that were part of the FOF. The unions of these three groups of women workers vehemently opposed the idea of health identity cards because they were associated with prostitution. Registered sex workers had to submit to frequent and humiliating tests for sexually transmitted diseases in order to qualify for identity cards, and health inspectors and the sanitary police conducted regular raids on both clandestine and registered houses of prostitution to search for untested women.[64] Sex workers who were arrested were tested, quarantined in the tuberculosis hospital, and subjected to poor treatment at the hands of authorities.[65] The city government demanded that market women, members of the Sindicato de Culinarias, and food vendors submit to the same testing as La Paz's sex workers before they could obtain an identity card.[66] The logic was that they ostensibly carried the same diseases as the sex workers.

The Sindicato de Culinarias opposed this requirement, arguing they were not like the sex workers: "[The office of hygiene] was designed to service women who do not work with their hands; this [fact] matters to the honesty of the proletarian women."[67] The union argued that since its members cooked in the homes of the wealthy, the doctors of those families should examine them.[68] Members of the FOF and the Sindicato de Culinarias recalled pitched battles against the police in their efforts to resist the implementation of stall taxes and ID cards. They used soap to "wax" the cobblestones around the markets to prevent the police from using mounted officers to disperse protesters.[69] The soap made it difficult for horseshoes to grip the cobblestones and thus made the mounted officers ineffective. The Sindicato de Culinarias and the market vendors' and food vendors' unions capitalized on the opposition to the health cards to recruit more women for the unions and to encourage women who had never participated in labor activism to join the protests in order to publicize their efforts to get a minimum wage and Sundays off.[70] The Sindicato de Culinarias also wanted to rename themselves "laborers of the household" instead of "domestics" because they believed that the term "domestic" undervalued their labor and their skill.[71] For several years, these three unions were able to resist the implementation of health examinations by arguing that theirs was "honorable labor" and that they had nothing in common with the prostitutes of La Paz.[72]

In addition to holding strategy meetings, giving speeches, and participating in protests, the FOF members took a series of petitions to the city government. In one case, they requested that Mayor Muñoz Cornejo fire the market inspector and curb the powers of the market police. Women who were in the Sindicato de Culinarias in the 1930s later recalled that Max Murillo Bocángel, the superintendent of the market, was ruthless in his treatment of market vendors, whose union was closely allied with the Sindicato de Culinarias. Bocángel encouraged the market police to fine the market vendors for all infractions and repeatedly tried to enforce stall fees. The market vendors pressured the mayor and Bolivia's president to remove him.[73] In 1945, the market vendors resisted the imposition of stall fees and license fees.[74] These efforts paid off: in 1949, the Sindicato de Culinarias and the market vendors unions convinced the city to reduce stall fees and abandon the requirement that *culinarias* carry health cards.[75]

The market vendors' union organized a congress to plan their strategies and address the concerns of all of their members regardless of their racial and social identity or language limitations. In August 1938, the vendors spoke at

> a proletarian parliament of the most extreme transcendence. The speakers spoke in Aymara, Quechua, and Spanish. "Are we not Bolivian? We are not Chinese or Turks. Have our husbands and children not burst like toads in the Chaco [War]

and now they want to take the bread from our mouths too? Is it a shame for the poor to sell in the city's streets?"[76]

A newspaper report emphasized the fact that the women spoke in Aymara, Quechua, and Spanish. The use of all three languages at this congress indicates that rural, urban, indigenous, and mixed-race women were involved in the unions and organizations that attended the congress. When they gave their oral histories in the late 1980s, women repeatedly emphasized the lack of discrimination within the unions.[77] Women responded to racism by noting ethnic differences among themselves and attempting to bridge them. Moreover, the women retained aspects of traditional dress, which seems to have been a component of labor and class solidarity, while men tended to adopt European style clothing in order to avoid police harassment.

The congress these unions held demonstrated that Aymara-, Quechua-, and Spanish-speaking women associated with and were allied with the male-dominated FOL. The FOF did not turn away any workers—even those who were not formally unionized—and its members helped one another when they faced the police or other authorities or presented petitions to the government.[78] While members of the Sindicato de Culinarias were insulted as "*cholas* and *indias*" and were discriminated against in theaters and shops on the Prado, the unions included everyone who attended their meetings regardless of ethnic difference or linguistic barriers.[79] The unions and federations associated with the FOL and the FOF (which included construction workers, the Sindicato de Culinarias, and market and food vendors) tried to avoid formal alliances with political parties. As a result, the Sindicato de Culinarias did not participate in mobilization on behalf of political parties in the post-Chaco period.[80] Politically active laborers and members of anarchist unions lived in the same neighborhoods and were members of the same families of workers who did attempt to participate in and influence party politics. In this period before the MNR revolution of 1952, the working class relied heavily on the discourse of the labor movement, and radical and exiled intellectuals for its ideologies. The labor movement developed as a way for workers to seek better working conditions, better lives, and more respect in their public interactions in La Paz.

Labor Activism in the 1940s

President Germán Busch committed suicide in 1939. His successor, General Carlos Quintanilla (August 1939–April 1940) purged leftist officers from army command posts and set about installing more moderate and conservative officers in positions of power. The Concordancia, an alliance of the pre-Chaco elite political parties, which pressured the army for a return to civilian rule, succeeded in getting the army to add traditional politicians to the cabinet, and secured a promise from Quintanilla to withdraw the army from the government as well as to schedule elections.[81] Quintanilla worked closely with the Concordancia politicians and dismantled many of the military socialist decrees.[82]

Despite the resurgence of traditional elite parties, the elections of 1940 demonstrated that elites did not control the nation's political apparatus to the degree that they had before the Chaco War. They ran a unity slate, as the traditional parties had done with Salamanca, and were able to elect General Enrique Peñaranda (a likable war hero) to the presidency, but they did not control the congress. These national level changes reflected broader processes of transformation on the local level. In La Paz, the activism of unions demonstrated that union members and residents of indigenous neighborhoods were part of this transformation of the city's culture and life. The military hierarchy's purging of leftists from its leadership positions and the reemergence of the elite political parties did not signal a return to the political or social status quo of the pre-Chaco period.

The continued organizing activity of unions and the rise of reformist parties were unintended consequences of the Concordancia's requirement that Bolivia return to electoral politics. The FOF organized unions in the sectional markets that opened in the city in the period from 1939 to 1943.[83] Construction workers expanded programs at a night school organized in the late 1930s.[84] *Culinarias* and market women organized a subsidized breakfast and lunch program and planned a childcare cooperative for working mothers.[85] In addition, in 1942, the MNR was founded and began working with other leftist organizations. Political mobilizations across the political spectrum, from the elite Concordancia to the reformist MNR, enabled unions to avoid persecution and remain vocal in defense of their membership.

In 1940 and 1941, inflation caused the prices of basic household items to rise significantly.[86] The market vendors' union supported its members when the press and government accused them of engaging in speculation. The union argued that the true speculators were the wholesalers and the owners of large estates and that big capitalists were to blame for the high cost of food in the city. These wholesalers were the same men the city council asked for help in curbing speculation.[87] Women vendors defended their prices, noting that "we are the sole providers in our households."[88] They argued that direct sales from producers to market women and then from market women to the public would solve the problem and that the city government needed to ensure that the wholesale prices of basic goods be reduced by 50 percent. They wanted the government to include national products (such as potatoes, quinoa, and beef) in this scheme.[89] They analyzed price increases as a problem of supply and monopoly caused by the owners of large estates and wholesalers who controlled the flow of imported and domestic goods. As a result of pressure from consumers and market vendors, city governments provided government-subsidized wholesale warehouses for imported foodstuffs as the solution to inflation.[90]

In the post-Chaco period, union activism in the city expanded tremendously. The urban-based labor federations gave construction workers, cooks, and market vendors renewed impetus to strengthen their unions. At the same time, the political situation at the national level created links between labor federations, and city councils and the national government. The unions included all workers, even those who were low-skilled or unskilled. The unions allied with the FOL and the FOF fought for space on trams, for market stalls, for new market buildings, for public bathrooms, for subsidized prepared foods, and for childcare for market women, and rejected accusations that they engaged in speculation. They also protested against increased fees and taxes and health examinations they deemed invasive and unacceptable. Union activism continued beyond the military socialist period and the Concordancia, and extended into the repressive period just before the 1952 Revolution.

Conclusion

The mutual aid societies and unions of the early twentieth century helped integrate artisans and Aymara indigenous peoples into the fabric of the city. These institutions played a key role in the celebrations that took place in indigenous neighborhoods and helped organize the neighborhoods into craft-based guilds. They brought together Aymara, Quechua, and mestizo craftsmen and tradesmen in mutual aid societies and Catholic lay brotherhoods. The FOL united men and women as it supported *culinarias*, market women, flower sellers, construction workers, carpenters, butchers, and other craft workers who created unions and joined it or the FOF. The FOF became an important federation that organized market women, vendors, Sindicato de Culinarias, and several other groups of women in various crafts. These unions and federations supported each other's strikes, petitions, and activism.

Market women and members of the Sindicato de Culinarias emphasized that they were honest workers who were gainfully employed, but in their oral histories, market women and members of the Sindicato de Culinarias emphasized that although they were honest workers who were gainfully employed, they faced discrimination based on their race and gender. They recalled how other household laborers warned them against speaking Aymara or Quechua in the workplace because that was likely to generate discrimination and mistreatment.[91] The importance of including all domestic laborers regardless of their racial identity or ability to speak Spanish was fundamental in the ethos of the Sindicato de Culinarias. In the FOL and the FOF, women "could speak in Aymara, Spanish, or Quechua; [everyone] is much more apt to speak if she ha[s] the freedom to do it."[92] During their efforts to organize against market fees and identity cards, union members spoke in Aymara, Quechua, and Spanish.

Male and female union members were both workers and indigenous; people who identified as *cholos* or mestizos might speak mainly Aymara or Quechua. The FOF, the FOL, the Sindicato de Constructores y Albañiles, and the Sindicato de Culinarias included men and women who spoke Aymara and Quechua and the artisans whom elites classified as indigenous or *cholo*. The women and men's oral histories suggest gendered responses to the classism and racism that union members experienced. The women in the FOF and the Sindicato de Culinarias welcomed linguistic diversity within the union and at times used that diversity to demonstrate the broad base of support for their activities. The women advocated for food subsidies, better access to food, and childcare for their members, concerns that related to the welfare of their families. They seemed more cognizant of the struggles other laborers faced. They knew, for example, how hard it was for rural *pongos* to advocate for themselves as laborers in elite haciendas and homes. They recognized the difficult plight of ambulant vendors. In contrast, the men tended to focus on the importance of the union and their work identities. They reported that they learned not to wear "indigenous" clothing when entering the Plaza Murillo to avoid police harassment. Despite these gendered differences, women and men worked together and supported each other's activism and strikes. Unions provide one avenue for understanding how popular classes expanded the boundaries of the discourses elites had created. They used their involvement in the *sindicato* to assert their right to public space and their rights as workers, as men and women, and as individuals.

Saavedra's discourse about workers opened up possibilities for them in new ways and made it possible for workers to organize unions and engage in other forms of activism. This discourse was vague and was limited to Saavedra presenting himself as a "revolutionary" leader and an "ally" of the laboring class. In real terms, Saavedra was not willing to extend his "populist" stances beyond these vague statements. It is true that he decreed the eight-hour workday and the six-day workweek, and that his coup, his discourse about workers, and the labor legislation he passed helped initiate the transformation of the political system. Nevertheless, as unions and labor federations challenged Saavedra to support their efforts, Saavedra demonstrated he was more interested in intimidating his opponents than in instituting far-reaching reforms. Workers responded by continuing to organize labor unions and labor federations.

The private sector largely ignored many of Saavedra's proposals. Workers remained unprotected, and when they acted independently, Saavedra repressed the labor movement. Ultimately, the small number of workers organized into labor unions could not hope to gain control of a government that kept the elite minority in power by catering to itself and to a small, middle-class urban sector. Despite these obstacles, unions continued to organize and extend their influence within the city.

The military socialist experiment of the post–Chaco War era was the culmination of earlier processes in the 1920s. It was also a reimagining of Bolivian society along a corporatist model.[93] The military socialists reiterated laws that Saavedra had passed in the 1920s such as the eight-hour workday, the six-day workweek, and restrictions on the labor of women and children. They legalized unions, granted amnesty to deserters, and refused to prosecute members of the military high command for their failures in the conduct of the Chaco War. Amnesty for the military was part of a larger effort to bury the conflict between junior officers and the high command and to avoid discussions of the army's failures in the Chaco War. As Busch became impatient with the slow-moving political apparatus, he used executive orders to push government policies in radical directions. He closed the congress in 1938 and ruled by decree.[94] His actions became increasingly radical. For example, he passed decrees to enforce the mandatory unionization of all sectors of society.[95]

For government officials and other elites, class-based discourse created an artificial division between workers and *indígenas*. They were unwilling to entertain the idea that identities among workers and indigenous people in La Paz were fluid, insisting, instead, on a sharp contrast between rural and urban residents rather than the flexible social, economic, and political relations that actually existed in the city. For reformist political elites, the shift to class-based discourse did not completely erase their belief that race was immutable. Nor did it speed up the slow transformation of *indígenas* into acceptable elements of society in their minds. La Paz's "popular classes" of *indígenas* and mestizos used their occupations to access honor, as the market vendors did by distinguishing themselves from dishonorable individuals such as prostitutes. These residents emphasized their honest labor, their reputation, and their participation in national events and in the collective life of their neighborhoods to demonstrate their status as *Paceños*.

4

Alternative Identities

Negotiated Modernity and the Building of the Indigenous Neighborhoods, 1900–52

Introduction

Bolivia's working-class and ethnic-based activism is often examined in the context of land dispossession and the oppression of rural indigenous people or as part of the history of activism in the mines.[1,2] However, the ways working-class and ethnic migrants to La Paz transformed the city politically, socially, and physically are less well understood. The social, political, and spatial discrimination that migrants faced is the subject of this chapter. One essential aspect of this transformation is an overlooked fact: residents truly built their own neighborhoods by negotiating with the city and national governments for the infrastructure and services they needed.[3] In so doing, they worked with government officials to create what I refer to as a negotiated modernity.

The indigenous neighborhoods were home to recent indigenous migrants from rural areas, migrants from other cities, and mixed-race and socially and economically diverse people born in La Paz.[4] To call them indigenous neighborhoods is somewhat misleading, yet this is the label by which they were known, partly because they were so strongly associated with Bolivia's indigenous populations. Indigenous neighborhoods were the most densely populated in the city. According to census data published just after the Chaco War, nearly 40 percent of the city's 150,000 people lived in Gran Poder, San Pedro, San Francisco, and San Sebastián. By early 1942, nearly 60 percent of the city's 250,000 residents lived in indigenous neighborhoods. By 1950, the city's population had reached 350,000 people and the majority of the people living in indigenous neighborhoods were mixed-race and Aymara. Geographically, these neighborhoods had once been traditional indigenous villages, and many of the migrants (though by no means all) were of an indigenous background.[5] In addition, the activists living in indigenous neighborhoods employed many of same strategies labor activists—many of whom were also indigenous—used in the mines and indigenous activists used in the countryside.

In the twentieth century, Bolivia, like much of Latin America, experimented with liberalism and populism and experienced a nationalist revolution—one of three nations to have such a revolution. Politically, one of the pivotal moments of the century was the Chaco War (1932–5) between Bolivia and Paraguay, which Paraguay won. The social, political, and economic aftermath of the war laid bare the racial discrimination inherent in Bolivian society and drew attention to the possibility of class-based social reforms. After the war, the national discourse on race changed to open a pathway to greater involvement in Bolivian society for indigenous people. This change coincided with the urbanization of La Paz. Residents of indigenous neighborhoods became activists who seized the opportunity to build their neighborhoods as part of the modern Bolivia that political elites envisioned.

Postwar neighborhood associations drew on networks that had been formed before the war. In Villa Potosí, which was originally settled by migrants from Potosí province, the neighborhood association illustrates the evolution of indigenous neighborhoods and the activism of their residents. Justo Román, the president of the association in 1945, recounted how the association grew out of the neighborhood's Catholic lay brotherhood, which coordinated the yearly May 4 celebrations commemorating the Intervention of the Holy Cross. In early 1940, Villa Potosí's residents organized a "true neighborhood association with a new mission to bring progress to the neighborhood."[6] Postwar neighborhood associations, Román said, let the government "know the sad conditions in which the worker lives and [that] he is the true nerve and muscle of the nation."[7] The language Román used linked workers, the "nerve and muscle" of the body politic, with the health and progress of the nation as a whole. Without the workers who lived in the indigenous neighborhoods the nation would not be able to move forward. The muscle and nerves moved neighborhoods forward and brought progress to the city.

In Bolivia, lay religious organizations and craft-based unions were a source of popular urban activism and civic engagement in the first half of the twentieth century. Lay brotherhoods, unions, and neighborhood associations brought together a diverse group of residents who identified variously as indigenous people and as workers. Before the Chaco War, these institutions held meetings, organized petition campaigns, and called strikes to assert the rights of residents, pressure government institutions, and claim membership in the Bolivian nation. These tactics have a long history in Bolivia and remain important tools in the repertoire of politically marginal groups in Bolivia.[8] Even though some historians argue that the Chaco War constituted a major rupture in Bolivia's history, there was great continuity in the organizing work brotherhoods and unions engaged in before and after the war.[9]

After the war, the military social governments, inspired by fascism in Europe, made laws and promulgated decrees that stipulated that corporate institutions be created to represent groups of people before the government. This led to the creation of various bodies. During the military socialist dictatorships of Col. David Toro Ruilova (1936-7) and Col. Germán Busch Becerra (1937-9), neighborhood associations developed the Federación de Juntas Vecinales (Federation of Neighborhood Associations; FEDJUVE) to demand goods and services from the city government.[10] From the late 1930s through the 1950s, FEDJUVE was the umbrella organization that mediated between residents and local and national political structures.[11]

The associations skillfully pushed urban officials to follow through on their stated agenda of making La Paz a modern city. Together, neighborhood activists and urban officials forged what I refer to as a negotiated modernity, one that was negotiated from below by activists who wanted to better their neighborhoods. Government officials had their own reasons for wanting to improve neighborhoods; their desire to create a modern nation and a modern city was rooted in a longer process of building a coherent and unified nation out of Bolivia's diverse population. Their desire to overcome racial divisions, poverty and its associated diseases, and backwardness drove government officials' push for modernization. After the Chaco War, the focus of La Paz's elites shifted from beautification and projects in the city center to a more comprehensive project of creating infrastructure and remodeling the city.

Indigenous neighborhood residents pushed government officials toward this shift with demands for infrastructure and services in their neighborhoods. In the period from 1936 to 1952, urban leaders focused on a holistic plan that saw the city as connected. During this period, municipal elites saw the city as a "living and integral organism." Mayor Muñoz Cornejo argued that the city's housing and its markets "must function in an ordered fashion and should be clean" and that the infrastructure "should be remade and its proper functioning ensured" for the benefit of the entire city.[12] The political importance of indigenous neighborhoods increased because of these goals.

In the post–Chaco War period, military socialist dictators oversaw the professionalization of urban bureaucracies. The military socialist governments and the governments that followed them also made sure that some career public servants at the municipal level stayed in office in La Paz. The longevity of their service helped these men implement urban planning programs that included massive additions to urban infrastructure, such as building roads, providing electricity and potable municipal water, channeling the valley's rivers underground, constructing sewer systems, and building new markets.[13] The city government's postwar modernization project coincided with rapid population growth, including in indigenous neighborhoods.

Racial Discourses and Activism after the Chaco War

In early twentieth-century Latin America, indigenous people's capacity for political participation was undermined by the discourse of racial exclusion. In Guatemala, indigenous peoples were considered legal minors and were required to carry work papers or risk being forced to work in sugar-cane fields in the lowlands.[14] In nineteenth-century Mexico, governments eroded communal landholding rights and marginalized indigenous peoples politically. After the revolution there, the revalorization of Indians focused on the great civilizations of the past (the Aztecs and Mayas) and sought investment in education to prepare the Indian of the present for assimilation into the "cosmic race."[15] Similarly, in Bolivia the discourse of indigenous incapacity and inability was a legacy of nation-state formation in the nineteenth century. Bolivia's creole elites answered questions about indigenous peoples' intellectual and political capacities with empty platitudes of liberal equality that failed to hide the real politics of exclusion and marginalization. In addition to these long-term issues, the 1899 Civil War, in which Bolivia's Liberal Party elites betrayed Aymara allies, helped shape portrayals of indigenous peoples as savages.[16]

While Bolivia's defeat in the Chaco War engendered a fundamental transformation of the nation's political organization and discourse, it is important to acknowledge that those changes were limited.[17] The Chaco War and its memory catalyzed a series of transformations that took place in the period from 1936 to the outbreak of the MNR revolution in 1952. As political and social leaders began to expound the discourses of classism and nationalism, a middle-class movement developed that sought to replace and reorganize Bolivia's political structures in ways that excluded certain elements of the traditional creole political elite.[18] Reformists among Bolivia's political and intellectual elite began to see the structure of the nation's economy and political system as the reason why Paraguay was able to win the war. Their analysis suggested that Bolivia had lost because its political leaders had neglected its indigenous peoples and then sent poorly trained, uneducated Bolivians into a war that slaughtered them. According to this analysis, the blunders of Bolivia's out-of-touch traditional politicians and elites before and during the war had led to defeat.[19] For reformist elites, defeat in the Chaco War was a consequence of Bolivia's racial divide, a direct effect of creole elites' failure to incorporate indigenous peoples into their definition of the nation. In order to address the structural inequality that had fractured the nation, these leaders pushed for an inclusive Bolivian nation.

The reformers' cultivation of new allies helped broker alliances between workers and the middle class and created a platform for the development of mass politics. For instance, the military socialists mandated that unions, occupation-based associations, and federations be created as part of an attempt to reconfigure the makeup of the Congress by giving proportional representation to each corporate body (labor unions, lawyers' associations, doctors' federations, and so on) in the law-making chamber. In La Paz, several craft unions created a labor federation, the number of neighborhood associations increased, and both unions and neighborhood associations cultivated connections and relationships with politicians and government officials. Through these alliances, residents of indigenous neighborhoods (many of whom did not identify as indigenous), military socialists, and reformist politicians reshaped the city's form, politics, and social composition in profound ways. For example, residents contributed labor to several of the new plazas, roads, police stations, and sectional markets the city built. They also worked on electrification projects and helped build a sewer system and canals under the city to channel the valley's rivers. Through this labor, they reshaped the city and its traditional physical divisions. For example, the Choqueyapu River and its twenty bridges, which traditionally divided the city between its Spanish and indigenous halves, could no longer serve as a visual border and marker of social distinction. Residents of indigenous neighborhoods were pivotal in the transformation of La Paz. They participated in the expansion of the city not only as laborers but also as citizens who extracted resources from governments and as activists who negotiated for rights and resources in the city.

New Infrastructure for Neighborhoods

As the Chaco War ended, veterans returned from the front and several thousand rural people migrated to cities.[20] Across Latin America, the factors that influenced rural-to-urban migrations were varied and complex.[21] For example, new opportunities enticed people to Mexico City after the Mexican Revolution.[22] In the 1930s, the hardships of the Great Depression demonstrated to many elites that the countries of Latin America needed to industrialize and decrease their dependence on goods and credit from North America and Europe if they were to protect their populations and their sovereignty. In the aftermath of the First World War and the Great Depression, populist governments throughout the region grappled with the problems of the urban underclass and worked to create more inclusive political structures. In Bolivia, both push and pull factors led to migration to cities. Extensive consolidation of rural land pushed many people out of their homes. Many soldiers who had served in the Chaco War returned home with broadened horizons and a new awareness of the possibilities that lay beyond their rural homes. Government efforts to industrialize also drew people to cities.[23]

Right after the Chaco War, La Paz was on the cusp of becoming a major urban center. Before the war, the city government had spent most of its resources on beautifying the city, rebuilding the Alameda (a major traffic artery but also a boulevard in the city center that served as a place for the elite to see and be seen), developing an electrical grid and tram service in the city center, rebuilding several plazas, and building the national stadium in an agriculture area and suburb called Miraflores. These projects focused on the city center and on the wealthier residential areas of La Paz. However, elites' attempts to divide the city along racial and class lines were not completely successful. Divisions between indigenous and nonindigenous spaces were not as clear as some elites attempted to make them: residents of indigenous neighborhoods worked in the city center and in elite homes throughout the city. While elites typically linked outbreaks of disease and natural calamities such as flooding to the filth and lack of infrastructure in indigenous and *extramuro* neighborhoods, outbreaks of disease were common in many areas of La Paz. In addition, the city's most popular markets were located in indigenous neighborhoods. Clearly, there was much movement between indigenous neighborhoods and the city center and thus many opportunities for diseases to spread throughout the city regardless of where they allegedly originated.

Both national and local government authorities sought to prevent rural-to-urban migration. Urban leaders and politicians considered rural-based migrants to be socially inferior and dangerous additions to the cities they were trying to modernize. The national government even discussed the possibility of imposition of fines and the requirement of internal passports to prevent *indígenas* from moving to cities.[24] The fact that these proposals were not implemented demonstrates that the realignment of Bolivian society after the war was filled with uncertainty.

Bolivia's military socialist national leaders, inspired by European fascism, envisioned modernization as a top-down process led by heads of urbanization councils and technocratic departments that they appointed rather than by elected city council members and political parties. The national government forced La Paz's prefecture and municipality to expend resources to create a modern city in which to live and work.[25] Some of the funding came from the national coffers and loans, but a great majority of it came through bond measures that allowed the government to sell bonds in exchange for capital. For Bolivian elites and government functionaries, "modernity" meant building infrastructure and creating a level of industrialization that resembled that of the cities of the Global North. This push for modern cities coincided with the development of a nationalist discourse that lumped a diverse group of characteristics (rural, urban, mixed-race, and working-class identities) into categories based on class—*campesino* (peasant) and *obrero* (worker). This meant putting aside Bolivia's historical and cultural roots, especially the identities and experiences of indigenous peoples, in order to reframe identity around a racially undifferentiated class identity. This was an idealized vision of a population that did not conform with the reality of the people who lived in the urban centers of Europe or North America.[26]

The modernization discourse in Bolivian cities was not unique in the mid-twentieth century. Romulo Costa Mattos's work on Brazil's shantytowns demonstrates a similar dynamic in which modernity was the metric city officials used to determine the value of working-class housing.[27] Juxtapositions of traditional and modern that led to "othering" of people who did not conform to desired ideals occurred in the capitals of modernity. For example, Parisian officials sought to confine sex workers to the Latin Quarter. London's officials struggled with the visibility of women in public after the First World War.[28] The United States, especially New York City, grappled with the effects of immigration from southern and eastern Europe.[29]

The Latin American context serves as an enlightening comparative frame for understanding how politicians and elites dealt with racially diverse populations. Sarah Chambers examines how indigenous and working-class people laid claim to identities as honorable citizens during the birth of the Peruvian republic. Even though elites believed that honor was a discursive category reserved for themselves, invoking honor became a primary way for lower-class residents to assert their belonging in the republic. The question of honor and political rights continued to structure national belonging in Peru in the twentieth century, but those attributes became components of racial identity. Marisol de la Cadena demonstrates that indigenous peoples in Peru faced a racialization that rejected them as indigenous in the present but valorized Indians in the past. Thus, honor and belonging were wrapped up in questions of racial identity and worth.[30] Similarly, in Mexico, those engaged in nation building valorized the indigenous past and created a fabled Mestizo nation.[31] In contrast, for many Bolivian political and social elites, indigenous identity was an obstacle that was almost insurmountable. Bolivian elites regarded indigenous people as threats to their project of creating a modern city and nation. Neighborhood activists pushed back against the racialized dimensions of the elites' conceptions of them. By participating in the expansion-of-modernity discourse, the supposedly backward *indígenas* defied elites' conceptions of them and were instrumental in negotiating extensions of the city's modern infrastructure.[32]

The Dance of Power

The growth of neighborhood associations was accelerated by the birth of FEDJUVE in 1937 and the influence of the associations increased through the collective power that FEDJUVE represented. The executive boards of neighborhood associations constituted a pool of candidates for FEDJUVE's board, who were elected by the associations.[33] As a power broker between neighborhood associations and governments, FEDJUVE played a key role in negotiated modernity: it enabled neighborhoods to stake their claims to resources. However, the city government also had power. For example, it limited the number of associations to one per neighborhood. It gained even more power during the Concordancia dictatorship (1940–3), when it began to fund FEDJUVE's activities and influence its policies.[34] Despite these dynamics, FEDJUVE was able to negotiate significant gains for the city's indigenous neighborhoods. In the Villa Potosí neighborhood, residents acquired water lines from the city. The municipality approved the plans, supplied an engineer to oversee the work, and provided the materials. In exchange, neighborhood residents provided the labor. The neighborhood association organized the laborers' schedules and expected those who did not provide voluntary service to pay for laborers to take their place.³⁵ Similarly, the Nuevo Potosí neighborhood association offered the government an exchange of labor for the city's provision of waterlines. When this work was complete, the association requested that the city also extend electrical lines, streetlamps, sewer lines, and roads into the neighborhood.³⁶

From the end of the Chaco War to the mid-1940s, neighborhoods continued to grow and the influence of FEDJUVE became more pronounced. But the city also gained in power. For example, the city government could use its power to grant charters to dissolve local associations and could nullify a neighborhood association's elections. In addition, starting from 1946, FEDJUVE's funding came directly from the city. This was a change; before that, the member associations provided funding for the federation. Using funding from the national government, the city government provided a stipend for each neighborhood association that FEDJUVE distributed.³⁷ This centralized channel concentrated a significant amount of power within the federation, even though the associations still controlled how funds were disbursed within their neighborhoods. The benefits of such a system, according to FEDJUVE, was that it incorporated the residents into their neighborhoods by making them stakeholders in neighborhood projects and made the city more responsive to neighborhood needs.³⁸ The city government endorsed the system because it channeled many issues to government officials through one mechanism. FEDJUVE helped the city attain political power and influence in neighborhoods and it helped individual neighborhood associations increase their power in their interactions with the city government and in the neighborhoods. Thus, neighborhood associations and FEDJUVE came to serve as intermediaries and managers in the process of urbanizing the indigenous neighborhoods of La Paz.

Neighborhood associations used their connections to FEDJUVE and the city council to acquire materials and expertise from the city government. The 14th of September Neighborhood Association, for example, pressured the city council to provide an engineer for a project to repave the plazas in its neighborhood.³⁹ It also wrote to the president of FEDJUVE to ask for the federation's "help in acquiring the necessary materials" from the city council.⁴⁰ These efforts were successful: the neighborhood association and the city government rebuilt the Plaza Riosinho and the 14th of September Plaza. Such evidence suggests that neighborhood associations did not relinquish power to FEDJUVE but used it as a vehicle for petitioning and making demands on the city government.

Neighborhood associations frequently engaged with city officials through petitions and requests that the city extend services and infrastructure to their neighborhoods. The La Paz municipality inaugurated water services in many indigenous neighborhoods through a process that involved a copartnership between neighborhood residents, who provided labor, and the city, which provided expertise and materials. During the dedication of the water lines in the Nuevo Potosí neighborhood, Félix Salazar, an association member, referred to the sacrificial and patriotic act the mayor had performed on behalf of the city. He reported that he and his neighbors could see that "the water lines were evidence of [the mayor's] favor."[41] The mayor stated that he was happy to "give" the water lines to neighborhood residents and that prior to his administration the city government had "not once in fifty years ... learned of [the indigenous neighborhoods'] needs." It was the mayor's desire, as it was of all men of the Villarroel revolution (1943–6), to "help ensure the well-being of the working classes that generally live in the 'suburban area.'" Providing clean water, he said, fulfilled a promise to "neighborhoods that were once abandoned, [and] now have sixty water lines."[42] City officials and neighborhood leaders framed the extension of these services as gifts or benevolence brought on by the government's desire to extend progress and modernity to the indigenous neighborhoods. However, the city government "gave" the water lines only after neighborhood associations petitioned for and demanded them. Moreover, "gifts" could be reframed as a quid pro quo for residents' attending political rallies or doing the preparatory work on a project like the water lines at no cost to city government. This exchange had the potential to blunt activism and rein in neighborhood activists with the promise of future "gifts."

It is also evident that neighborhood associations used the same discourse as city officials: they referred to a neighborhood's favored status, to its extensive "needs," to the political "charity" of the city, and to municipal "gifts" in their petitions to acquire improvements. In their petitions, neighborhood associations framed their own goals in language that suited the modernization ideals of these men and the new racial project of the nation as they demanded infrastructure improvements. The speech of each side was carefully coordinated and specially crafted.

The Legacy of La Paz's Catholic Lay Brotherhoods

Many postwar neighborhood associations organically adopted the structure and membership of lay brotherhoods. In fact, in the neighborhoods of Rodríguez and Nuevo Potosí, there was no clear boundary between lay brotherhoods and neighborhood associations. Although the leaders of the lay brotherhoods in these neighborhoods organized labor for religious festivals and the leaders of the neighborhood associations organized labor for secular projects, often these leaders were the same people.[43] In many neighborhoods, associations were the primary social outlet.

Some associations emerged through links with lay brotherhoods and indigenous parishes, which planned, managed, and carried out the rituals for the local saint's day festivals in the La Paz Valley in the early twentieth century. The brotherhoods also maintained the parish by cleaning the church, helping with repairs, improving the grounds of churches, raising funds, and maintaining saints' images and their altars. These brotherhoods, whose members were neighborhood residents and craft union members, provided leadership for neighborhoods and parishes.

Neighborhood associations were formed in relationship to local lay brotherhoods. In some neighborhoods, the neighborhood association arose in opposition to a brotherhood. In other neighborhoods, there was a direct transfer of the leader and members of a brotherhood into a new association. In some places, neighborhood associations were the first civic organizations in the region. Regardless of a neighborhood association's relationship with the local lay brotherhood, these associations developed organically within neighborhoods. They were formed by groups of neighbors who knew each other well and had socialized and worked together in other public settings. They were not imposed by external authorities.

The leadership structure of lay brotherhoods and associations was inspired by Aymara practice. In La Paz, both groups practiced something resembling the cargo system that Aymara communities used to organize saints' day festivals.[44] In that system, the leaders of urban lay brotherhoods were the only members who were active throughout the year; they mobilized other members for collective work only during peak times in the religious calendar.[45] In the twentieth century, part of the task of organizing these festivals was petitioning the city government for the right to carry out public celebrations.[46] Thus, petitioning the government was not an unfamiliar practice to neighborhood residents in the postwar years. By the late 1940s and early 1950s, expanding on tactics they had developed in these festival-related negotiations with the city, lay brotherhoods were claiming an increasingly important role in the social and political life of La Paz. Hence, they grew into more permanent and expansive organizations.

Similarly, residents of indigenous neighborhoods were important leaders in craft guilds and unions. Often, the members of these labor organizations were also members of the same lay brotherhood.[47] For example, in Challapata, the butchers were organized into a guild that participated in a lay brotherhood.[48] Like the lay brotherhoods, craft unions also helped mediate between neighborhood residents and city officials, especially in the efforts of indigenous people to acquire infrastructure and services for their neighborhoods. Unions petitioned the city for services such as water lines, electricity, sewerage, schools, daycare, marketplaces, larger and more conveniently located markets, better housing, and better working conditions for neighborhood residents. The principal leaders in the Nuevo Potosí neighborhood were also active in the anarchist Federación Obrera de La Paz (Workers' Labor Federation).[49] The overlapping memberships of neighborhood associations, unions, and lay brotherhoods facilitated the easy transfer of strategies for laying claim to goods, services, and rights.

Once city authorities officially recognized a neighborhood association, the latter began pressuring the city authorities to participate in making improvements such as housing and schools, markets, roads, water and sewer lines, and electricity. In 1934, as soon as the charter of the Miraflores Neighborhood Association was approved, it requested that the council close several houses where the "shameful practice of clandestine [prostitution] occurred near the major hospital zone."[50] The activism of members of neighborhood associations refutes the characterization of indigenous people as lazy, backward, and disinclined to participate in civil society. As soon as they could, indigenous neighborhood residents formed labor organizations and petitioned the city government to make improvements in their neighborhoods.

Indigenous Citizens

In 1945, even though the city of La Paz was the entity that controlled the extension of the electrical grid, several neighborhoods joined forces and appealed to the national government to provide electricity for them.[51] This tactic was designed to gain external support for their cause and pressure local authorities. Urban officials were often resentful when national authorities involved themselves in local affairs and neighborhood residents could play the two sources of power against each other. The national government provided funding for various construction projects and national ministries solicited bids, reviewed contracts, and paid vendors in the process of constructing the city's water, sewer, and drainage networks, including in indigenous neighborhoods.⁵² The strategy of appealing to national officials drew upon the tactics unions and rural indigenous activists used to gain access to title to land and relief from taxation.⁵³ They had also turned to the national government to serve as an intermediary between indigenous communities and their antagonists in the countryside. Much like the indigenous activists historian Laura Gotkowitz investigates, neighborhood residents and associations petitioned specific politicians and competing institutions to ensure that their demands would be met.⁵⁴ In one petition to the La Paz prefect—whose authority in the case was marginal at best—neighborhood residents asserted their national belonging by stating that they were "*indígenas* and residents" who required the "guarantees and protections" of the indigenous rights laws of 1945.⁵⁵ In another instance, residents played on the concerns of national political elites that indigenous and working-class people were backward by arguing that if the national government were to extend infrastructure to indigenous neighborhoods, it would bring them "progress."⁵⁶

Political battles regularly occurred among residents of indigenous neighborhoods as they competed for control of neighborhood institutions and local power. Despite the fact that these areas were known as indigenous neighborhoods, indigenous people were not their only residents. The populations of many neighborhoods included creoles, mixed-race people, and people who preferred to identify with their profession or craft rather than with racial labels. This diversity was sometimes the cause of conflict. For example, in 1945, a group of "neighbors from Chijini Alto and Chocata" argued that the Los Andes Neighborhood Association had used its influence with the city government to intimidate them.⁵⁷ They stated that the Los Andes association had "carried out all manner of threats as the authorities of that supposed association," which included the attempted "theft of our lands" using the "pretext of opening new streets." The letter writers asserted that the Los Andes Neighborhood Association had carried out plans for urbanization without permission "from the [municipal] authorities in whose name they abuse our condition as peaceful *indígenas* and neighbors" in order to take the homes that the "neighbors of Chijini and Chocata" had acquired through "work and honest sacrifice." As Bolivians, they requested "guarantees [*garantías*] [from the prefect]" and the prefect's "protection [*amparo*] and guarantees in light of the laws protecting the *clase indígena*."⁵⁸

In this case, members of two indigenous neighborhoods asserted their right to protection based on the rights the Bolivian state extended to the "*clase indígena*." According to the military dictator Gualberto Villarroel's May 1945 decrees, indigenous Bolivians would not be subjected to forced labor and to the labor service that wealthy landowners had traditionally demanded from their sharecroppers and laborers. The judicial guarantees the neighborhood residents cited were those the constitution granted all Bolivians plus the extra guarantees they received as result of their indigenous status. The residents of Chijini and Chocata demanded the prefect's protection not just because they were indigenous but also because they were Bolivians and full members of the nation. This letter illustrates strategic deployments of indigenous and Bolivian identities. Their use of the terms "*indígenas* and neighbors" suggests that the residents of Chocata and Chijini conveyed the idea that they were asserting the right to Bolivian as well as indigenous identity.[59]

I argue that neighborhood residents were asserting the right of belonging to the nation through this meaning of the concept of vecino. In the colonial era, that word included the right to belong in urban spaces and the responsibility to help govern the municipality. In effect, it referred to a citizen. Despite the national context, however, residents were asserting the two identities separately because they were members of the nation by definition even as indigenous peoples. The two identities also suggest diversity in the neighborhoods; the indigenous neighborhoods were also home to people who were nonindigenous. Some craftsmen did not identify themselves by race. Thus, the use of both "neighbor" and "*indígena*" is significant for understanding the activism that emerged from within these neighborhoods. Understanding the word "vecinos" as akin to "citizens" shows that residents of indigenous neighborhoods saw themselves as helping the municipality govern those places. As with any system of government, conflicts emerged over who had power in the neighborhoods.

These conflicts were a regular occurrence and demonstrate both the central role the municipality played in deciding the legitimacy of an association and the diversity of people who participated in neighborhood associations. The associations formed after 1938 usually created an executive board structure similar to that of a private corporation and then requested that the municipality recognize their charter. The city government used its power to favor one association over another when it issued charters.[60] For example, in the Chijini neighborhood, two associations vied for official recognition. They fought over which of them was legitimate in the eyes of municipal officials. The historical documents suggest that members of the two associations were members of different racial groups and had different political connections. The Chijini association that claimed it had a right to protection and guarantees from the prefect on the basis of indigeneity did not receive official recognition.[61] The members of the Chijini association that did receive a charter had several connections with the boards of the Gran Poder and Los Andes associations.[62] In that association, the lowest positions of leadership, neighborhood inspectors, seemed to be filled by members with indigenous surnames (Quispe, Nina, Limachi, Huanca, Apaza, and Mamani), and thus the association was nominally indigenous in character.[63] However, the executive board was dominated by members with Spanish surnames (Bedoya, Keiffer, Pozo, Quintín, Meave, Velasco, Villarreal, Mercado, Cáceres, Landaeta, and Sanjines).[64] Unlike its less successful counterpart, this association was able to leverage the creole-identified portions of its board membership to claim a greater degree of legitimacy.

Negotiated Modernity

Members of neighborhood associations had their own definition of modernity that went beyond the provision of basic infrastructure. Activists sought to improve the lives of their children by seeking improved access to recreational activities, green spaces, schools, and electricity in their neighborhoods. Residents argued that the city needed a children's park, sports fields, and camps for children.[65] They appealed to the fears of government elites by arguing that indigenous children needed healthy diversions to prevent idleness and criminality. They argued that building schools would "help their children become members of society."[66] In all of these developments, urbanization was a contested and negotiated process in which local residents used the tools at their disposal, including playing on popular notions of race and class and their status as recent migrants. They strategically manipulated government officials' notions that indigeneity signified backwardness and an absence of modernity.

Neighborhood associations and city officials reshaped the valley's landscape as they reshaped neighborhoods.[67] By 1945, residents in indigenous neighborhoods had improved access to water, improved access to electricity, new roads, several public bathrooms, new schools, and new markets. In their capacity as laborers and union members, neighborhood residents continued to pressure the municipal government for subsidized meals at the markets for workers, and members of anarchist unions sought to organize evening schools for workers and proposed a daycare scheme for working mothers.[68] However, despite the city's apparent concern for the residents in indigenous neighborhoods, it faced resistance from residents over the actions it took while completing infrastructure projects. For example, the population was so dense in indigenous neighborhoods that some residents had built homes on marginal lands behind the La Paz cemetery near a major river. When the city government increased the size of the cemetery, it used eminent domain to level "improperly built houses" along the banks of the river. The occupants who were forced to relocate filed complaints with the prefecture and attempted to sue the city.[69] In another instance, housing inspectors sought to remove tenants from street-facing rooms because of the dangerous state of the building. One tenant, a carpenter by trade, refused to vacate and petitioned the housing department head for relief.[70] The city government, the prefecture, or the national government could also force residents to sell a property for less than the market rate. Urbanization in the indigenous neighborhoods was a continuous negotiation between the needs of individual residents, the goals of the government, and the goals of neighborhood associations.

Government officials in La Paz were willing to improve infrastructure and re-envision indigenous neighborhoods because of their aspirations regarding hygiene and modernity.[71] Dirty neighborhoods with unkempt children wandering the streets with nothing to do did not fit their vision of what a modern city should look like. The improvements the city made required the active participation of the residents of indigenous neighborhoods, who saw the opportunity and pressured the city government to make improvements that benefited their lives. They also provided the labor to make these improvements possible. Ceremonially conceding credit to the city's authorities, neighborhood leaders sought to encourage continued improvements and cement political relationships that they could use to their own advantage and the advantage of their communities. Neighborhood associations played a pivotal role in that negotiated process of reform.

Conclusion: A Negotiated Modernity

Neighborhood associations, in conjunction with unions, shaped the development of the indigenous neighborhoods of La Paz.[72] The associations connected neighborhood residents to the city government and enabled city officials and their national counterparts to extend their reach into neighborhoods. The discourse of modernity and progress shaped how neighborhood associations interacted with and framed their petitions to government officials. By the late 1930s, government elites were responding to the needs of a broader cross-section of La Paz's residents.

In the context of a new racial discourse following the war, elites considered modernity and progress to be important yardsticks for measuring the worth of indigenous neighborhood residents after the war. These concepts had important implications for the social and political developments city officials wanted to see in La Paz. Residents of indigenous neighborhoods exploited the ideas of modernity and progress in the language they used to request goods and services. The associations tended to emphasize how improvements in infrastructure brought them "progress" and exposed their members to modernity. In doing so, neighborhood residents pushed back against prewar perceptions of indigenous people as incompetent. Both indigenous neighborhood residents and government officials pushed their needs and agendas in these interactions. The content of modernity in La Paz was thus part of a negotiation in which both sides had something to gain.

The city government's cultivation of FEDJUVE inserted another layer of administration between city officials and neighborhood associations. The municipality tried to control FEDJUVE's leadership. It also controlled which neighborhood associations could participate in the modernization project in La Paz. However, even though FEDJUVE became an arbiter of power and the channel through which neighborhood associations acquired resources, it was the neighborhood residents' drive to acquire schools, electricity, markets, pavement, water, and sewer connections that pushed the city to respond to their basic needs. Ultimately, the associations went as far beyond basic needs as they could in order to secure a better quality of life for their children.

The evidence presented here illustrates how government actions and discourses continued to mark many indigenous neighborhood residents as different, despite the development of unions and neighborhood associations. The speeches at the dedication of the new water lines in the Nuevo Potosí neighborhood demonstrate that government officials thought in class terms and saw themselves as benevolent benefactors when they provided resources that put basic infrastructure into indigenous neighborhoods. Neighborhood association members sometimes framed their receipt of government resources as acceptance of that benevolence and at other times asserted their right to such resources as *indígenas* and Bolivians. However, neighborhood activists were not content to receive occasional gifts. They continued to seek more improvements for their neighborhoods. Neighborhood associations were successful because they did not overtly advocate the destruction of one class or caste or assert the power of one group of residents over another. The key to the success of the neighborhood organizations was their willingness to adapt to the political context and their ability to frame demands in ways that would elicit government action. Their willingness to adapt to the viewpoints and goals of city officials is what led to their success as the two sides negotiated modernity. For neighborhood residents, modernity meant a better quality of life for their families, particularly their children. Their horizons were much more local than the world stage La Paz city officials were thinking of when they contemplated a modernized city.

5

"Social Worries, Not Legal Theory"

Race, Class, Gender, and Space in the Indigenous Neighborhoods, 1935–6

Introduction

In 1937, Pastor Loza, a milliner who lived on Buenos Aires Street in the Gran Poder indigenous neighborhood, had a disagreement with Felipe Endara, who lived on Tumusla Street in the same neighborhood, over a loan Endara had made to him. Their argument led to a fistfight and both were arrested. Although Loza and Endara supposedly reached an amicable solution, a few months later Loza filed a suit against Endara for failing to respect him and for besmirching his honor. The occupations of the people who testified about the words and blows the men exchanged before the police arrived reveal the types of jobs available to members of La Paz's working classes: market vendor, weaver, electrician, domestic worker, tailor, and porter. The appeal to honor illustrates the vital importance of reputation to indigenous neighborhood residents.[1] Honor and race were central in another incident that happened in May 1942. That month, Andrés Chinahuanca filed a criminal complaint in La Paz Superior Court, accusing the patriarch and sons of the Choquehuanca family of murdering his father. Although the murder had happened in Irpa-Chico, a rural indigenous community in La Paz province, Chinahuanca filed the suit in the city of La Paz because he believed he "would not find justice" in his local township, where the authorities—Chinahuanca claimed—were all relatives of the Choquehuancas.[2] The two families had been enemies due to boundary disputes. After the Chaco War, Andrés had moved to an indigenous neighborhood in La Paz, where he joined the police force. However, he maintained usufruct rights to agricultural lands in Irpa-Chico.[3] Honor and reputation were integral to Andrés's decision to file the case in La Paz, where he was well known as a policeman, and reputation and honor and race became central to the Choquehuancas' arguments regarding their innocence. This chapter builds a portrait of the texture of life in indigenous neighborhoods. It focuses on how economic, social, and political rules and institutions shaped these neighborhoods and how residents interacted with and used these institutions in their social lives in La Paz.

In their interactions with legal institutions, residents emphasized reputation, right behavior, and honor as they asserted their presence and demanded recognition and rights in a rapidly urbanizing city. Any effort to understand La Paz's neighborhoods from the perspective of residents requires creative use of limited sources. Although documents produced by police and the courts tended to privilege elite perspectives, they yield insightful data when one has the context to read them properly.

Court records offer insight into how everyday actors perceived correct behavior and how they chose to justify their actions. Moments of conflict—over space, identity, or behavior—reveal that the process of urbanization was messy and conflictive. In those moments, residents revealed the social glue that kept indigenous neighborhoods functioning and the reasons why that functioning broke down. An arrest record can reveal names, physical characteristics, residence, and occupation of the participants. Although narrative reports differ in the level of access they offer to the voices of the voiceless, they reveal how neighborhood residents interacted with the state and with each other and how they used physical space.[4]

The literature on honor in the Latin American colonial period is extensive and the literature on honor in the national period is growing. For example, in *The Tyranny of Opinion: Honor in the Construction of the Mexican Public Sphere*, historian Pablo Piccato builds on Julian Pitts-Rivers's classic definition of honor in the Mediterranean ("honor is someone's estimation of his own worth, but it is also the acknowledgement of that claim, his excellence recognized by society, his right to pride") by arguing that honor is local and is tied to relations people have in the public sphere.[5] Piccato argues that if nationalism is a collective venture, then honor is the individual's value and worth to the state. Honor helps create the permissible boundaries of public and private and shapes what behaviors are honorable vis-à-vis the collective.[6] Thus, honor is directly related to issues of citizenship, nationalism, urban residency, and claims on public spaces. Piccato notes that as the Mexican state grew, it became more involved in resolving disputes over reputation.

Building on these insights, I argue that in Bolivia, ideas about honor, gender, nationalism, and citizenship shaped the public and private lives of the residents of La Paz's indigenous neighborhoods and that honor was crucially important in a rapidly urbanizing city. In La Paz, honor underwent a broad transformation from a colonial category in which all social groups had different rights and responsibilities in a highly structured social hierarchy to a republican idea in which everyone was supposed to be equal under the law.[7] In the public sphere, honor was invoked in the name of rights and guarantees that had been valid in the colonial period. Honor was a way for the poor residents of La Paz to create a collective identity and a common culture. In other words, honor and reputation constituted social capital in the indigenous and other neighborhoods. Court records from La Paz from the early 1920s through to the 1940s indicate that police and judicial institutions handled more and more cases related to reputation. As the role of the state expanded after the Chaco War, the state became the primary arbiter of social reputation.[8] The importance of honor is evidenced in case after case where residents invoked honor—even when police officers and judges rejected that as proof of a person's pure intentions or legal strategy.[9]

The previous chapters covered the dominant discourses about workers and race. They emphasized the importance elites and state institutions assigned to race and the distinction elites made between workers and Indians. However, in the police and court records, race and class identities affected residents' interactions and shaped their claims to honor, a good reputation, and moral behavior. Poor Paceños used their access to legitimate employment to construct honorable identities; they focused on their occupations and honor without necessarily disavowing their indigenous identity. These records also provide insight into residents' construction of themselves as honorable workers, respectable neighbors, and good *indígenas*. Police and the courts focused on different issues: they often defined people by race and class. These identities influenced the decisions judges made about people's trustworthiness as witnesses and about the validity of their arguments.

The interactions recorded in police and court records illuminate how residents of indigenous neighborhoods legitimated their presence in urban spaces. Court records indicate that neighborhood residents built robust and complex relationships in the city and in the countryside.[10] The political, social, and cultural developments of La Paz were all influenced by these urban and rural connections. Both court and police records illustrate how individuals built identities as urban or rural residents, as indigenous people, as mestizos, and as whites and how they combined these identities with notions of reputation, honor, and moral behavior as a way of creating social and political spaces for themselves in La Paz. These records help us understand how neighborhood residents combined seemingly contradictory notions to build identities and validate their actions. The cases I use in this chapter reveal details about conflict, abuse, and murder in La Paz. At the same time, they also reveal the myriad ways that neighbors made lives in the city, the values that structured their interactions, and the relationships between people who lived in indigenous neighborhoods and those who lived in the countryside.

Discourse and Practice in La Paz's Indigenous Neighborhoods

The residents of La Paz built urban neighborhoods in several overlapping discursive and physical layers. Each of the court cases I examine in this chapter illustrates how social interactions and values linked people to their neighbors, their relatives, and their coworkers. The evidence shows that the facile divisions elites made between indigenous and nonindigenous spaces failed to take into account the actual texture of indigenous neighborhoods, which were complex spaces that housed people of multiple classes and ethnicities. Honor and moral behavior gave residents a common language they could use to establish legitimate urban identities.

Brazil provides points of regional and historiographic comparison that make it possible to create a nuanced picture of race in La Paz and Bolivia. Nation builders in Brazil used the myth of racial democracy to address the supposed intellectual and moral weaknesses of Brazilians of African descent.[11] Brazilian scientists of the late nineteenth and early twentieth centuries assumed that darker individuals were more likely to have been slaves or to have had recent slave ancestors. In the racial thought of these men, darkness was a sign that people of African descent were indolent, and lacked the intelligence and the (white, capitalist) drive of Northern Europeans. Brazilian intellectuals rejected idea that the race could not be improved through education and supported the idea that people could improve through environmental factors. Brodwyn Fischer, who has examined how race, class, and gender intersected in court cases in Brazil, found that although the ideology of racial democracy masked certain elements of race in court records, race still played a role in outcomes and judgments.[12]

In La Paz, some attorneys used race to explain innate character flaws or the role instinct played in the actions of litigants. Attorneys argued that rage had blinded Carlos Monje, a white wealthy merchant, so completely that he had shot a man while defending his family's honor. In another case, an attorney argued that a mixed-race mechanic was so focused on preserving his honor that he could not consider the possibility that he had committed premeditated murder. All he could think about was the fact that the code of honor had forced him to defend his family's name.[13] According to defense attorneys in another case, the indigenous origins of the actors explained and justified kidnapping and murder. Another litigant pointed to his indigenous origins to buttress his claims to honor. While it seems that race was not central in the discourse that took place in courts, it was important to the people who passed through them as plaintiffs and defendants.

The intersections of honor, race, class, and gender were key to the urbanization of La Paz and were important to the residents of La Paz's indigenous neighborhoods. Different combinations of identities influenced perceptions and, thus, outcomes in court cases. Sue Ann Caulfield demonstrates that in Brazil, race shaped how gender and sexuality were perceived in court. She demonstrates that working-class men and women used the category of honor to assert their right to public space.[14] Laura Gotkowitz demonstrates that mixed-race market vendors in Cochabama, Bolivia, asserted that they had made sacrifices for Bolivia and had defended its independence, just as the *heroínas* of the independence era had done. Thus, even though they were not considered white, they were honorable.[15] La Paz court records that focused on honor, calumny, and other constructs related to reputation reveal how ideas about honor shaped race, gender, and class.[16] Even though race rarely made a direct appearance in court documents, it is clear from the content of these sources that it shaped the public and private spheres and played a role in how belonging and citizenship were defined in Bolivia.

Honor and Race, Class, and Gender

Despite the fact that reputation mattered a great deal among neighbors, in their occupations, and within neighborhood institutions, reputation mattered little to judges and police officers. When they saw a poor, indigenous, or mestizo neighborhood resident, they often discounted their testimony. Police and judges routinely considered such people to be inherently suspect. For instance, the judge in the two murder cases cited earlier gave a harsher sentence to one man over another even though both had used handguns to commit violent acts. The defendant in one case, a university-educated factory manager who had business and family ties to rural La Paz, belonged to a different social milieu than the working-class defendant in the other case.[17] The two men lived in the same area of Sopocachi. The working-class defendant was a "respected mechanic" in his neighborhood, but for the judge, his reputation was not a mitigating factor in the way it had been for the university-educated defendant.[18] And although women could claim honorable status as workers, neighbors, and members of labor unions, judges often rejected their testimony based on their marital status (they were dependents and thus legal personhood was defined or attacked differently for women based on their gender).[19]

Court records provide a great deal of information about residents and about the transformation of La Paz in the first half of the twentieth century. They offer data about the marital status, occupation, place of birth, residence, and details about the lives, activities, and work of neighborhood residents.[20] The cases referenced here all took place in Second District Superior Court in La Paz in the transformative period of 1900 to 1956.[21] Few sources have focused on this crucial period. Despite all the changes that took place in these years, it seems that deep-seated discrimination and relatively inflexible social norms were two constant themes.[22] The 171 court cases I examined contained information about personal and economic relationships, connections and conflicts among neighbors, and the movement of people between urban and rural areas. Residents mixed work and leisure, they loaned each other money, they invested together in business ventures, and they provided references for jobs and tools friends needed for their work. They joined each other for drinks in neighborhood *chicherías* and participated together in neighborhood festivals and other events. While these economic and social relationships show how people cooperated, they could also be the source of conflict among neighbors and work colleagues.

Honor and reputation were important to the Paceños who appear in court cases. Their reliance on honor or reputation to justify particular actions was not simply a function of legal discourse. Pablo Piccato argues that honor was a "right to be defended" and that it not only "signified social status, but also reliability, resourcefulness, and loyalty."[23] Poor residents of La Paz fought to have their honor validated: often when they lost a case in a lower court, they filed a claim in a higher court, where they reiterated their claim to honor or an unsoiled reputation even though an earlier judge had rejected such arguments.[24]

In the 1930s and 1940s, La Paz was in a boom cycle that brought capital and people to the city. Rapid urbanization forced people into cramped living quarters, new occupations, and new social settings and surroundings. Residents of La Paz's indigenous neighborhoods belonged in the city and by extension in the nation because their neighbors could attest to their honorable actions and good work ethic. Thus, in this era, urban life was no longer the exclusive privilege of a white elite. Indians and rural folk had flooded in and changed the dynamic of the city and the nation. This dynamic played out in the streets of indigenous neighborhoods and raised new questions: Could Bolivia be modern and Aymara? Could Aymara Indians be honorable?

In several cases, people who identified as workers, *indígenas*, and residents of La Paz argued that their reputations and previous behavior made their criminal actions aberrations rather than patterns of behavior. These statements suggest that ideas about honor, reputation, and moral behavior had real meaning. People believed that adhering to them would affect the outcome of a court trial. Even though some institutions were changing, many remained discriminatory and mobilizing the categories of honor and reputation as indications of a moral nature was one way indigenous people and other neighborhood residents could assert that they were members of larger communities—indeed, of the nation.

Honor

Honor was contested terrain. When Andrés Chinahuanca claimed that he had renounced violence in the court case I mentioned at the beginning of this chapter, he may have been trying to distance himself from the discourses that posited that the Aymara were violent because of the harsh climate they came from. Many whites believed that the Aymara people's environment of origin had a "degenerating" effect on the race.[25] However, Andrés disagreed with such views. He claimed that his service to the nation in the Chaco War had proved his honor, that his neighbors could "vouch for [his] reputation," and that his supervisors could provide "letters of good conduct."[26] He used these claims to establish that his testimony and documents were truthful. He also said that the members of the Irpa-Chico community knew that the Choquehuanca family did not hesitate to "steal, lie, and turn to violence" whenever it suited them.[27] Honor provided a mantle La Paz's residents could use to protect their interests and prove their credibility.

However, some people used the concept of honor to justify violent acts. When Sabelia Monje, a resident of Corocoro in rural La Paz, became pregnant with her boyfriend Armando Méndez's child and thus "dishonored" her family's name, her brother, Carlos Monje, sought out Armando in La Paz to "make things right."[28] Monje lived near the factory where he was a manager, in the indigenous neighborhood of Challapampa, northwest of the city center. Méndez owned two stores, one in rural La Paz and the other in the city. According to Monje, the two lawyers for the case, and a clerk, initial negotiations between the two families had gone well. After a lunch break, Monje and Méndez were waiting in the office of Méndez's lawyer for the lawyers to return. As they were waiting, Méndez decided that he did not want to recognize the child on the way, he refused to issue an apology in the local papers, and he said he would not pay the sum that Monje had demanded. Monje stood up, pulled out a revolver, and shot Méndez three times at point-blank range.[29] In his defense, Monje argued that Méndez had taunted him by saying there was no way of knowing if the child was his because Sabelia "was with many different men." Monje claimed that he was blinded by rage by this disrespect for his family's name and his honor when he killed Méndez.[30]

Monje and Méndez were clearly of a middle-class social status: one managed a factory and the other was a businessman. The judge in this case found that he believed that Monje had committed the violent act as a "crime of passion" and that he had lost control of his faculties in defense of his family's honor. He sent Monje to prison for three years instead of the usual sentence of eight years. The judge cited the defense of the family's honor as the reason for the lenient sentence.[31] Méndez's widow appealed against the conviction, claiming that the sentence had not "followed the precepts of the law." Her attorney argued that Monje's claims to defending the family's honor were "outside the legal framework and constituted social worries and not legal theory," although the prosecution did concede that protection of the family's honor must "nonetheless be respected as [one of the] norms in society."[32] The appeals judge rejected the petition and, instead, ordered San Pedro Prison to release Monje for time he had already served while awaiting the resolution of the case.[33]

While honor was usually considered to be outside the law and judges generally rejected it as a legitimate defense, in Monje's case, the claim that he had acted to protect his family's honor softened the penalty. Monje brought several witnesses who stated that he was the sole provider for his siblings and that he had always put their needs above his own—an honorable action. When Monje's parents died, he took a management job in La Paz and sent money back to the family in the town of Corocoro in provincial La Paz. He visited when he could manage time away from his job. All of the witnesses Monje presented stated that he was honorable (*honrado*) and that he had become "like a father to his brothers and sisters."[34]

Monje cited the multiple ways that he had wanted to handle the situation without resorting to violence. He had tried threatening Méndez's reputation by saying he would go to local newspapers with the story. He had forced him to recognize the child and to negotiate terms of payment. Monje stated that all of these efforts were peaceful, honorable, and reasonable attempts to resolve the issue at hand. His defense hinged upon his efforts to negotiate in an honorable way; his lawyer argued that Monje had not intended to kill Méndez but that passion had overtaken him. The defense brought in an expert witness, a medical doctor, to argue that like all human males, Monje was susceptible to fits of rage that could cloud judgment.[35]

The legal claims of La Paz residents show that honor was also a gendered concept. While both men and women had access to it through reputation and occupation, women's sexuality helped determine if they were "honorable."[36] Sabelia Monje had jeopardized her own marriageability, her family's name, and her family's class status when she became pregnant and her affair was exposed. In La Paz, residents linked women's honor to their sexual practices and their perceived chastity. Neighbors' questioning of the sexual activities of a woman, married or unmarried, directly influenced the perception of her reputation and her honor. Women could "lose" their honor through sexual intercourse.[37] Laura Gotkowitz found that in Cochabamba, honorable status was one way that women made claims on public space.[38] One common way women tried to put a woman "back in her place" was to insult her by saying she was promiscuous and provided favors to local authorities and other people in power. Some of the anxiety that sexually manipulative insults revealed was connected to the belief that only women could use their sexuality to influence politics. In La Paz, these beliefs enabled women (and sometimes men) to question how other women acquired their resources and position in society. Like honor, then, gender contributed to performative identity. How a person looked, what they did for a living, and who people knew them to be in their neighborhood were the bases of that person's identity.

The social currency of an honorable identity gave residents the incentive to invest in it even though it constituted a "social worry" and not a legal principle. Even though claiming an honorable identity did not always compel judges to change the decisions of a lower court, residents of indigenous neighborhoods pointed to their good reputations, their honor, and their moral behavior before the judges. In the Chinahuanca murder case, the Choquehuanca family appealed against their convictions two times, presenting witnesses who stated that the Choquehuancas were known for their honorable behavior and participation in the Irpa-Chico community. The judges in both instances rejected these arguments.[39] In several other cases, "known" thieves, "habitual" criminals, and prisoners pointed to their behavior and their reputation among social superiors, neighbors, and work colleagues to establish their honor and trustworthiness. José Castro, a tailor who was a "known thief," presented a letter from the prison warden about his work as evidence of his moral behavior. During his trial for murder, Domingo Luna presented evidence of his outstanding work record to counter his criminal record. Another resident pointed to his participation in a neighborhood association and his occupation as a mechanic to support his claim that he had shot a man in self-defense.[40]

These notions of honor and reputation could reinforce social hierarchy. For example, the 1955 version of the penal code made striking someone of higher social status, a category that included a person's father or mother and others "with honorable status," in the presence of witnesses a crime that was punishable with a minimum of one year and up to ten years in prison.[41] While this law ostensibly reinforced the social hierarchy, people also challenged the social order, since people of all classes made honor-based claims.

Legal cases show that ideas about honor, status, and reputation remained important in the context of a city undergoing transformation. And even as the city's population was growing rapidly, its neighborhood residents did not experience the anomie and anonymity that was said to characterize many large urban centers. In La Paz, one resident asked his neighbors to testify to his "calm nature and inability to slander others."[42] The Choquehuanca family urged witnesses to attest to their honor and service in the community of Irpa-Chico. When José Rodríguez accidentally killed his son-in-law, he petitioned the court for release from prison, asserting that his honorable status as a shoemaker was endangered because he was unable to work.[43] Ideas about honor were connected to the pride and strength a person derived from his work or from belonging to a union. Bonds based on shared occupations, socializing, economic links, and lay religious celebrations gave La Paz's indigenous neighborhood residents many opportunities to build a reputation that their neighbors, coworkers, and city government politicians and officials acknowledged.[44] These bonds enabled them to make common cause with their neighbors. Religious and neighborhood associations constituted the social glue that bound neighborhoods together.

Race, Class, and Gender

Indigenous identity was malleable, and city residents could and did manipulate their identities to serve their interests. In the case I described at the beginning of the chapter, Pastor Loza presented himself as an "honorable *indígena*" to the court. He claimed that his identity did not detract from his status as an honorable person or his reputation as a competent milliner. His opponent, Felipe Mendoza, was not as sanguine about indigenous identity. He argued that his identity as an honorable indigenous person was unusual and cast indigeneity as generally negative. The strategies these two men used suggest that they worked to shape their identity in order to serve their own needs in court.

This did not mean that judges or courts gave these efforts or ideas credence. The courts relied on the dominant discourse about the backward racial attributes of indigenous people and *cholos*. In the Choquehuanca case, the dominant discourse about indigenous peoples shaped the judge's decision. The judge argued that it was common for indigenous people in Bolivia to kidnap women as a negotiation tactic in arranging marriages. He stated that because this "custom" was part of the indigenous peoples' "culture," his ruling was valid. In many cases, elite jurists used racial discourse to maintain social hierarchy and discriminate against *indígenas*. Given this climate, it is surprising that a few litigants defined themselves as "honorable *indígenas*." This suggests that indigenous identity had some positive currency for *indígenas*.

When litigants used race and class in court to construct their own identities, to lay claims to their honor, or to insult one another, they demonstrated how they lived race and class in their neighborhoods. For neighborhood residents, occupation seems to have been primary in constructing identity. Honest work was crucially important to residents of indigenous neighborhoods because the legal system continued to use anti-mendicancy and vagrancy laws to harass and arrest them. Pastor Loza claimed that his occupation made him honorable despite his indigenous identity. When Octavio Mendoza, an indigenous apprentice painter who lived on Avenida Baptista in an indigenous neighborhood, took a job without his master's approval and the Croc family accused him of theft and had him arrested for stealing, Mendoza claimed that his indigenous identity made him honorable and that he was thus above stealing.[45] However, the Chinahuanca and Choquehuanca murder case, in which the patriarch of the Choquehuanca family kidnapped a daughter of the Chinahuanca family, reveals that the judicial attitude toward indigenous peoples remained discriminatory. The judge ruled in favor of releasing the Choquehuancas (the father and the eldest brother had been jailed for the crime) because the "cultural" traditions of local communities dictated that the people involved be given the license to violate laws that supposedly applied to everyone.

The use of indigenous identity to highlight positive or negative characteristics illuminates how in the 1930s and 1940s in La Paz, race was simply an empty vessel. Indigeneity was relational and contextual. In this society, indigenous and rural identities overlapped. Both rural and urban indigenous peoples also sought to define their own identities in positive ways. Behavior, reputation, and profession all influenced how people defined indigeneity as positive. In addition, education in a trade or profession and literacy also played a role in racial and class definitions. At the same time, middle-class and elite Bolivians deployed a whole series of characteristics that explained the social hierarchy by justifying Bolivian society's inequities as part of the natural order and as the logical outcome of innate biological superiority and history.

The Chinahuanca murder case demonstrates judicial attitudes toward race. The Chinahuanca family filed a complaint against the Choquehuancas for murder because the family patriarch had disappeared. Fidel Chinahuanca was found dead in an abandoned building near his home in rural La Paz province. His son Andrés filed charges in La Paz because he believed that his suit would have more success if the authorities were not from or living in Irpa-Chico. The suit alleged that the Choquehuanca patriarch Humberto had "stolen" Rosa Chinahuanca, the youngest of the Chinahuanca children in order to marry her. In the aftermath, Humberto's eldest son Jose met Rosa's father to negotiate for Rosa's hand in marriage on behalf of his father. At this meeting, Jose Choquehuanca killed Fidel Chinahuanca in an altercation and members of the family helped hide the body in an abandoned building. The Choquehuancas' third appeal convinced the judge to overturn the conviction. According to the judge's decision, it was a custom among the "*clase indígena* and among the *cholada* to steal women and then negotiate their hand in marriage."[46] Therefore, the "theft" of Rosa was a typical and accepted way for *indígenas* and *cholos* to form marriage alliances.[47] The judge's decision relied on the idea that *indígenas* and *cholos* had customs that were primitive and backward. This and other cases reveal how malleable and blurry the lines between *indígenas* and *cholos* were for some elite whites. It is not clear from the text of this case if the judge saw all Aymara Indians who moved to the cities as *cholos* or whether the land and livestock the Choquehuancas had accumulated made them *cholos*. It is also noteworthy that Inocencio, a boy who lived with the family but who was likely a servant, was marked as indigenous in the court records. By contrast, the race of the Choquehuancas was never part of the court records until the third appeal, when the judge suddenly "explained" the problem and the solution by referring to indigenous and *cholo* "customs" as the mitigating factor in the murder.[48]

Judges seem to have weighed social class heavily in their decisions about the validity of litigants' claims. The ruling in the *Méndez v. Monje* murder case is an example of how social class influenced the decision made by a judge. The judge considered Monje's claim to honor to be valid. Monje's witnesses emphasized his role as the family's patriarch and primary breadwinner. Monje's social class, which derived from his education and his position as a manager at a factory, influenced the judge's decision to regard his honor as a mitigating circumstance.[49] The judge did not see the fact that Monje had carried a gun to an arbitration meeting with lawyers as an indication of premeditation. Perhaps he accepted the idea that carrying a gun was a sign of manliness. Monje's racial status is conspicuously absent from all court documents, which suggests that his white racial status was never in doubt.

In another murder case that was decided by the same judge, the defendant's social class did not seem to help his claims to honorable status or his argument that he had acted in self-defense. Gregorio Rentería, who was born in rural Bolivia, had become a clerk in a mining company and had served in the Chaco War. After the war, he had settled in La Paz and established a mechanic's shop. Antonio Moreno had allegedly attacked Gregorio because he felt that Gregorio had besmirched his honor. Moreno had entered Rentería's workshop and tried to strike him. Rentería had avoided the blow, ducked behind the counter, and crawled toward the storage area and workshop behind a partition where he had a loaded gun. Rentería had fired at Moreno three times and hit him twice, once in the chest and once in the torso. In his defense, Rentería claimed that his honor had been questioned when Moreno accused him of sexually harassing his wife. Gregorio Rentería pointed to his participation in a neighborhood association and his occupation as a mechanic to support the argument that his decision to shoot Antonio Moreno was in self-defense and that he was an "honorable mechanic and neighbor."[50] Rentería's social class did not aid his claims to honor. The judge ruled that the murder had been premeditated despite the fact that the case rested on weak circumstantial evidence. The witnesses who lived near the scene of the crime and who attested to Rentería's good behavior and good conduct did not persuade the judge to issue a lenient sentence. Curiously, Rentería's social class seems to have influenced the judge to reject his claim to honorable status; he ruled that "reputation and good conduct" were not "important" factors in the circumstances of the murder.[51] However much defendants tried to shape their own identities in court records, it was the judges who had the most power in this context because they could adjudicate and shape racial, class, and gender discourses as well as discourses about honor and reputation. Although the dominant racial discourse may have exerted a heavy influence in society, actors living their quotidian lives sometimes pushed back against the social hierarchy. While socioeconomic class sometimes enabled actors to use honor as the justification for their behavior, at other times it did not. In some cases, the testimony of neighbors and coworkers in the indigenous neighborhoods convinced judges about the character and identity of a defendant. Thus, actors from all social classes helped build and negotiate questions of honor in urban La Paz in the period from 1936 to 1956.

Urban Spaces

Honor, race, class, and gender have spatial dimensions. The behavior and social interactions of neighborhood residents occurred in tight urban spaces. Artisans and vendors vied for living spaces that faced the street. Alfredo Ríos, a tailor in Sopocachi, had rented two front rooms: one was his tailor's shop where he employed two apprentices and the other was a small store where his neighbors purchased everyday items.[52] A resident of Gran Poder who had rented two rooms put up at a "structurally deficient home" in order to keep his carpentry shop in a central location.[53] In the same neighborhood, a tailor and a carpentry shop operated in the front rooms of one house, while two back rooms on the first floor functioned as storage for a separate business and the second floor of the building was home to several tenants.[54] In the Los Andes neighborhood, the front section of one house was a convenience store, the back rooms functioned as a leather shop, and the second floor consisted of residential rentals. The owner of the house lived a few blocks away.[55] In several sections of the indigenous neighborhoods, bars, *chicherías*, *tambos*, houses of prostitution, and gambling houses coexisted alongside markets and convenience stores. Thus, indigenous neighborhoods were mixed-use localities and it was not uncommon for residents to mix in their workplaces and entertainment venues.

The internal architecture of urban structures constituted an additional layer in the social and physical composition of neighborhoods: common patios and courtyards were spaces where people exchanged gossip, children played, and conflicts played out. In 1938, tenants at the house of Alfredo Ríos's mother-in-law chased him away after they discovered him trying to break in.[56] The response of the tenants suggests that they were familiar with his behavior, and, in fact, Ríos had a bad reputation.[57] His neighbors testified that he had "abused" women from the neighborhood.[58] One day, Raquel Barragán, Ríos's neighbor, looked out of her window because she heard screaming. She assumed that Ríos was beating his wife again, but it turned out that he had pushed a *cholita* out of his tailor's shop. Raquel Barragán stated that Ríos was "known" (*conocido*) to be a rapist of minors.[59] Barragán also claimed that Ríos and his wife fought regularly in public in view of the whole neighborhood.[60]

Yet court records suggest that Ríos was also an integral part of the neighborhood. Several neighbors testified that they regularly purchased items from him and employed him to mend clothes for them. Ríos presented witnesses who testified that he was an honest tailor and a hardworking man.[61] His attorney used the ability to examine and cross-examine witnesses to argue that Ríos was always respectful and that he was known as a well-mannered ("*educado y lleno de gentileza*") person and was not involved in criminal activity. Ríos asked his character witnesses to "attest whether or not I have conducted myself, my work, and my shop with respect and honor."[62] However, his witnesses could not attest that he was honorable. They avoided answering questions about his treatment of women and limited their testimony to his work ethic and his reputation as a tailor.[63] Ríos's attempt to claim honorable status through the testimony of his neighbor-witnesses suggests that he thought work-based honor would shield him from accusations of vandalism and assault. Ríos's claims to honor did not save him; he was found guilty and sentenced to three years in San Pedro Prison and three years of exile from the city, with the sentences to be served consecutively.[64] His own witnesses' avoidance of questions that focused on his personal behavior is fascinating. The unwillingness of his neighbors to answer direct questions about those topics suggests that honor was negotiated.

Neighbors intervened in internal family dynamics when they deemed it necessary to curb abuses.[65] A recent migrant to the indigenous neighborhoods named Domingo Luna was known to enjoy his "cups of *chicha* [corn beer]." According to police reports, his landlord and neighbors testified that Luna liked to drink and that he was employed as a porter. In 1946, Domingo was arrested for murder. The arrest file stated that he was originally from Challapata in rural La Paz province and that he was an "*indígena*" with "precarious residence in [La Paz]." Domingo Luna's son, Félix, worked for several neighborhood businesses. He delivered meat for the neighborhood butcher, collected money on behalf of the milkman, and worked as a shoeshine boy.[66] According to another witness, Félix had "been misbehaving" since his mother's death, which had happened several months before Félix and Domingo moved to the Cemetery District.[67] In a previous transgression, Félix had stolen money from a local milkman and disappeared for over two weeks. Félix had good reasons to hide from his father, Domingo, who beat him regularly.

Domingo's neighbors had grown "accustomed to intervening when the beatings [of Félix Luna] had gone too far."[68] One night, Domingo, "obviously dizzy from *chicha*," came home and asked his landlady if Félix had finished trimming the garden hedges around their house.[69] She told him that Félix had not completed the chore. An angry Domingo went to his room and soon she could hear Félix crying and begging Domingo to stop hitting him. The crying eventually ceased, and neighbors assumed that Domingo had passed out and that everything would be fine in the morning.[70] In fact, Domingo had killed his son. He tried to cover up his crime by taking Félix's body to the Choqueyapu River.[71] This case demonstrates other more mundane aspects of daily life in La Paz. Domingo Luna worked as a porter at the central station, his son worked odd jobs in order to help the family, and the neighbors knew him well. His misbehavior, several witnesses explained, was only because he "missed his mother," and they felt that his father knew only "one way to correct the boy." Domingo had migrated from the countryside with the boy after the mother's death. According to the neighbors' testimony, they knew enough of Domingo's behavior patterns to know how he would react to Félix's failure to finish gardening and that his drinking influenced the excessive discipline that had forced them to intervene on previous occasions. The Lunas' case demonstrates how neighbors' had intimate knowledge about each other. Yet, it is also clear that as new neighbors, the Lunas were not yet fully integrated into the urban fabric; the police report described Luna as having "precarious" residence in the city.[72]

On the streets of La Paz, Paceños engaged in various activities that centered on neighborhood life. Activities such as drinking, gambling, gossiping, shopping, and participating in religious and civic celebrations were integral parts of life, as were protests, fighting, and interventions by police and other officials. When residents' celebrations turned to fights, the police and the courts quickly became involved in minor and major disputes. Residents of La Paz's indigenous neighborhoods were no strangers to police stations and courts. They mobilized tried and tested strategies in Bolivian history when they appealed to judges, police, and local politicians: drafting petitions, writing letters, and participating in lawsuits.[73] These are similar to the strategies rural people used when they sought legal protections and justice. These strategies bridged the nineteenth and twentieth centuries.[74] Indigenous communities petitioned for the return of communal lands by using colonial documents and early national-period taxation records, and by filing lawsuits as individuals or as communities. The

Cacique Apoderado movement is one major example of this kind of activism. The strategy is reminiscent of the indigenous neighborhoods' residents who described themselves as "*indígenas* and residents" and who took recourse to the "guarantees and protections" of the indigenous rights laws of 1945. As historian Rossana Barragán shows, social and political elites and officials of the Bolivian government often read these strategies as duplicitous.[75] Nevertheless, residents used the courts to challenge social superiors and fight perceived injustices.

Conflicts over space were common in La Paz. Residents of San Pedro regularly witnessed two neighborhood women clashing over a prime corner for selling small-ticket items.[76] Residents and vendors of Gran Poder feared police patrols and regularly accused police officers of abuses and mistreatment.[77] Informal vendors often worked together and helped each other when police threatened to confiscate their goods or fine them for violations of health laws.[78] These were just some of the everyday conflicts over space and the right to that space.[79]

Elite discourses about racial and class uniformity in La Paz's indigenous neighborhoods contrast sharply with the evidence presented here. Residents' uses of urban space point to socially mixed areas. Indigenous neighborhoods housed racially diverse peoples who were engaged in many different occupations. Socially marginal residents had few resources to draw upon beyond their word and their work to demonstrate their value in society, and they used both in the courts. Residents wove together narratives that included reputation, honorable behavior, and work. Moreover, conflicts over the right to public space show the implicit values residents held and deployed strategically and the boundaries of acceptable behavior. The testimony of neighbors often revealed the complex nature of the relationships and conflicts among family members, neighbors, and coworkers.

Rural and Urban Connections

While drinking brought conflict to the fore and violence erupted during even minor disagreements in these court cases, efforts to find justice or punish neighbors reveal the deep roots of rural and urban socioeconomic networks. Some families settled in the city in stream migration patterns, in which one family member served as an anchor and others followed. Some men had come to the city after the Chaco War, while some families lived in rural areas close to the city where they worked. Sometimes women came to the city in search of work or to escape from conditions back home.[80]

The networks of some residents included family, friends, and neighbors in both the city and the countryside. Some migrants to the city also continued to earn part of their livelihood from rural businesses or lands. Andrés Chinahuanca, a former police officer and factory worker, held lands in his native community and lived in La Paz. He continued to have access to land in the community of Irpa-Chico that his father, mother, and sister continued to work in his name. Members of the Choquehuanca family had provisional liberty (bail) while in the city for over three years, as they battled the case against them. They had enough property to pay the required bail and they had reputable contacts in La Paz who vouched for their continued attendance at trial. They converted livestock they owned to cash in order to pay their lawyers.[81]

The case of the Choquehuanca family illustrates that the division between rural and urban was more complex than many white elites were willing to acknowledge. Elites tended to minimize difference and categorize everyone living in La Paz's indigenous neighborhoods as indigenous. After the Chaco War, they referred to all residents as the "popular" class. Court discourse was a different matter. The classical liberal ideal of equality perhaps explains why court records might have avoided labeling persons by race and why one must read against the grain to parse the racial identities of individuals.[82] Uncovering the perspective of neighborhood residents by reading for their voices helps us understand how residents saw themselves and each other.

Conclusions: Social Relations, Race, and Reputation in La Paz

Court cases reflect many of the changes in La Paz that developed in the aftermath of the Chaco War: increasingly crowded conditions, housing shortages, crime and conflict, unpredictable police responses, and cohesive internal neighborhood organizations. While these records focus on crime, they also reveal that the ideas elites propagated about indigenous neighborhoods as disorganized dens of disease, crime, and chaos were inaccurate. Such attitudes reflect the outsider position of the writers, speakers, and government officials who promulgated race-based theories.

What we know about life in La Paz after the Chaco War demonstrates that residents did not conceive of their spaces as disorganized dens of iniquity, nor did they see themselves as criminals. Honor and reputation connected urban residents to their neighbors and coworkers and legitimated their presence in public spaces. Urban spaces shaped residents' interactions and the development of urban identities. Court records reveal how residents interacted and engaged with the officers of the court and the social values that shaped their lives. In the city of La Paz, both trivial and substantial issues involved honor, moral behavior, and reputation.

During the first half of the twentieth century, La Paz's urban neighborhoods were vibrant, evolving communities that were sites of activism, migration, conflict, and cooperation. La Paz's indigenous neighborhoods were also economically and socially diverse, despite the fact that elite and middle-class jurists, officials, intellectuals, and political activists homogenized their residents as "popular classes" and their spaces as "indigenous neighborhoods." Examining the spaces where people lived and how these spaces influenced social interactions enables us to understand how people became politically active and to investigate how residents' social identities shaped urban spaces. The residents who settled in the indigenous neighborhoods knew each other intimately and they earned their livelihoods, socialized, and fought over real and perceived slights in their neighborhoods. Neighbors were knowledgeable about each other's behavior and reputations in the city's streets and public spaces. Despite their crowded living conditions and ethnic diversity, residents built cohesive neighborhoods.

La Paz's indigenous neighborhood residents transformed the culture, infrastructure, geographical spread, and heterogeneity of La Paz. They used the police and the courts in their efforts to legitimate their claims to space and social acceptance in the city. The evidence in court records of neighborhood networks, conflicts, and socialization reveal how new migrants and native residents negotiated the process of integrating into the life of the city.

The evidence examined here also suggests that the relationships neighborhood residents built between the city and the countryside were complex. The boundary that elite theorists constructed between urban and rural was simply inaccurate. The networks migrants cultivated with rural friends and family complicate the elite notion that rural signified indigenous and urban signified white or *cholo*. The social, economic, and political relationships between urban and rural residents were central to how La Paz urbanized in the first half of the twentieth century. In a very real sense, the economic and social resources rural families had built subsidized the urbanization of the city.

La Paz's neighborhoods were tight-knit communities where space shaped peoples' interactions. The records illustrate how knowledgeable neighbors were about each other's behavior and how this knowledge determined how people constructed public social identities. In addition, residents were well acquainted with government institutions and used them to adjudicate disputes and resolve conflict in neighborhoods. Information about residents' social interactions, alcohol consumption, fighting, work, theft, and market exchanges reveals how they built cohesive lives in the city. These records also reveal the limits of unacceptable behavior and the values that residents prized in their neighbors. They help us understand how neighborhood residents combined seemingly contradictory notions to build identities and to derive legitimacy from their actions.

6

Race, Class, and Political Power

Urban La Paz before and after the Chaco War, 1900–52

At "a proletarian parliament of the most extreme transcendence" that took place in August 1938, the female market vendors of La Paz discussed the sacrifices they had made for the nation and their right to earn a living. The women at this workers' congress spoke Aymara, Quechua, and Spanish. One demanded to know: "Are we not Bolivian? We are not Chinese or Turks. Have our husbands and children not burst like toads in the Chaco [war] and now they want to take the bread from our mouths too? Why should it be a shame for the poor to [be] sell[ing goods] on the city's streets?"[1] These women linked their labor and their status as Bolivians to argue that they had the right to work in an honorable fashion and earn a living wage.[2]

The market vendors' statement demonstrates the complex interplay between notions of race, class, and gender in urban La Paz. Their claims on the state occurred in the context of the social and political transformation that took place after the Chaco War. Before the war, the Liberal and Conservative parties and a small group of elite politicians dominated Bolivia's politics. These politicians rotated between municipal, congressional, and executive government positions, depending on the party in power and the various favors these politicians owed each other. The parties closely guarded their power and the vast majority of the population remained disenfranchised. Suffrage did not expand significantly until after the 1952 Revolution. Historian Herbert Klein estimates that there were only about 10,000 voters in a nation of two million in the late 1920s.[3] In 1926, after several mobilizations and demonstrations, the city's master artisans gained the right to vote. Even this concession was highly restrictive; the ordinance included only those who owned their own shops.[4] Historian Pilar Mendieta suggests that before the extension of universal suffrage in 1954, about

7 percent of the population was eligible to vote; after the expansion of suffrage, almost one in three Bolivians could vote.[5] Elites' poor conduct of the Chaco War discredited traditional politicians and their parties and paved the way for transformations in workers' activism, their role in Bolivian politics, and in their role in the urbanization of La Paz.

The evidence presented in this chapter suggests that many post–Chaco War reformers were active in politics before the war. This is yet another reason to see the Chaco War as a moment that laid bare Bolivia's racism and inequality for elite and middle-class reformers, but it was not some wholesale transformation of Bolivian society. Some politicians, like Juan Bautista Saavedra, reinvented their political personas and political discourse to fit the postwar context. All of the main founders of the MNR were active in government before the war. Víctor Paz Estenssoro, an influential leader of the MNR, served several presidents, the military socialists, and the military dictators of the 1940s.[6] Moreover, pre–Chaco War politicians drafted and implemented some of the reforms associated with the military socialists, long before the advent of their populist programs. Many of these initiatives had emerged in the 1920s under Bautista Saavedra. When the military socialists (1936–39) were in power, they redeployed the same labor reforms because they believed they would help Bolivia modernize. The military socialists' efforts gave the residents of La Paz's indigenous neighborhoods another basis for organizing and strengthening their labor unions.

The Chaco War shaped Bolivian collective memory of the Liberal period (1900–20), of the 1920s, and of the military socialist populism of the late 1930s. It also shaped how Bolivians remembered and wrote about the military socialists and the Villarroel dictatorship (1943–6), and it was seen as a natural transition point that was necessary for the success of the 1952 Revolution. In the history and historiography of Bolivia, the Chaco War marked the transition from a society organized around race to one *seemingly* organized around class. The history of the urbanization of La Paz illustrates how that apparent transition from race to class occurred, how race and ethnicity continued to matter even though they were submerged in official discourses, and how the people who settled in the city helped shape urban and rural political activism. It also helps us understand the continuities in politics and policies before and after the Chaco War.

Much of the earlier scholarship on the post-Chaco period reproduces the MNR's mythology of its origins and historical genesis.[7] The roots of these middle-class reformers' political evolution lie in the elites' disastrous conduct of the Chaco War, and this historical analysis has colonized subsequent historical scholarship.[8] This history posits that urban-based reformers provided the impetus for reforms and paved the way for revolution and relegates rural-based and working-class movements to a supporting role in the awakening of political elites.

More recently, historians have begun to analyze other important aspects of the first half of the twentieth century such as the role of the military in social and political life; the role of land reform in Bolivia; gender, sexuality, and reproduction in Bolivia; and the history of medicine. This recent turn in the historiography reframes the political participation of indigenous people and pressure from below as central to Bolivia's political and social history.[9] Some of this literature argues that the revolution was a longer process that had antecedents in the nineteenth century. These scholars argue that the pre-revolutionary era was the product of longer processes of organization and legal challenges that indigenous peoples pursued to push the government to return communal lands expropriated in the nineteenth century.[10] The more recent scholarship—of which my work is a part—reassesses the influence of popular actors on twentieth-century Bolivian politics. My work approaches the history in a similar manner: I respect the militancy of activist Aymara scholars and the importance of battling the colonialist nature of the Bolivian state. However, an overemphasis on the colonial tendencies of the Bolivian state tends to lead to a reductionist understanding of the interactions between the state and Bolivian people of all social groups.[11]

One scholarly current seeks to revalorize the contributions of indigenous people to Bolivian history.[12] Other scholars writing in this vein raise valid critiques of the Bolivian state and seek to discover and valorize the experiences and contributions of indigenous people to the politics of the nineteenth and twentieth centuries. Silvia Rivera Cusicanqui, for example, argues that indigenous people who engaged with the projects of the Bolivian state had a larger vision of what they could achieve in terms of political power and autonomy than the vision of political elites.[13] Roberto Choque demonstrates the importance of education as an extension of the colonial project and the efforts of indigenous people to articulate alternate visions of citizenship and national participation through education. In a similar vein, Esteban Ticona highlights Aymara separateness and a different history of the Aymara people than the dominant models of the historiography offer. Ticona shows how Leandro Condori Chura, a scribe of the *caciques apoderados*, participated in the efforts to regain lost communal lands by pursuing colonial land titles, petitions, and lawsuits in the early twentieth century. Through his work as a representative of indigenous community interests, he also formed part of the growing number of urban and rural activists that emerged in the twentieth century. He wrote many petitions for indigenous activists, worked as an educator, and participated in strategy meetings with other *caciques apoderados* and other rural-based movements.[14] These works are part of a larger political project to preserve indigenous history and knowledge.[15] This book expands upon these lines of inquiry by analyzing the urbanization of La Paz's indigenous neighborhoods and the political participation of neighborhood residents in the first half of the twentieth century.

This chapter contributes to this revision of historiography by advocating for a more nuanced vision of the Chaco War and its effects.[16] It is true that the Chaco War represents a break in the history of Bolivia. The war caused dislocation and drove migration to La Paz. After the war, many ex-combatants left their homes in rural Bolivia and settled in the north and west of the city, the areas known as the indigenous neighborhoods. However, some things did not change after the war. Racial discourse and the indigenous racial identity continued to structure postwar nation-building projects. In addition, discrimination was a continuous theme before and after the Chaco War.

Aymara indigenous migrants shaped the urbanization of La Paz. They settled in, built, and expanded indigenous neighborhoods. Anthropologist David Guss argues that "within 30 years [1900–30] the population tripled. It was becoming an Indian city once again with most of its new inhabitants monolingual Aymaras from the altiplano."[17] This process began before the war; in 1929, the city was home to 100,000 people; by 1948, the population had exploded to over 350,000. The claims residents of indigenous neighborhoods made that they were "*indígenas*," "neighbors" and "Bolivians" were problematic throughout the first half of the twentieth century because elites consistently rejected the idea that indigenous and mixed-race people were capable of functioning as full citizens and members of the nation. According to Bolivian elites and local and national politicians, the people living and settling in the indigenous neighborhoods were not citizens and were not part of the city and their invasion of La Paz was something the local and national government had to manage and control. The manner of that management changed over the course of the twentieth century, a process that people living in indigenous neighborhoods influenced.

The changes in Bolivian politics after the Chaco War and the expansion of the city's population empowered activists in La Paz. They took advantage of the freedom the military socialists, the elite-oriented Concordancia (1940–3), and the reformist dictatorship of Gualberto Villarroel gave parties, unions, and associations to organize and agitate for labor reforms and improvements to the city's indigenous neighborhoods. Unions organized and became more active in the 1920s through to the 1940s; union members were often also active in the neighborhoods, and this, in turn, enabled residents of indigenous neighborhoods to organize associations. By the late 1940s, these associations were pressuring the city government to make improvements in their infrastructure and to consider these neighborhoods—long considered marginal and outside the city—as part of La Paz proper.

Scholars have determined that the migration after the Chaco War was largely Aymara but that some Quechua-speaking peoples also migrated and that the majority of the initial migrations were enlisted soldiers and their families and those most affected by the Chaco War.[18] The sources on the migration from the provinces are vague.[19] Although the 1942 urban census provides some data about the place of birth of city residents, it did not record where people had lived before they migrated to the city. This is significant, since that census revealed that at least 40 percent of the people living in La Paz had been born outside the city.[20] Moreover, the census made no mention of rural or urban migration patterns. Evidence from court records and police files reveals that many migrants came from rural areas and that the majority were from the highland regions of Bolivia. In part, our lack of knowledge about where migrants came from is the result of the fact that the city and national governments conducted censuses in 1929 and 1942 and thus did not capture the migrations that took place during and just after the Chaco War. That is why migration and urbanization—key processes of transformation---—are auxiliary in explanations of this period. Even though the explanatory power of these quantitative sources is somewhat limited, this book analyzes the importance that migrants and other popular actors had on politics, urbanization, and reform movements in the first half of the twentieth century in Bolivia.

The dispossession of indigenous communal lands in the period from 1880 to 1920 coincided with broader transnational debates about the effects and ostensible immutability of race and the obstacles that indigenous peoples posed to the nations of Latin America.[21] In Bolivia, the period of the heaviest attacks on communal lands coincided with the legitimation of racial science, social Darwinism, and eugenics in the 1870s through to the 1890s.[22] This was also the time when liberal economic thought pervaded Bolivia's national politics. The Liberals sought to turn communal lands into individually held plots, turn indigenous people into smallholders, and reduce the power of collective indigenous identities. Racial discourses and Liberal economics hardened the social division between whites, mestizos, and indígenas and made including indigenous people as full members of the nation difficult.[23] In the early twentieth century, the label "indigenous" placed rural and urban Bolivians on the lowest rung of the social ladder.[24]

Even though race was a central social category of difference before the Chaco War, the historical terminology that shaped discussions of indigenous people in La Paz is problematic.[25] In the twentieth century, elites did not maintain a consistent distinction between *indio* and *indígena* and sometimes used them interchangeably. In addition, elite writers reduced the diversity of the indigenous population to a single male archetype when they discussed indigenous peoples. As Laura Gotkowitz has argued, in the context of early twentieth-century Bolivia, "elite politicians and intellectuals . . . imbued the term 'Indian' with notions of poverty, ignorance, or savagery and . . . intrinsic inferiority."[26] Gotkowitz also shows how elites also referred to indigenous people as *colonos, comunarios, indígenas, raza indígena*, and *campesinos*.[27] Thus, we must carefully analyze these categories.

The content of these racial definitions also changed over time. The development of the intermediate categories of mestizo and *cholo* originated in colonial-era castes.[28] The mestizo identity was theoretically an intermediate category between the Bolivian *criollo* (white) elite and the category of *indio*. As Rossana Barragán has argued, the mestizo identity served different purposes at different times. The 1880 census of La Paz included mestizos and whites in the same category to increase the proportion of nonindigenous peoples in the city. By the time of the 1902 census of Bolivia, the category of mestizo was separate from the category of white. The 1929 census of La Paz also distinguished between mestizo and white; by that time the number of mestizos in Bolivia had increased. In addition, Paceño intellectuals shaped the content of these categories in confusing and unique ways. Rigoberto Paredes, for example, posited a noticeable difference in behavior between whites and mestizo, arguing that the offspring of a white person and an indigenous person would "retain the negative traits of each race." He also argued that a *cholo* was an *indígena* who lived in the city and took advantage of "his own kind."[29] Other intellectuals differentiated between *cholos* and mestizos using various class-based mechanisms to create differences. The distinctions elites made between whites and mestizos and mestizos and *cholos* were often made for politically expedient reasons, as the example of the 1880 census demonstrates. The mutability of these categories demonstrates the contextual and relational nature of race and the supposed innate characteristics associated with race.

Popular usage of the labels *indígena* and *cholo* during the period under examination demonstrate that non-elite actors both worked within the confines of elite discourse and expanded it. Indigenous neighborhood residents did not automatically associate negative attributes with indigenous identity and used the term *cholo* in both negative and positive ways.[30]

Elite individuals and government officials used the term "popular classes" to describe residents and spaces of indigenous neighborhoods, further muddling the distinctions between the labels mestizo and *cholo*. In particular, "popular classes" was widely used in reports about the physical appearance and hygienic state of La Paz's indigenous neighborhoods, markets, and the city's streets from the 1920s onward.[31] For example, one publication reported that the city government "distributed mutton, fuel, and coal for the benefit of popular classes in the neighborhoods of Chijini, San Pedro, and the Chocata."[32] In another example, the same publication reported that the city's police fined the owners of "popular-class markets for dirty stalls and price speculation."[33] In justifying its investment in the Rodríguez Street sectional market, the La Paz city government argued that "[the market] sits at the intersection of three popular-class neighborhoods, the Chocata, the Nueva Paz, and Chijini."[34] The city also sought to expand funding for the "popular cafeterias" that existed in three sectional markets in 1943 and provided "a humanitarian and efficient service to the poor population of the city." The feeling was that these cafeterias should be established in the "other densely populated popular-class neighborhoods such as 14 September, Churubamba, Villa Victoria, Avenida Buenos Aires, some areas of Obrajes, Cemetery district, Tembladerani, Caiconi, and Alto de La Paz (meant to service the traveling *indígenas* of the provinces)."[35] In 1946, government officials noted that "popular-class housing is a huge problem that needs resolution in the city."[36] The "older neighborhoods in the city were full of dark, unhealthy alleyways; [and] an infinity of properties that exist in ruinous conditions." However, those properties could become "good, popular-class housing" if the city were to create "new housing in the old neighborhoods and destroy those things that are not modern and useful for the city."[37] In the first half of the twentieth century, elites used the label "popular class" as a means of erasing racial and class markers. It also seemed to have been a shorthand way to mark lower economic and social status.

Urban Growth, Urban Planning, and Municipal Government Expansion

From 1900 to 1930, migration to the neighborhoods of La Paz west of Plaza Murillo expanded the geographical area elites defined as indigenous neighborhoods. The areas of most growth were Challapampa near the rail station and Sopocachi in the southwest.[38] Challapampa, Pura Pura, and Achachicala were the site of the city's industrial zones. San Francisco, Santa Barbara, and San Sebastián came to house many workshops, markets, *tambos*, and warehouses of the city.[39] In San Pedro and San Francisco, residents built workshops, small stores, and larger commercial enterprises. They worked in several light industries that produced matches, cigarettes, condiments, and textiles, and in a bottling plant and artisan workshops. Elites lived in Sopocachi, on the Alameda (El Prado), in San Jorge south and west of the city center and, later, farther south, and in Miraflores. The Plaza Murillo and central La Paz housed the city's most important department stores, government buildings, convents, churches, and elite housing.[40] San Francisco, the main indigenous *reduccion*, had a large church and a plaza. It was located close to the Plaza Alonso de Mendoza, the first Spanish settlement in the valley, and was home to a monastery, a convent, markets, and artisans.[41] During this period, migrants settled in parts of Gran Poder, Sopocachi (southwest), north of Plaza Murillo, and in the south, San Jorge and Obrajes. The Alto de San Francisco north and west of the cathedral (later called Gran Poder) was the location of several *tambos*. The Garita de Lima was an important geographic and social nexus in the heart of the indigenous neighborhoods; it contained several *tambos*, small shops, artisan workshops, and housing. It was also a central node for all the major rail lines in the area.

From 1900 to 1925, the government of La Paz and the national government invested in the infrastructure of the city center. As the city and national governments prepared for the centennial celebration of the nation's independence, they invested in the infrastructure of the central district. The city government used contract labor gangs, prison labor, and forced labor to complete buildings, statues, sidewalks, electrical lines, and tramlines. The railway station that connected La Paz and Guaqui was completed in 1920. The Soligno, Forno, and Said textile factories were built in Challapampa, and the city and national governments paved roads and extended electricity to the area.[42] In Miraflores, the national government completed two civilian hospitals in 1925. The municipality, the prefecture, and the national government improved water and sewage lines and built floodwalls along rivers.[43] The city also built a small workers' neighborhood in Challapampa near the rail terminals.[44] In 1930, the city government connected the indigenous neighborhoods, the Garita de Lima, and the railway stations by completing Buenos Aires Avenue, which crossed all of the indigenous neighborhoods and connected Sopocachi to Challapampa without crossing the center of the town.[45]

In the 1920s, labor unions began to recruit workers in La Paz's principal industries, government ministries, and artisanal crafts. At the time, there was no national labor federation, but regional and local federations were popping up in the principal cities. Efforts to organize miners also occurred at this time.[46] In the 1920s, President Juan Bautista Saavedra (1920–5) employed a vague pro-worker discourse and gave tepid support for workers' rights in an effort to strengthen his nascent Republican Party.[47] Workers used Saavedra's vague discourse as a basis for expanding their unions. After the Chaco War, the military socialists and the Gualberto Villarroel regime openly supported efforts to unionize and sought to use the unions to gain influence in the city's indigenous neighborhoods.[48]

Progressive social welfare laws, labor reforms, the changes in the political base of the national and city governments, and the growth of the city's population provided new avenues of social inclusion for mestizo and indigenous city residents. It was still the case that when indigenous residents entered the city center, creoles and elites marked them as indigenous, but popular actors often used the changes in the political and class discourses in Bolivia to blur the differences between rural, urban, mestizo, and indigenous identities.

Before the Chaco War, mutual aid societies and early craft unions faced government repression and persecution. The new political alignments that developed during Bautista Saavedra's administration made unionization safer. In this more open climate, both the city government and the national government faced challenges from urban unions.[49] Saavedra also faced challenges from miners and rural workers.[50] Urban labor activism challenged Saavedra's government to fulfill the promises of his pro-worker discourse and helped build strong regional labor federations.[51]

When supporting workers suited his political needs, Saavedra encouraged labor activism. When the alliance no longer served him, he abandoned or repressed unions. In theory, Saavedra supported the workers of Bolivia, but in practice, his government withdrew that support any time workers challenged it or private industry to meet workers' demands about wages, work hours, or other issues.[52] Labor movements and indigenous organizing in the countryside suffered similar fates: as long as they were under Saavedra's control, he used them. However, when unions became liabilities, he repressed their activism.

During Saavedra's presidency and "revolution," whenever workers threatened to move beyond the confines of Saavedra's programs or posit independent actions, the government repressed movements, jailed leaders, and controlled the course of union activism. However, the changes Saavedra made to the labor code (instituting the eight-hour workday and the six-day workweek and providing a legal framework for union recognition) and his courting of worker leaders inadvertently helped union organization grow. Evidence suggests that unions developed both independently of and in conjunction with a more permissive post-Saavedra political climate. Workers continued to organize during the pre-Chaco War period despite the difficult political climate.

Unions continued to grow after Saavedra was overthrown in late 1925. A printers' union gained members and strength and a construction workers' union grew stronger and allied with the FOL, an anarchist labor federation. The FOL supported the emergence of the FOF and the Sindicato de Culinarias (cooks' union) in 1927. Hernando Siles Reyes created the Nationalist Party and ascended to the presidency in 1926 after Saavedra's attempt to manipulate the 1925 elections and topple his handpicked successor's government. Siles's administration did not cultivate alliances with workers or enforce the labor codes passed during Saavedra's tenure.

Labor and Indigenous Identities in La Paz

In addition to organizing various industries, many union members also engaged with the lay brotherhoods of their local parishes, which were the ceremonial centers for the old indigenous *ayllus* of La Paz. Members of unions tended to live in neighborhoods where workers in their craft clustered. For instance, many members of the butchers' union lived in Challapata and Villa Victoria. Members of the pork butchers' union tended to live in Entre Ríos near the cemetery district. Many construction workers lived in the Challapampa neighborhood. Members of unions and mutual aid societies participated in the religious and social lives of the different parishes and this sociability connected them to the religious and social calendars of other neighborhoods and unions. El Día de los Reyes Magos (January 6) was the traditional day of construction workers. On that day, they celebrated a mass and then held a procession that included the other guilds. They usually met near the Plaza Riosinho and the Av. Perú near the railway station. For May Day, the guilds and the neighborhood associations held meetings, danced, and participated in another procession. All of this took place in the context of three decades of political chaos—the government's wild vacillation between reformism and reactionary politics in the period from 1920 to 1950.

The Chaco War and Postwar Realignments

The war and its perceived failures marked all sectors of Bolivian society and shaped activism within indigenous neighborhoods. As result of Bolivia's defeat in the Chaco War, the Liberals, the Conservatives, and others associated with that period were portrayed as part of the elite that had led the nation to disaster. Yet, Saavedra's break with the Liberal Party and his efforts to incorporate workers, albeit in a limited way, opened new spaces for activism in La Paz.

The collapse of the tin market in 1930 significantly affected the Bolivian state's coffers and its ability to maintain its debt payments. Moreover, President Daniel Salamanca's administration (1931–4) employed a rather regressive economic strategy: his government cut spending, devalued the currency, and employed regressive taxation schemes to extract more revenue. He tried to squeeze revenue from market vendors and itinerant vendors in the city's markets. This did little to alleviate problems for the poorest sectors of society and eroded the earnings of the middle class. Cuts in spending meant less economic activity within the city, and since Bolivia was a major food importer, imports became more expensive and the cost of everyday items rose rapidly.[53]

The regressive response to the economic crisis led the nascent unions and reformist political organizations to criticize the government's approach to the economic situation. Like Saavedra had done in the 1920s, Salamanca chose repression instead of negotiation. In 1932, the government telegraph workers' union went on strike to demand improvements in wages. The union asked the rail workers' FOT to support the strike, but Salamanca declared the strike illegal and had military troops occupying all of the nation's telegraph offices. He refused to negotiate with the FOT and successfully stifled the strike.

The shambolic conduct of the war demonstrated to political elites, military officers, middle-class intellectuals, and common soldiers that the structure of Bolivian society had failed Bolivia's people, and many argued that this failure led directly to the country's defeat in the Chaco War. This defeat gave renewed impetus to the development of alternative political parties, the re-formation of unions, and rejection of the prewar political system. In addition, the war heavily influenced the generation of politicians who challenged the political system after the war. As soldiers on the front, these politicians had witnessed the highly unequal class and race systems that led to the needless death of many mestizos and *indígenas*, and they had experienced the ineptitude of many army officers and political elites. As journalists and political operatives after the war, these leftist politicians and future MNR leaders helped bring about the realignments of the postwar period.

While the Chaco War caused a break with aspects of the past, it was not a clean break. The basis for class and race discourse changed after the war: while race had been more important before the war, class became more central after the war, although it did not displace the importance of race. Before and during the war, the national government stripped unions of formal recognition and persecuted their leaders, but the war did not eradicate activism within the crafts or the alliances the unions and guilds had forged before the war.

Many of the postwar migrants to La Paz after the war were veterans and rural people who had joined the FOF and the FOL. National government officials and local officials on the altiplano sought to prevent this migration. The government tried to legislate against labor recruiters who traveled to rural areas and recruited people to work in Argentina and Chile. All levels of the government sought to limit the impact that migrants had on the city. The government discussed the possibility of fines and the use of internal passports to prevent *indígenas* from moving to cities. These proposals did not come to pass, but nevertheless they demonstrate that the realignment of society after the war was tricky and filled with uncertainty.

Despite the activism of the postwar period, many of the economic, social, and political bases of Bolivian society did not change. The government continued to rely on tin and on other extractive industries for much of its revenue. A small number of elite individuals controlled much of Bolivia's arable lands. Despite the fact that the war discredited the prewar political parties, many politicians remade their careers in the postwar period, including Bautista Saavedra, Víctor Paz Estenssoro, and Hernán Siles. Other politicians, especially at the municipal level, maintained a level of stability that was not possible in the national political arena.[54] Although the war created several breaks with the past, continuity prevailed in several sectors of Bolivian society.

The military socialists who took power in 1936 were junior military officers who had served during the Chaco War. Their political success signaled changes in La Paz's political arena. The dictatorship replaced the elected city council and mayor with appointed politicians and paved the way for a centralized municipal government that began investing heavily in the infrastructure of indigenous neighborhoods in an attempt to bring the entire city into its vision of a modern urban life.

The rise of the military socialists coincided with renewed labor activism. They actively courted workers and unions as a way to build a corporatist model of government. In 1935, the La Paz printers' union decided to strike after the government postponed a decision to address the union's demands for wage increases and food subsidies.⁵⁵ The FOL supported the strike and called for a general strike. The strike mobilized so many sectors of La Paz's working classes that the Tejada Sorzano government decided to withdraw all the police from the city. The military, under the leadership of Germán Busch, decided not to intervene as long as there was no violence.⁵⁶ After this victory, the printers' union, the FOL, and the FOF pressured the government for wage increases and improvements in working conditions for women and children. They also requested that the government suppress monopolies on consumer goods, suspend the state of siege, allow freedom of association and the press, allow legal organizations for workers, draft new social legislation, and provide jobs for veterans. They also presented petitions asking for support and aid for the mutilated victims and orphans of war.⁵⁷ Activism from below continued despite government repression.

Conclusion

The mutual aid societies and unions of the early twentieth century helped integrate a population of artisans and Aymara indigenous peoples into the fabric of the city. These institutions played a key role in celebrations in indigenous neighborhoods and helped organize neighborhoods into craft-based guilds. They brought together Aymara, Quechua, and mestizo craftsmen and tradesmen in mutual aid societies and lay brotherhoods. The FOL united men and women as it supported the *culinarias*, market women, flower sellers, construction workers, carpenters, butchers, and workers from other crafts who created unions and joined the federations. The FOF organized market women, vendors, *culinarias*, and several other groups of women in various crafts. These unions and federations supported each other's strikes, petitions, and activism. In the early 1920s, Bautista Saavedra sought to exploit this active labor movement.

The military socialist experiment in Bolivia was a reimagining of Bolivian society along a corporate model.⁵⁸ Military socialists analyzed Bolivia's problems in terms of class dynamics and international capitalist exploitation.⁵⁹ They established the eight-hour workday, the six-day workweek, and restrictions on women and children's labor; they legalized unions; and they gave amnesty to deserters. The labor laws were a reiteration of the laws Saavedra had passed in the 1920s. The amnesties for the military were part of a larger effort to bury the conflict between junior officers and the high command and to avoid detailing the failures of the army in the Chaco War. As Busch became impatient with the slow-moving political apparatus, he began to push the government in radical directions. He closed the congress in 1938 and ruled by decree.[60] He also passed decrees to enforce the mandatory unionization of all sectors of society.[61]

The period from the Chaco War through to April 1952 has often been discussed as one coherent period. The traditional historiography portrays it as a time of natural progression toward the triumph of the nationalist revolution. This progression has in many ways been teleology: the MNR triumphed and thus it must be that it was a mass movement that enjoyed widespread support and controlled the masses in the city and in the countryside. More recent scholarship has reassessed that history to show that there was more diversity of action and more long-term activism and that the MNR's triumph was not a foregone conclusion. My work supports this historiographical revision by showing that indigenous neighborhoods developed politically, socially, and physically quite independently of the MNR and its structures. That the MNR enjoyed support in the neighborhoods and factories and among some indigenous neighborhood residents does not mean that it monopolized all working-class activism. In La Paz and in Bolivia, that activism had deeper roots.

7

Urban Revolution

Indigenous Neighborhoods, the MNR, and Those Three Days in April 1952

Around midnight on April 8, 1952, MNR militants arrived at the Universidad Mayor de San Andrés and linked up with student leaders of the youth wing. Armed MNR militants took their stations at predetermined locations in La Paz. In La Paz's indigenous neighborhoods, MNR militants were tasked with taking control of a small garrison in Caiconi and a weapons depot at the train station in Challapampa. The youth elements of the MNR and workers affiliated with the MNR had two charges: (1) to take the university's main building and prevent possible reinforcements from the military college south of the city center from entering central La Paz; and (2) to prevent military units stationed in Miraflores, southeast of the city center, from crossing into central La Paz. As the MNR youth made their way to their meeting points, they "pretend[ed] to be groups of young men on their way to serenade [their girlfriends and sweethearts] carrying instruments, singing, joking, and hiding their weapons in the cases of the instruments" to throw "[Police Chief Donato] Millán's bloodhounds off the scent."[1] According to this account in *La Nación* from 1955 on the third anniversary of the triumph of the MNR Revolution, "The mothers of the young militants ensured their sons had the weapons they needed by serving as runners and messengers, and not one forgot to give her young nationalist his weapon to fight and possibly die for National Independence."[2] At 4:00 a.m., the student leaders returned to the university and under the direction of Jorge Arze and the "MNR comrades Raul A. Garcia, Carlos Mendizábal, Javier Lorini, Mariano Baptista, Luciano Urquieta, N. Villarroel, Daniel Quiroga, and Enrique Mariaca along with unnamed members of the workers' movement[,] awaited further instructions."[3] By the early hours of April 9, other party militants had dispersed throughout the city.

In the heavy fighting that followed on April 9, the students, the MNR militants, and other belligerents held off the cadets and military units stationed in Miraflores and in the south of La Paz. Just before daybreak on April 10, when the Lanza Regiment and the Colegio Militar cadets made their way toward the university to attack the belligerents there, "comrade [Hernán] Siles engaged in an emotional farewell with the university students." The students urged Siles to "go to take charge of the revolution and command it, we will stay here and fight," promising him that the armed forces of the "feudal-mining order shall not pass."[4] University students and workers defended the university and held it even though they came under heavy fire. On April 9 and 10, MNR militants and residents of indigenous neighborhoods defeated the military units in charge of the garrison and arms depot. This enabled insurgents to reinforce those fighting in other parts of the city. From the mobile insurgents, those who were fighting at the university learned that the depot and garrison in the indigenous neighborhoods had just fallen to the belligerents in Villa Victoria. The ammunition and weapons insurgents acquired in Villa Victoria enabled them to continue fighting and resisting the military's efforts to retake La Paz.

> The people were now armed and following the instructions from the leaders of the MNR who had helped repel the murderers [*massacradores*].[5] The miners [from Milluni], young members of the military [who were loyal to the MNR], the national police [who were loyal to the MNR], and members of the MNR zonal commands made their way to El Alto with the intention of preventing the military from bringing reinforcements to retake the arsenal, the weapons, the depot, the city center, and the Estado Mayor.[6]

At this point, the military

> units attacking the university, who just one day prior had taunted the university students by suggesting to them that they should ask for a truce so [they] could evacuate their injured and dying comrades, were now lost completely. They were ashamed [that they had lost] and [had] lost their arrogant stance of abuser. Many rank-and-file soldiers—sons of the people—who had not wanted to fire on their "brothers" had been cruelly assassinated—shot in the back by these abusers.

This evocative language again makes the MNR the protagonist and assumes that many rank-and-file soldiers identified as "brothers" with the insurgents. It also fails to detail why many deserted the army and makes the military sound much more prepared than it was for the fighting that occurred on that day.[7]

An essential component of the mythology of the MNR was its relationship to the Villarroel government (1943–6) in which the MNR were protagonists until they were expelled from the government for pro-fascist sympathies. This ascent to power for the MNR under Villarroel shaped its activism, its rise to power, and its triumph in 1952. The MNR commemorated his tragic death and tied themselves to the reform that characterized Villarroel's administration:

> These nights of holy week [April 9–11] had been the brightest the Bolivian people had ever witnessed.... And on the day of Christ's resurrection when the bells rang out across the city in remembrance, the people venerated the lamppost where Villarroel had been sacrificed, where a crown of red roses had been placed in the middle of the battle by the MNR youth wing.

These actions "attest to the loyalty they showed to those who had fallen in the struggle for Bolivia's economic independence."[8] It seems highly unlikely that in the middle of firefights taking place around the city, anyone engaged in them would have taken the time to lay down a wreath of roses or "venerate" a lamppost. Moreover, many of the people engaged in the fighting could have been at the protests in 1946 and may have witnessed this horrifying act of mob violence against Villarroel and his aides.

The period between July 1946 and the triumph of the MNR-led uprising on April 9 through 11, 1952, looked on the surface to be a continuation of the post–Chaco War shifts between reform and reaction. However, the triumph of the MNR's revolt was not preordained nor was the MNR the only possible alternative to the reactionary Partido de la Unión Republicana Socialista (Socialist Republican Union Party; PURS), which had won the elections in 1947 and held power until May 1951. In May of 1951, President Mamerto Urriolagoitía gave power to the military instead of respecting the outcome of the elections in which the MNR had received a plurality of votes but not an outright majority. There is no doubt that the MNR was a leading reformist faction in Bolivian politics, but the political activism of miners, urban workers, and Paceño residents did not move in tandem with the MNR. In fact, the evidence I have presented suggests that many residents of indigenous neighborhoods continued their activism in the face of repression in the period between 1946 and 1952 and did not rely upon the MNR and its party structures to support their activism. Moreover, the triumph of the MNR did not alter the strategies of the residents of La Paz's indigenous neighborhoods, and they continued to press for their rights or asserted their right to occupy public spaces as they had since the 1920s and 1930s. The continuity in organizing and the pressure the neighborhood associations put on the government remained rather consistent, although they became more acute and radical as time passed.

This chapter demonstrates that the MNR's triumph tapped into a long-standing process of resident participation that superseded the MNR and its structures and had deeper roots than the MNR's history of this period suggests. In fact, the MNR's triumph relied on political activists who were already engaged in challenging the government and its power. It also analyzes the period from July 21, 1946, when Gualberto Villarroel was assassinated, to the MNR uprising in April 1952. It focuses on the contribution of indigenous neighborhoods to the urbanization process and the relationship of that process to the larger political context. Thus, it complicates the MNR's mythology of its success in April 1952.[9] This MNR-centered historiography posits a central role for reformers linked to the MNR and relegates rural-based and working-class urban movements to a supporting role in the awakening of political elites. I posit that the triumph of the revolution is more complex and not as clear as the MNR and its sympathizers claim.[10]

1946–51: An Overview

Gualberto Villarroel had a well-known history of supporting reform, having seen the disastrous consequences of the Chaco War. He was a supporter of the military socialist governments of 1936–9. He also belonged to the Razón de Patria, a progressive military lodge that sought the structural reform of Bolivia's politics and economy. When Col. Germán Busch, who had lost the support of the military and faced increasing pressure from subaltern groups in both the city and the countryside, committed suicide, Villarroel continued to serve in the military and subscribe to the ideals that Busch had fought for during his presidency. The presidential elections of 1940 returned the traditional elite and those associated with powerful mining interests to power. The latter were often referred to as La Rosca (the ring). In 1943, Villarroel led a group of military officers in a coup to remove Gen. Enrique Peñaranda from power. When he assumed power, Villarroel chose to work with the MNR, the Nationalist Party that had been founded in 1942. The MNR's founders Víctor Paz Estenssoro and Hernán Siles Zuazo had been politically active since at least the Chaco War. Both served in government as junior ministers in the 1930s and early 1940s before the MNR made an alliance with Villarroel.

The alliance between Villarroel and the MNR was fraught with tension because of the MNR's purported sympathies with Nazis and its increasingly independent actions. The Villarroel government was unable to control the MNR and the MNR sought greater independence and reform. The MNR leadership began to support labor in the growing labor movements of miners and workers in the city.[11] In late 1943, the Villarroel government, under pressure from the United States, expelled several members of the MNR from the cabinet, but it brought the MNR back into the fold one year later. After that, the MNR set about developing a much more ambitious plan of reform. Villarroel's regime legalized unions and delineated the rights of workers. In response, the miners' confederation formed the Federación Sindical de Trabajadores Mineros de Bolivia (Sindicalist Federation of Mine Workers; FSTMB) in 1945.

Villarroel's co-government with the MNR also gave unions and neighborhood associations the legal recognition and right to organize and agitate for labor reforms and improvements to the neighborhoods of La Paz. Villarroel's reformist ideas included several projects to help indigenous Bolivians and workers attain further rights. His administration passed a union rights law, a Christmas bonus law, a law that gave workers paid vacations, and an urban rent reduction law.[12] It also established cooperatives for public employees.[13] The Villarroel government also made major advances in the area of indigenous legislation. Villarroel decreed the end of indigenous forced labor (*ponguaje*), the end of unpaid labor, the construction of new schools on rural properties, and the preparation of a rural labor code. He also helped sponsor the first National Indigenous Congress in Bolivia in 1945.[14]

On July 21, 1946, President Villarroel and several of his aides lost their lives in an uprising rooted in increasing discontent with the economic and political situation among elites, the middle class, and sectors of the working class. Elite opposition appeared soon after Villarroel's rise to power in 1943. Mine owners had little patience for the kind of reforms Villarroel sought. Middle-class and working-class agitation emerged from slightly different places. Labor activism in the mines, in the agriculture sector, and in urban areas emerged as a result of the open political situation that enabled labor unions to organize and agitate for further reform. Discontent among the middle class stemmed from rising prices and economic stagnation.

The government responded to this combination of working-class unrest and elite agitation with repressive measures that included several shocking acts in the name of maintaining order. The government arrested middle-class protesters, rejected petitions from urban labor unions, and murdered political elites because they feared these elites were laying the groundwork for a coup.[15] In response, the MNR withdrew from the government, leaving largely military personnel in charge. As a result of economic depression and widespread strikes, the government's coffers were drained and it struggled to pay for its programs. All of this eventually led to widespread anger and protests that culminated in a massive protest on the Plaza Murillo in front of the Government Palace on July 21, 1946. This protest turned violent when the crowds laid siege to the palace. Villarroel was forced to resign, but that did not end the protest or satisfy the crowds. Several dozen protesters pushed their way into the palace, where they assassinated Villarroel and several aides. They threw Villarroel's body from a second-story window and hung it and those of two aides from a lamppost just off the Plaza Murillo.[16]

The overthrow of Villarroel began a new period of reactionary politics. The leaders that emerged placed two career politicians in the presidency in order to prepare for new elections. Nestor Guillen Olmos served for just under a month, while Tomas Monje Gutierrez, a lifelong politician, served for just over six months while elections were being organized. The elections brought Enrique Hertzog—a solid member of the Rosca—to power. Hertzog had begun his political career in the 1920s as part of Daniel Salamanca's Partido Republicano Genuino (Genuine Republican Party), a splinter group of the Liberal Party and Bautista Saavedra's Republican Party. Hertzog had served in various government positions, including as the prefect of La Paz. He had served as minister of government and minister of education and communications during the Chaco War, and during Enrique Peñaranda's government he had served as minister of hygiene and health. When he was elected president, Hertzog faced a bleak economic situation. During his tenure, he survived several coup attempts and had to contend with activism and revolt from the countryside and in the cities.

Hertzog ruled from 1947 through to 1949. After he resigned, his vice president, Mamerto Urriolagotía, took over power and ruled until the elections of May 1951.[17] The press accused the government of targeting indigenous activists and agitators, allegedly by "convincing a good number of indigenous peoples to migrate to the lowlands only to leave them there to die." The excuse the government used was the improvement of agriculture and the expansion of production; it also said that the "altiplano Indian" had become accustomed to the heat of the lowlands. And yet, press reports suggest that indigenous peoples from the highlands were "transported by plane, dropped off with nothing, and left to fend for themselves."[18]

In La Paz, even though Urriolagotía's administration promised to be nothing like that of Gualberto Villarroel, the neighborhood associations continued to pressure the government for services and used the media to highlight their demands. The Nueva Potosi neighborhood association, which, as we saw in

Chapter 4, had celebrated the expansion of water lines and electricity with La Paz's mayor in 1944 and 1945, now used publicity to its advantage. In 1949, the association named Humberto Palza, the editor of the La Paz daily *Ultima Hora*, an "honorary member" because he maintained a great "interest in" their "progress" and in the "progress of the [city] and [Palza] had identified himself with [the Villa Potosí residents] due to his 'great sense of patriotism.'"[19] The Villa Potosí neighborhood association wanted more than water lines. Villa Potosí association members petitioned for roads, schools, and electricity in their neighborhood.[20] Other associations asked for and received schools, roads, water lines, and paved roads.[21]

At the same time, residents of indigenous neighborhoods fought against treatment they perceived as unfair. In 1949, the city government sought to remove several renters from a property in central La Paz in order to use it as an elementary school. A group of neighbors including the renters who were to be evicted visited the editorial office of *Ultima Hora* to explain that the government wanted them out within five days, a period of time the editors considered "too short." They also criticized the city's housing authority, arguing that the government had chosen a locale that was "falling apart" and "not apt for a school."[22] This was a continuation of the activism, which had gained in strength during previous administrations, that supported labor movements and indigenous rights.

During Hertzog's tenure and after his resignation, and the ascendancy of Vice President Mamerto Urriolagotía, the government seemed keen to turn back the clock to the pre-Chaco time when elites directed government policy. That was not going to happen. By early 1951, even *Ultima Hora*'s editors, who were not allies of the leftist parties or the MNR, had a prophetic warning for Urriolagotía and the members of the Rosca: "Those who plant winds, will harvest storms."[23] The editors argued that Bolivia's political machinery had not learned the "lessons of 1920 [the destruction of the old liberal order and the ascendancy of Juan Bautista Saavedra], the Chaco War, and revolution of 1943–46 and the 1946 overthrow." The political machine of the PURS was "doing a disservice to democracy." An editorial argued that a cycle of chaos had begun in 1932 and had continued into 1946 and that many people had believed that the [1946] "revolution would purify Bolivia." Instead, the people "have been deceived, and the nation fell into the hands of those who caused it harm and had led the nation to ruin," by politicians the editor characterized as vengeful, hateful, and small-minded. Although they claimed to be "saving the nation, . . . not the blood of the Chaco, not the blood of the revolutions, not sacrifices of thousands of citizens have served to restore or regenerate [the nation]. We have returned to 1920. This is the historical truth." The editorial accused the government of political manipulation and electoral fraud.[24] The reactionary turn Bolivian politics took in 1947 had not restored the old regime. Instead, labor agitation and discontent with the economy and the political situation continued and grew, and demonstrated that a return to the liberal order was not a viable option.

As the economic situation became more acute after the Second World War, both the government of La Paz and the national government continued to face significant challenges within and outside of Bolivia. The roots of the economic situation lay in a decision the national government had made during the Second World War, when Bolivia had agreed to sell its tin to the United States in solidarity with the Allies. This had created an imbalance because Bolivia sold its tin to the Allies at below market prices and when the market bottomed out in the late 1940s after the war, it caused severe economic problems through the mid-1950s. In fact, successive US administrations offered aid to prop up Bolivia's government. These economic problems spurred reactions from agriculturalists, miners, and urban workers. In March of 1949, for example, the Federación Obrera Sindical threatened to mobilize its affiliated unions in the city and other parts of the nation to protest the lack of materials for "all forms of manual labor." The shortage of supplies needed in the textile industry (in this case, wool and thread) was "acute" and in the "Soligno Factory alone 800 workers were idle." Other labor unions besides the FOS were considering actions. Union representatives had heard only "promises from the government ministers" despite the deteriorating situation.[25] In April of that year, the Associacion de Mutiliados y Invalidos de la Guerra del Chaco (Mutilated and Invalid Veterans of the Chaco War) decided to go on a hunger strike over the economic situation and the unwillingness of the national government to pay the promised stipends.[26] These strikes and other actions in the countryside by indigenous peoples were supposedly the work of the MNR according to the government.[27]

The Federation of Neighbor Associations (FEDJUVE) in La Paz continued to use its influence to pressure the government. It asked the police and the city government to help it engage in a campaign for moral uplift.[28] According to one journalist, the FEDJUVE was perceived as "one of the associations of the city that most benefits the common citizen" because it sought "moral urban improvements" and "the improvement of services for the entire city." It made "no distinctions" in social classes and thus was popular "in all of the city's neighborhoods." Thirty-three of its thirty-nine member associations regularly attended its meetings.[29] Despite the government's return to elite hands, the situation in Bolivia had transformed in such a way that elites could not turn back the clock to the heyday of liberal order. In fact, the bleak economic situation made such attempts appear more and more out of step with Bolivia's reality. La Paz's residents continued to petition, make demands, and protest in the period before the 1951 elections.

This economic situation led to strikes, government repression, and then, new waves of political activism. Major textile factories in La Paz struggled to import raw materials due to low levels of foreign currency.[30] Layoffs led to protests, threats of strikes, and petitions to the municipal and national governments. The MNR was believed to be behind some of the protests, which included "the explosion of a granary and arms depot."[31] The reality was more complex. Organizations such as FEDJUVE and FOS agitated for improvements to infrastructure and neighborhoods, wage increases, and food subsidies. Instead of negotiating with these groups, the government chose repression. It proclaimed martial law and put over 100 people in prison.[32]

During Urriolagotía's presidency, residents of indigenous neighborhoods deployed very similar language to the language they had used when governments that were more sympathetic to the working class were in power. For example, when the residents of Villa Pabon requested that the city government restore "potable water service," they argued that the progress of the neighborhood was being affected because the lack of water kept a "vital element of life from the [residents] of the neighborhood." They noted that communal water lines were essential because there was no "potable water service to the individual homes in the neighborhood" and that they had "asked innumerable times" for a water main, offering to supply all the "necessary" labor to complete the project.[33] The municipal government responded by sending an engineer to oversee the restoration of communal water lines.

Several unions and neighborhood associations sought government intervention and mediation in 1951. The Union of Free Seamstresses struck in solidarity with textile workers over the shortages of cloth and thread. Municipal workers sought increases in pay. The Milluni mining union sought pay increases, housing and food subsidies, and a new pay scale for miners as well as administrative workers. Landlords and tenants in La Paz were shocked to discover that the national government had decided to close the landlord-tenant dispute resolution office in the La Paz Housing Authority due to lack of funds.[34] The situation was dire.

As the political situation continued to deteriorate, the government's repressive measures worried even those who might have been supportive of an elite-oriented government. As the elections of 1951 neared, even those who nominally supported the government began to question its actions. The editors of *Ultima Hora*, for example, suggested that the government had "abandoned its moral obligations to govern for all Bolivian people" and stated that Urriolagotía and his government were "completely disconnected from the reality of the majority," and refused to admit their "own moral failings and errors." The government's behavior was that of "authoritarian governments."[35] Despite such criticism, Urriolagotía and his ministers refused to mediate disputes and to increase subsidies, and continued to choose repression. Even elite politicians wondered about the viability of Bolivia and its institutions.[36]

The Liberal Party, an elite party under the direction of Tomas Manuel Elio, questioned the government's actions regarding the May 1951 elections.[37] Distrust pervaded the political spectrum from the Liberal Party to the Falange Socialista Boliviano (FSB)—a far-right group also questioned whether the government would respect the outcome of the elections.[38] The official policy of the PURS seemed to be that it would open the elections to all opposition parties, including the MNR. However, the government refused to guarantee the safety of MNR leaders or to assure those in exile, like the MNR's presidential candidate, Víctor Paz Estenssoro, that they would not be arrested while campaigning. In addition, the campaigns took place in the context of martial law, which limited public meetings, included a curfew, and gave government forces significant power to detain and arrest residents.[39]

Instead of ensuring free and fair elections, the Urriolagotía government engaged in repression and accused opposition parties—even those that were largely made up of elites—of fomenting violence and instability. Government forces throughout Bolivia arrested "agitators" in the days before the elections. For instance, the government arrested a journalist on assignment in Santa Cruz and refused to reveal his whereabouts or the charges against him. He had gone to Santa Cruz for a family function and to report on campaigns there for a La Paz daily. He was arrested before he could even attend the family function.[40] In the run-up to the election, the government arrested opposition politicians and journalists and accused them of participating in "subversive plots."[41] This did not curb the activism of urban residents. Chaco War veterans planned a march and strike in support of opposition parties. The La Paz printers' union carried out a general strike. Oil workers in Camiri engaged in a wildcat strike over pay disputes. Students planned and carried out a general strike in La Paz. Thus, the government faced widespread opposition from all quarters in the run-up to the 1951 elections.[42]

The 1951 Elections

The elections took place on May 7, 1951. Despite reported irregularities and alleged fraud by the government, the MNR emerged victorious in the presidential contest and won a number of seats in the Bolivian Congress. Initially, it seemed that Mamerto Urriolagotía and his political allies would respect the outcome of the elections. The MNR celebrated its win and praised its adherents for resisting the government's efforts to incite them to violence. Its members declared that "agents of imperialism and the oligarchy have witnessed the high political and civic culture of the working classes," noting that the working classes had "behaved in an exemplary fashion despite the chaotic manner of the last elections."[43] *En Marcha*, the MNR's newspaper, published an article from Víctor Paz Estenssoro—exiled in Argentina at the time—that said that workers had demonstrated "discipline and courage in the face of difficulty," despite the former government's "anti-worker agenda." This conduct contradicted a government that had "accused our militants of bad behavior" and gave the lie to its characterization of the people as the "thugs, delinquents, and murderers of Villa Victoria, Av. Buenos Aires, and other popular class areas." Indeed, "[these workers] have instead demonstrated a high level of education, higher still than those who studied in Paris, higher than those who write odious editorials and who are in the university."[44] Highlighting those who studied in Paris was an allusion to Bolivia's tin barons and other elites who believed in the superiority of a European education. The MNR wanted to clarify that it stood with workers, sending "hearty congratulations to all of our working-class comrades" for "their exemplary comportment." These "militants of the MNR" had displayed "class consciousness" and had "acquired a sense of responsibility" in a difficult position as "soldiers in a revolutionary and popular" cause in the face of "libel and slander and provocations by those paid by the PURist government and the police."[45] This language ignored much of the agitation workers had engaged in before the election.

The same message from Victor Paz—who was still in exile in Argentina because the Urriolagotía government refused to guarantee he would not be arrested—also said that "the supreme elections tribunal—an arm of the people—has certified our electoral win. This will pacify the majority if the legal elections are respected."[46] However, the evidence suggested that the Urriolagotía administration would not certify the election. All across the nation, provincial governments detained and arrested opposition party members and candidates. The MNR went on the offensive in an attempt to convince authorities and the public that it would "justify the popular and national faith that the people have deposited in the Party. We will maintain peace by respecting the outcome of the election in its entirety."[47]

Then, to add to the uncertainty, the Liberal Party candidate, General Bilbao Rioja, accused President Urriolagotía of attempting to subvert the will of the electorate by trying to convince Rioja to "join a military junta."[48] The general had rebuffed the president because it was "important to respect the results of the election and the will of the majority."[49] The MNR tried to convince the government to respect the elections, arguing that "the entire population, including the military, urban police, and other forces of the public order, are required to follow the example of the general and respect the results of the election." It stated that the Bolivian people "are awake and alert in their position, which is clearly institutionalist" and that the people would defend "order, laws, rights, and the suffrage."[50] *En Marcha* published "uncertified results" that stated that the MNR had "collected 68,000 votes across the country—an absolute majority."[51] The official number suggested far fewer votes in favor of the MNR—about 38,000, which was not enough to achieve a majority. Using this lack of a majority as an excuse, Urriolagotía and his minister of government refused to certify the election and, instead, handed power to a group of military officers, who argued that they were simply going to guide Bolivia out of the "chaos" and that they would allow those who followed "the law and maintained public order" to live their lives. These officers promised that they would not allow Bolivia to undergo any kind of "sovietization." Their role would to protect Bolivia as a country that was "Christian and democratic."[52] It seemed that the military junta would have governed as the PURS had governed with the added caveat that it could deploy the military apparatus against the people. And like the PURS, it seemed that the military junta would seek to turn back the clock.

The political and economic situation exacerbated the problems Bolivians faced. The Hertzog and Urriolagotía governments and the military government of 1951 and 1952 were either unwilling or unable to respond in a way that would resolve the widespread agitation that gripped Bolivia in the period between 1947 and 1952. These governments attempted to quell dissent through violence and absolute control of the governing apparatus. They continued to construe the activism of workers as the result of some marginal group of agitators and political parties and did not acknowledge that workers had a broad base of support. Indeed, as we shall see, worker activism became integral to the triumph of the insurgency less than a year after the May 1951 elections.

Three Days in April: The MNR, Residents of La Paz's Indigenous Neighborhoods, and Unexpected Victory

The quotes at the beginning of this chapter show how the MNR had colonized the narrative of the events of April 1952 just three years after they occurred. Recall their statement that "no mother allowed her nationalist son to leave without his weapon" and the Christ-like place they assigned to the memory of Gualberto Villarroel: "And on the day of Christ's resurrection when the bells rang out across the city in remembrance, the people venerated the lamppost where Villarroel had been sacrificed, where a crown of red roses had been placed in the middle of the battle by the MNR youth wing." That narrative was published on the third anniversary of the revolution and explicitly focused on the actions of the youth section of the MNR in 1952. It mentioned some working-class activists but the ones it named were usually MNR allies. This is not the narrative that emerges from the evidence I have found. My evidence highlights how the insurgents benefited from residents' knowledge of the terrain of their neighborhoods, their long-standing and deep understanding of each other and their neighborhood, the residents' long-term political activism, and from some residents' participation in the Chaco War.

On the evening of April 8, 1952, at the request of the MNR's revolutionary committee, student members of the University Alliance of the MNR met at the law school of the Universidad Mayor de San Andrés in central La Paz. They were ostensibly there to attend a lecture by the head of the youth wing of the party, Mario Guzman Galarza, entitled "Strategy and Tactics of the National Revolution."[53] According to the MNR's narrative, the true purpose of the meeting was to coordinate the students' action in the revolt that was to begin that night. The MNR had been planning the insurrection for months with its allies in the police, the FSB, and the ministry of government, but the role that those not associated with the MNR were going to play was not clear. In fact, the plan seems to have been a "palace coup."[54] As we shall see later, this plan was weak because it largely relied on military commanders to support the coup and the base of the insurrection was relatively narrow.

According to the 1955 *La Nacion* account of the MNR's actions, after the lecture, the students divided into three groups. The first group remained at the university and a second group made its way to the MNR's weapons cache, which included "homemade grenades, weapons, and ammunition that would arm the militants of the Party."[55] The second group returned to the main building of the university and a third group made up of high school students made their way "very discreetly to the Confiteria Chic," a candy shop in Sopocachi (in central La Paz) to await further instructions.[56] While the MNR was preparing for its uprising, the chief of police, Donato Millán, ordered the political section investigators under his command to the home of MNR militant Jorge Arze to arrest members of the MNR's revolutionary command. According to contemporaneous accounts, Millán had been tipped off about the revolutionary actions and acted to thwart the plot.[57]

Other sources suggest that while the youth wing of the MNR was one component of the plan, the success of the insurrection relied upon the cooperation of several members of the military junta.[58] In his recollections of the insurrection, General Antonio Seleme, the minister of government at the time who controlled the police forces in La Paz, stated that the MNR's leadership had planned the uprising in coordination with him.[59] Donato Millán, who was Seleme's subordinate, supposedly also supported the MNR secretly. Earlier on the night of April 8, before the end of the university lecture, General Hugo Ballivián, the head of the military junta, had requested that the members of the junta tender their resignations so that he could confirm a new cabinet and government. According to his recollections, Seleme, fearing that he would lose the opportunity to overthrow Ballivián, counseled against forcing the junta to resign in that moment because it was Holy Week. Seleme supposedly pulled Ballivián aside and asked the president who would attend the Te Deum mass with him the following day. This apparently convinced Ballivián to postpone the resignations until after Holy Week.[60]

Knowing it would be his last opportunity before losing command of the police, Seleme did not waste any time. He mobilized two units of the national police and instructed 1,500 men to take up strategic positions throughout the city and distribute weapons to MNR militants. Seleme met with four other members of the military junta, including General Humberto Torres Ortiz, and they decided to carry out the overthrow of the government. This fact highlights the narrowness of the insurrection's principal actors: the MNR; 1,500 police officers; some FSB radicals; and several members of the military high command. It had all the hallmarks of a palace coup. Separately, Seleme notified the commanders of the five military battalions stationed in El Alto and in the Bolivian highlands about the plot. All agreed to support the coup. Next, Seleme notified the leaders of the MNR and the FSB that the plan had been put into action.[61]

Óscar Únzaga de la Vega, head of the FSB, then sent a message to General Torres Ortiz that said that both the MNR and the FSB had been notified about the plot and that Seleme was about to imprison Torres Ortiz. It is unclear if

Únzaga was privy to that kind of information or if this was an attempt to thwart the MNR–Seleme coup. Únzaga then sent Seleme a messenger and declined on behalf of the FSB to participate in the coup.[62] Meanwhile, Torres Ortiz made his way to the Bolivian Air Force base in El Alto, where he notified the battalions stationed there and in other parts of highland Bolivia of Seleme's plot. He received the support of these military units to form a new government under his own command. He ordered the units in the other highland regions to El Alto and the Escolta Regiment garrisoned in the Estado Mayor in Miraflores to head toward the city. He also instructed the cadets of the Colegio Militar to head north. These orders effectively encircled La Paz.

The complicating factor was the actions Seleme had taken to mobilize his civilian allies, which put him at odds with the military commanders and junta members who knew nothing about the MNR's involvement or its role in the insurrection. Seleme and the police had distributed 4,500 arms to the MNR and other belligerents and had taken over the radio stations announcing that Seleme was Bolivia's new president. The original idea had been to cut off the Estado Mayor headquarters in Miraflores from the garrison and arsenal located in the indigenous neighborhoods, take control of the university and the Government Palace as well as all the radio stations in the city, and proclaim the overthrow of Ballivián. The acquiescence of the generals in El Alto and in the other highland regions was an essential component of the plan because these military divisions posed a significant threat to any attempted overthrow. Now Seleme would confront a situation where the military hierarchy no longer backed him or his civilian allies.

Unbeknownst to Seleme, Torres Ortiz and the other generals no longer backed his coup. Just before sunrise on April 9, Seleme called General Blacutt, who was in charge of several battalions in the Bolivian city of Oruro, and was shocked to learn that Torres Ortiz had control of the air force base and had mobilized the highland units to help defeat Seleme, the police, the MNR, and the other belligerents. Torres Ortiz refused Seleme's offer to form a joint government, and believing that defeat was inevitable Seleme fled and sought asylum in a foreign embassy. Despite the fact that Seleme gave up, the plan was already in motion and it would go off without his direct participation or that of the FSB. The police, the MNR, and other actors were thus able to defeat the military.[63]

By the morning of April 9, before a single shot had been fired, all of the city's radio stations were under the control of the MNR's student wing and the working-class militants. Radio Illimani, the station with the most emitters, was the first to announce the triumph of the revolution. It was "the workers on the frontlines manning the radio stations that enabled a communication network to take shape in the city and across Bolivia."[64] Radio stations and police units with radios were able to effectively connect "the university to the revolutionary command to the militants in the various parts of the city including the national palace and the ministry of government."[65] All of the weapons the MNR had acquired up to that point had been distributed and the students at the university "only retained a few weapons and some dynamite."[66] Pitched battles occurred throughout the day in various parts of the city. Workers and students defended the university from the cadets of the Colegio Militar. Meanwhile, workers who were attempting to take control of the garrison in Villa Victoria were turned back. However, when military units pursued the workers, reinforcements in the Villa Victoria neighborhood ambushed the soldiers and soundly defeated them.

On the night of April 9, the revolutionary command met and analyzed the situation: they had few weapons, they were low on ammunition, they would surely face a counterattack from the military, and they now knew for certain that Antonio Seleme had sought asylum in the Chilean embassy instead of fighting.[67] After the status report was given by "comrade Hernan Siles Zuazo, a long and embarrassing silence enveloped the room until comrade Adrián Barrenchea breached the silence stating definitively that he preferred suicide to inaction or another defeat."[68] Comrade Siles's statement steered the meeting, which had threatened to turn "into a marathon session of arguments and counterarguments," back on course. He said that he would "assume all responsibility for their failure" and that he wanted the members present to decide what they were going to do now. At that moment, members of the university vanguard stated plainly that the university members and the workers would carry the revolution forward come what may. Guzman Galarza's proposal in favor of fighting to win or die carried the room and the situation was resolved."[69] Here again, the MNR is the protagonist that saves the day. The only speakers and the only identified actors are men. The most important protagonists are in that room, while the actors located throughout La Paz are an afterthought. Apparently, according to this account, it was down to the leaders of the MNR whether or not to keep fighting.

The fighting in and around Villa Victoria, along the slopes leading to El Alto, in El Alto itself, and between Miraflores and central La Paz required the participation of residents of La Paz's indigenous neighborhoods and other residents not associated with the MNR. Some of these residents were surely MNR militants. The success of the insurrection depended on all of these actors. In Villa Victoria, on April 9, a combined force of police and workers attempted to take control of the garrison controlled by the Calama division. The military repelled the attack and turned these forces back. Seeking to press their advantage, the army pursued the combined force of police and workers into Villa Victoria. Residents, workers, and police worked together to establish defensive positions in Villa Victoria before the military entered this indigenous neighborhood. Many male residents had kept their weapons after the Chaco War. In pursuit of the fleeing belligerents in Villa Victoria, the military moved across the Puente Villa, where the waiting workers ambushed and defeated the soldiers. Residents used their defensive positions, their knowledge of the neighborhood's topography, and the neighborhood's strategic location along the only viable route into La Paz to pin down military units and prevent reinforcements from reaching other sectors of the city.[70]

At the same time, another contingent of workers and police farther west near the Cementerio General de La Paz established strongholds in order to prevent military units from using footpaths into La Paz. Although the fighting was fierce in this sector, it was at a distance. Army units used light arms, heavy machine guns, and artillery to attempt to displace the men holding the cemetery. The contingent did its best to return fire and eventually took the slopes leading to El Alto and moved into El Alto to defeat the military units based there. Using the cover of night on April 9, the contingent of fighters in Villa Victoria and near the cemetery would have used their knowledge of the terrain and their paths up to El Alto to move in to attack the air force base.

A fundamental turning point for those fighting in the indigenous neighborhoods was the arrival that night of 500 miners from the Milluni mines near La Paz. These men divided into two groups and "walked along the rail lines"[71] to La Paz under the cover of darkness, arriving sometime before daybreak on April 10.[72] The miners and those who had been fighting in Villa Victoria joined forces and decided to take the arsenal and a garrison in La Paz's indigenous neighborhoods. Few of the fighters had weapons and ammunition was running low, but the miners had brought dynamite and charges with them. The miners came "strapped like Pancho Villa [the Mexican Revolutionary often pictured with crossed bandoliers] with dynamite."[73] They led the attack because they knew how to use dynamite. One Milluni miner recalled that "[t]here were many workers, and they were well organized, but had no weapons, and as you know bravery is useless with empty hands."[74] The men surrounded the garrison and arsenal in six groups and the miners detonated the dynamite. The surprise attack caught the arsenal unawares: a Milluni miner recalled how "[w]e ... surprised them and caught them in their underwear."[75] The soldiers put up little resistance and the miners and workers took a significant cache of weapons in their attack. This enabled them to begin their assault on the military forces holding positions in El Alto. Another contingent of Milluni miners attacked the air force base and the military battalions from behind. The combined maneuver of the two contingents of fighters from Villa Victoria, the miners who had come to La Paz to assist them and the second contingent of miners who attacked the armed forces in El Alto, finally led to the defeat of the soldiers at El Alto. Rank-and-file soldiers who supported the insurgents "turned their military caps backwards and their military jackets inside out." [76]

The revolt succeeded and the MNR installed Víctor Paz Estenssoro as president on April 12. The party called for several reforms that would become signatures of the revolution: land reform, universal suffrage, nationalization of subsoil rights (tin, oil, and natural gas), and the creation of a robust national internal economy. The party created civic groups that looked much like groups that already existed. For instance, the MNR created party cells throughout Bolivia and set up MNR commandos that in some ways resembled a mix of police and neighborhood associations. Applications for party membership increased tremendously.[77] The party rewarded its most loyal supporters by giving them government jobs.

The fact that the MNR benefited from, and then carefully masked, the roles of masses of miners, urban workers, army conscripts, and peasants is not all that surprising. The party has historically claimed that it had the support of the masses but had to "maintain secret structures" to avoid persecution. And yet the party was not particularly successful in elections before the revolution.[78] One possible reason, of course, is that supporters would have denied any association with the MNR because they feared persecution. A second plausible explanation for the lack of mass support for the party would be the suffrage: in a country where less than 10 percent of the population had the vote, a political party supported by the masses was not possible. A third reason for the lack of mass support is that the MNR was an elite party that suppressed those who did not strictly adhere to its policies, even though it benefited from the support of unions and the working class. Perhaps we can classify the pre-revolution MNR with Bautista Saavedra, the military socialists, and Villarroel as an elite-directed group that attempted to wrest control of politics from an oligarchic political apparatus but did not respond directly to the groups it purported to support.

Once in power, the party tried to co-opt and control many areas of political and social action. For example, the development of an activist women's group named after one Maria Barzola, an activist miner who was killed in the 1940s, was one such attempt. The Barzolas could be counted upon to swell the ranks of pro-MNR actors, but according to some union members who were not affiliated with the MNR, they could also be used as pro-government counter-protesters in violent confrontations.[79] One MNR leader—Lydia Guelier—thought the MNR relegated these women to an undignified role as agitators. After breaking with the party, Guelier said that she should have pushed harder for the MNR to take the Barzolas and women generally more seriously than they did.[80] The development of the MNR militias is another case that requires further elaboration and research. After the revolution, when the military faced an uncertain future, the MNR chose to rehabilitate the military and reorganize it. Bolivian revolutionaries chose to work with the military. The continued role of the military made the Bolivian revolution similar to the Guatemalan revolution: reformist military officers were key to the new government's stability and success.

The development of *comandos zonales* (zonal commands) was part of the MNR's strategy for ensuring its presence throughout the country. The structure of the *comandos* seems to have mirrored that of the neighborhood associations and other existing district institutions. In La Paz, the *comandos* played an intermediary role and served as a conduit for people to make requests to the party and government. For example, the Comando Zonal of Sopocachi of the MNR requested that the mayor and municipality "reward it with the proceeds of the sale of 22 quintiles of sugar and four new rubber tires plus 100%" of the fine imposed on the "owner of these products for his attempt to sell the items on the black market." It promised to use the income to purchase a used vehicle for "the use of the Comando in the service of the national revolution."[81]

Two very important themes emerge in the historical sources for the post-1952 period: the first is the proliferation of party-affiliated governance structures such as the *comandos* and the second is the continued activism of neighborhood residents through their associations and unions and by appeals to others who might help relieve their situations, including the MNR and its party structures.[82] The MNR rewarded unions and other adherents with land, new buildings, and political power.[83] For instance, the FSTMB received permission to build a large facility for its unions in La Paz, a building and organization that continues to exist today. Workers were given the option of purchasing land in urbanizing areas. Residents continued to engage with the structures that had historically worked for them and their neighborhoods. FEDJUVE continued to pressure the city, prefectural, provincial, and national governments for goods and services and does so to this day. In contrast, the MNR's structures are mostly, if not totally, defunct.

Conclusion

The MNR was able to control the history of the revolution, reserving heroic roles for itself and its adherents. However, it relied on neighborhood residents who could not have risked becoming members of the party, however sympathetic they might have been with its politics. The battles in Villa Victoria and El Alto demonstrate this. The MNR planned and executed a coup that succeeded because everyday people joined the insurgency. I argue that multiple strategies indigenous neighborhoods used for asserting their rights as residents of the city—including activism at home and at work—built long-term social and political relationships. In thinking about the success of the insurrection, residents of La Paz's indigenous neighborhoods, despite the fact that they may or may not have been part of the MNR or allies of it, were perfectly placed to help the MNR succeed. In addition, several scholars, including Mario Murillo, have asserted the importance of military training in the Chaco War for neighborhood residents as another key factor in the triumph of the insurrection.[84] My work helps lay the foundation for a reassessment of the relationship between the MNR and La Paz's indigenous neighborhood residents. My work also demonstrates that the sustained activism in La Paz's indigenous neighborhoods over the long term may influence how we should view the revolution. In addition, as I have shown throughout the text, residents of La Paz's indigenous neighborhoods had a long tradition of "doing politics" without relying upon the MNR or its structures, and they continued to engage in politics long after the decline of the MNR.

Mario Murillo has argued in his reconstruction of the revolution that the MNR has made the acts of everyday people difficult to recover because most sources have focused on the actions of its own militants and the party's leaders. In addition, the source base is extremely limited. Murillo sought to unearth and elevate the unnamed heroes of the revolution. In a similar vein, I have sought to document the importance of the residents of La Paz's indigenous neighborhoods to the physical, social, and political development of the city. This is the basis from which we must continue to research *how* and *why* the residents of the indigenous neighborhoods helped the revolution triumph.

Conclusion

The Mobilization of Indigeneity in Bolivia, 1900–52

By 1952, indigenous neighborhood residents had transformed La Paz as a physical, social, and political space. The city's indigenous neighborhoods became rich social spaces where residents joined lay brotherhoods and made urban festivals their own. They became places where unions, brotherhoods, and neighborhood associations gave both migrants and lifelong residents mechanisms for participating in the development of the city.

Bolivian political elites often characterized indigenous neighborhoods as disease-ridden, dirty places, the source of the ills that affected La Paz. The residents of indigenous neighborhoods used these expectations to pressure city government officials to provide goods and services that would improve their neighborhoods. They also added their labor to the expertise and materials the city provided so projects could be completed. They used their organizations to advance an agenda that benefited themselves and their neighborhoods.

Lay brotherhoods were also integral to the development of indigenous neighborhoods; they offered migrants institutions that were similar to those they knew from life in the countryside and provided a vehicle that helped them integrate into their neighborhoods. Lay brotherhoods became the first neighborhood associations. The Catholic Church and its lay institutions played a fundamental role in helping the neighborhoods develop and these lay brotherhoods continued a rich tradition of religious syncretism and cultural production from within La Paz's indigenous neighborhoods.

Craft guilds offered neighborhood residents examples of how to build labor unions. As the people settling in La Paz demonstrated in their oral histories, workers found that entering central La Paz as indigenous people could be very problematic. Male members of construction unions recalled having their ponchos ripped and experiencing general harassment from the police when they entered the Plaza Murillo. Women union members recalled similar discrimination: businesses on the Prado refused them service, their employers treated them poorly, and the police and market inspectors abused them. Unions gave people who were largely excluded from direct power and dismissed as incapable of meaningful participation in Bolivian society mechanisms for exerting greater control over the circumstances of their lives and participating in the construction of both La Paz and the Bolivian nation.[1]

The urbanization of La Paz was a process of conflict, adaptation, and adjustment for the city's elites and political leaders and for the people of La Paz's indigenous neighborhoods. The presence of indigenous people among the city's neighborhood residents was constitutive of urbanization, and defining who and what *indígenas* were was part of that process. There is no timeless definition of the *indígena* in Bolivia. The contingent and relational nature of racial labels and identities in La Paz was evident in the various ways elites consistently tried to situate what they defined as the city's problems as emanating from and belonging to La Paz's indigenous neighborhoods. While elites and others privileged class identities over racial ones after the Chaco War, race continued to play an important role in the construction of urban identities. Workers and indigenous peoples in the city continued to use these identities in their interactions with city officials and with each other despite the transformation of the national discourse about race after the war. For neighborhood residents, artisans, workers, and *indígenas*, indigeneity had much to do with the social rejection and harassment they endured in La Paz. The indigenous racial identity persisted under layers of urbanity; even after the war, elites and employers saw workers as peasants.

For some elites, *indígenas*, cholos, and mestizos were screens onto which they could project their anxieties about the inadequacies of the Bolivian population for the task of building a "modern" and "civilized" nation.[2] In the pre-revolution era, elite intellectuals argued that most indigenous peoples were incapable of participating in the nation unless elites controlled their education and their gradual incorporation into the nation.

Despite the desire of elites to control the discourse on race, Bolivia's indigenous majority shaped it. They rejected the biases of elites and, instead, associated indigenous identity with positive attributes such as honor and righteous behavior. In addition, attempts to define who was indigenous complicated indigeneity for political leaders, indigenous peoples, and mixed-race populations. Deconstructing the definitions of *indígena, cholo,* and mestizo reveals the problems with the divisions elites, institutions, and popular actors made between these identities. Exactly who *indígenas* and mixed-race people were was unstable. The category of mestizo is a complex category because for many government leaders and intellectual elites, socioeconomic class generally improved the mestizos' social position within Bolivian society and placed them closer to the ideal of whiteness.³ In the countryside, the archetypical mestizos lived in towns and served as merchants and intermediaries between agriculturalist indígenas and urban life.⁴ As a type, the mestizo was often labeled as *cholo* in intellectual discourse and was not highly regarded in Bolivia. According to elites, *cholos* were not the raw material for a more inclusive nation.

Using physical attributes to attempt to define these populations reveals the ambivalence and instability of racial classifications. In early twentieth-century Bolivia, *indígenas* were described as having "bronze skin and almond shaped eyes."⁵ A variety of markers defined the male *indígena*: he wore homespun cotton pants and shirts, a wide-brimmed hat or perhaps the *lluchu*, and the "traditional" poncho. Elite Bolivians said that the speech of the Aymara poeples was harsh and guttural and extrapolated from that that the people also were cold and harsh.⁶ But they argued that the Quechua spoke a "soft," "sweeter and more melodic" language and saw them as more malleable. Out of this ambivalent theorizing, racial hierarchies emerged that classified Bolivia's indigenous peoples according to their "natural" characteristics and thus their future abilities and utility.

This racial hierarchy placed the Quechua peoples closer to the Incas. In an effort to "rehabilitate" the Aymara, Arturo Posnansky connected the Aymara indigenous people to the advanced civilization that built Tiwanaku, arguing they were the precursors of the Incas and perhaps even the ancestors of the Incas and were possibly related to a long-lost Aryan tribe.⁷ These efforts allowed people to employ a "whitened" and acceptable Inca-related identity in Bolivia.

Elite Bolivians' rejection of indigenous peoples reflects the ambivalence and instability of the definitions of urban and rural. The intellectual efforts of the prerevolutionary period identified *indígenas*' place as outside the city, not within it. *Indígenas* were not urban. Even after indigenous people had built thriving neighborhoods, Bolivian elites considered them to be part of the extramuro. Yet, these neighborhoods were clearly part of La Paz. They housed the laborers, warehouses, shops, railway hubs, tambos, and markets that were necessary for the economic functioning of the city. La Paz was never solely an elite city, nor was it solely an indigenous one.

The prevalence of *indígenas* made elites and national authorities want to deal with them in a variety of ways. There was no clear progression from exclusion to inclusion, despite large changes in the nation's political culture.

Even after the Chaco War, when it seemed that class and nationalism might overcome racial divisions, intellectuals such as Vicente Donoso Torres and Luis Terán Gómez continued to assert that indigenous people were racially different and should be separated from mainstream society. Luis Terán Gómez also wanted to keep indigenous people separate and suggested educating them to participate in the modernization of agriculture and keeping them in their "best field." For Torres, this meant making *indígenas* literate in their own language, not Spanish.[8] This suggests that while the Chaco War changed many things about Bolivia's social and political life, racial discourses remained a consistent part of the national discussion. Both reformist and oligarchic elites subscribed to such racialized views.

In addition, for elites, indigenous neighborhood residents continued to embody difference and the absence of modernity. Postwar Paceño elites argued that the indigenous neighborhoods were unhygienic and that indigenous people spread disease when they entered the city. While government officials admitted that bars, houses of prostitution, gambling dens, and *chicherías* existed in the central city, they argued that the best place for them was the city's indigenous neighborhoods.[9] Prohibitions after the war were not explicitly racial; instead, they targeted vagrants, mendicants, and *mal entretenidos*.[10] The government also attempted to control indigenous workers by enforcing laws that required identity cards and to manage market women and those who worked in domestic service by enforcing new taxes and health regulations.[11] In response to these efforts, indigenous Aymara speakers who had unionized pressured the government to overturn such laws and to recognize them as full citizens.[12]

Indigenous and mestizo people who settled in the La Paz's indigenous neighborhoods took elites and government officials at their word when they said they wanted a modern Bolivia. When they asked the city council for improvements to their neighborhoods, they skillfully manipulated the racist stereotypes elites and officials embraced. They used the "worker" discourses Bautista Saavedra espoused to pressure the city to provide the roads and transportation services they needed to get to and from work in the city center. They turned concerns about unhygienic neighborhoods into requests for running water, electricity, and hospitals that city officials could hardly turn down, given their great concern about how their nation's capital was perceived around the world. When they pushed for additional schools in their neighborhoods, city council members, who publicly subscribed to the racialist arguments of elite thinkers about "lifting up" indigenous people, could hardly refuse them.

Police reports and court records provide a window into how indigenous people defined themselves. It is clear from the evidence that they did not accept the negative identity elites tried to impose on them. Instead, they promoted the concept of the honorable *indígena*. In one particular case, one man could fit three different identities. Carmen de Chusi accused Santiago Quispe of attempted murder in La Paz when he struck Carmen de Chusi on the head over a boundary dispute in their rural home community. Chusi's witnesses defined Quispe as an indígena; the police report defined him as a laborer with "precarious" residence in La Paz; his petitions for release defined him as a colono; and he defined himself as "a poor and ignorant indígena" in court testimony. Quispe was one man, yet he was variously a "poor and ignorant indígena," a "colono," and a "laborer" precariously residing in La Paz. The overlap among these identities illustrates the fact that the same man was at once a rural laborer, an indígena, and a marginal urban resident. Quispe's alleged violence ensnared him in the system of justice. The case reveals several of the ways in which institutions and the actors classified residents of La Paz's indigenous neighborhoods regardless of their racial or ethnic identity and participated in the construction of their identities, which were often situational and relational. One person could identify himself as a laborer when the police asked him who he was, a "poor and ignorant indígena" when he wanted a jury to believe his story, and a *colono* when he petitioned the court for his release from jail.[13] The ways historical actors used these labels illustrates how fluid they were and how skillfully indigenous people mobilized them.

Urbanization and the Neighborhood Associations

Neighborhood associations played a significant role in shaping the urbanization of La Paz. My investigation of the process of urbanization reveals how the city government adapted the infrastructure to existing settlement patterns and began to do business with the populations that government officials and elites had previously regarded as outsiders to the urban environment. These organizations succeeded because their members adapted to the political context and framed their demands skillfully and perceptively. The associations tended to emphasize how improvements in infrastructure contributed to their own "progress," exposed neighborhood residents to modernity, and brought positive influences to their neighborhoods.

The city and national governments used unpaid labor service, prison labor, temporary labor, and contract labor as they urbanized La Paz. These labor regimes served both the city and the neighborhood associations. The city government also used lay brotherhoods and free labor from neighborhood association members. The associations skillfully leveraged their access to labor to gain the expertise and materials they needed to improve their neighborhoods. Thus, the lay brotherhoods, unions, neighborhood associations, and FEDJUVE all worked with city government officials to shape the development and modernization of La Paz.

In this process, rural and urban activists did not belong to separate movements. Rural populations and urban dwellers shared political strategies, economic networks, and common culture in their daily lives. The activism and political participation of neighborhood residents in La Paz emerged from within the neighborhoods as people embraced and took full advantage of the broader political changes of the first half of the twentieth century. The activism of indigenous neighborhood residents, the persistence of racial discourses and the ways indigenous people pushed back against them, and the social and economic links between the city and countryside all point to complex interactions between the neighborhoods and the political elite of the post-Chaco period.

Indigenous Neighborhoods and the Revolution

Inspired by works that look for deeper roots of the social transformations of Bolivia, I have sought to investigate and analyze the importance of indigenous neighborhood residents to the physical, social, and political development of the city. As a result of my findings, I posit some reasoned speculation about how and why the insurrection triumphed in April 1952. I suggest that the decades of activism on the part of the residents of the indigenous neighborhoods were as important for the triumph of the insurrection as the acute repression of the late 1940s and early 1950s. The multiple strategies those residents used to assert their rights as residents of the city, which included activism at home and at work that built long-term social and political relationships, made indigenous neighborhood residents effective allies in the MNR insurrection. Several scholars have also asserted that the military training veterans had received during the Chaco War was another key factor in the triumph of the insurrection.[14]

The fighting in and around Villa Victoria, along the slopes leading to El Alto, in El Alto itself, and between Miraflores and central La Paz all required the participation of La Paz's indigenous neighborhood residents and other urban residents not associated with the MNR. Some of these residents were surely MNR militants and some were not. The success of the insurrection depended on all of these actors. In Villa Victoria on April 9, a combined force of police and workers attempted to take control of the garrison controlled by the Calama division. The military was able to repel the attack and turn these forces back, and seeking to press their advantage, pursued the combined police and worker force into Villa Victoria. Veterans of the Chaco War who had kept their weapons, workers, police, and women all worked together to establish defensive positions in Villa Victoria in preparation for the entry of the military forces. The military units pursued the fleeing revolutionaries, and made their way across the Puente Villa, where the ad hoc rebel unit ambushed and defeated them.

In addition, residents used their knowledge of the neighborhood's topography and its strategic location along the only viable route into La Paz to pin down the military units and to prevent reinforcements from reaching other sectors of the city from El Alto. At the same time, another contingent of workers and police established themselves further west near the cemetery in order to prevent military units from using footpaths into La Paz from El Alto. The fighting was fierce in this sector. Using the cover of night on April 9, the contingent of fighters in Villa Victoria and near the cemetery used their knowledge of the terrain and paths up to El Alto to make their way up and attack the air force base there.

As a result of their experience with neighborhood associations and unions, residents of La Paz's indigenous neighborhoods had organizational structures that they could use to mobilize in support of the MNR. Indigenous Paceños knew how to petition and strike when they felt were they right to do so and they saw themselves as full citizens. The women of FOF asserted their rights based on the service and sacrifice of their husbands during the Chaco War. The residents of the indigenous neighborhoods were a population that could help the nation achieve its goals. The residents of Villa Potosí successfully pressured the city to provide water lines, electricity, roads, and schools in their neighborhood. It doesn't require any great stretch of imagination to understand that they were ready to step forward to correct the political course of Bolivia in April 1952. Their decades of work to integrate themselves into the fabric of the nation, as workers, as citizens, and as honorable people, had prepared them for that role. Despite the negative stereotypes some elites tried to use to control the conversation about indigenous people, neighborhood residents responded with actions that proved those ideas false. In 1945, the president of the Villa Potosí neighborhood association reminded the politicians and neighbors gathered to celebrate the dedication of the water lines of the importance of the indigenous neighborhood residents to La Paz. Without the workers who lived in the indigenous neighborhoods the nation would not be able to move forward. Villa Potosí's residents, through their activism, made the government "know the sad conditions in which the worker lives and [that] he is the true nerve and muscle of the nation."[15] The language Román used linked workers, the "nerve and muscle" of the body politic, with the health and progress of the nation as a whole.

Notes

Indígenas, Vecinos, and Residents

1 The *ayllu* is a unit of governance and social identity. For some basic background, see Klein, *A Concise History of Bolivia*. For the importance of *ayllus* as a source of revenue and a political unit in the national period, see Tristan Platt, *Estado Boliviano y ayllu andino: Tierra y tributo en el norte de Potosí* (Lima: Centro de Investigaciones Sociales de la Vicepresidencia mayo de 2016, 1982). For the importance of *ayllus* in the colonial era, see Brooke Larson, *Cochabamba, 1550–1900: Colonialism and Agrarian Transformation in Bolivia* (Durham, NC: Duke University Press, 1998); Sergio Serulnikov, *Subverting Colonial Authority: Challenges to Spanish Rule in Eighteenth-Century Southern Andes* (Durham, NC: Duke University Press, 2003); and Sinclair Thomson, *We Alone Will Rule: Native Andean Politics in the Age of Insurgency* (Madison: University of Wisconsin Press, 2002).

2 For the importance of changes in land tenure patterns for the *ayllu* in La Paz province, see Rossana Barragán and Dora Cajías, eds., *El siglo XIX: Bolivia y América Latina* (La Paz: Muela del Diablo Editores, 1997). Liberal land laws were not implemented as much in the La Paz region as they were in other Bolivian regions. Much of the change in land tenure patterns in the nineteenth century depended on the ability of the communities to resist fragmentation of communal land in the colonial period. This played a role in the ability of communities to resist fragmentation in the national period. The type of agricultural products cultivated and the importance of the products in the world economy also played roles in land commodification. For a historical study of communal land fragmentation, the development of wheat as a commodity, and the importance of Cochabamba's production in the regional economy, see Larson, *Cochabamba*. All of these factors influenced the effectiveness of *ayllus* as important social, political, and economic institutions in the nineteenth century.

3 Eloy Salmón, *La Paz en su IV centenario, 1548–1948* (La Paz: Comité Pro IV Centenario de la Fundación de la Paz, 1948), 67.

4 Historian Brooke Larson argues that the city was the bastion of elite culture and knowledge; see "Forging the Unlettered Indian: The Pedagogy of Race in the Bolivian Andes," in *Histories of Race and Racism*, edited by Laura Gotkowitz (Durham, NC: Duke University Press, 2011), 134–56. In the colonial period,

La Paz was the regional nucleus of Spanish administration and power. In the nineteenth century, La Paz and other Bolivian cities were the *criollo* face of Bolivia. Elites looked to Europe and North America for inspiration in ruling Bolivia and emphasized their own differences from the large indigenous populations of the Bolivia's rural areas.

5 Marta Irurozqui, *La armonía de las desigualdades: Élites y conflictos de poder en Bolivia, 1880-1920* (Cusco: Centro de Estudios Regionales Andinos: Bartolomé de Las Casas, 1994).
6 Erick Langer, *Economic Change and Rural Resistance in Southern Bolivia, 1880-1930* (Stanford, CA: Stanford University Press, 1989).
7 Rossana Barragán, *Espacio urbano y dinámica étnica: La Paz en el siglo XIX* (La Paz: Hisbol, 1990); Marta Irurozqui, *A bala, Piedra y Palo: La construcción de la ciudadanía política en Bolivia, 1826–1952* (Seville: Diputación de Sevilla, 2000).
8 Platt, *Estado Boliviano y ayllu andino*.
9 Brooke Larson, *Trials of Nation Making: Liberalism, Race, and Ethnicity in the Andes, 1810–1910* (Cambridge: Cambridge University Press, 2004).
10 Larson, *Cochabamba*; Laura Gotkowitz, *A Revolution for Our Rights* (Durham, NC: Duke University Press, 2008).
11 María Luisa Soux, "El problema de la propiedad en las comunidades indígenas: Patrimonio y herencia 1825-1850," in *El siglo XIX: Bolivia y América Latina*, edited by Rossana Barragán and Dora Cajías (La Paz: Muela del Diablo Editores, 1997), 497–508.
12 Larson, *Trials of Nation Making*.
13 Serulnikov, *Subverting Colonial Authority;* Thomson, *We Alone Will Rule*.
14 Tristan Platt, "The Andean Experience of Bolivian Liberalism, 1825–1900: Roots of Rebellion in 19th-Century Chayanta (Potosí)," in *Resistance, Rebellion, and Consciousness in the Andean Peasant World, 18th to 20th Centuries*, edited by Steve J. Stern (Madison: University of Wisconsin Press, 1987), 280–326; Brooke Larson, "'Forging the Unlettered Indian,'" 134–56; Gotkowitz, "Introduction," in *Histories of Race and Racism: The Andes and Mesoamerica from Colonial Times to the Present*, edited by Laura Gotkowitz (Durham, NC: Duke University Press, 2012), 1–39; Rossana Barragán, "The Census and the Making of a Social 'Order' in Nineteenth-Century Bolivia," in *Histories of Race and Racism: The Andes and Mesoamerica from Colonial Times to the Present*, edited by Laura Gotkowitz (Durham, NC: Duke University Press, 2011), 113–33.
15 Larson, *Trials of Nation Making*.
16 Stephen Jay Gould, *The Mismeasure of Man* (New York: Norton, 1981).
17 Larson, "'Forging the Unlettered Indian'"; Barragán, "The Census and the Making of a Social 'Order' in Nineteenth-Century Bolivia"; and Seemin Quayum, "Indian Ruins, National Origins: Tiwanaku and Indigenismo in La Paz, 1897–1933," in

Histories of Race and Racism, edited by Laura Gotkowitz (Durham, NC: Duke University Press, 2011), 159–78.
18 See Erwin P. Grieshaber, "Survival of Indian Communities in Nineteenth-Century Bolivia: A Regional Comparison," *Journal of Latin American Studies* 12, no. 2 (1980): 223–69.
19 Álvaro Cuadros B., *La Paz* (La Paz: Facultad de Arquitectura, Urbanismo y Artes, Universidad Mayor de San Andrés, 2002), 122.
20 Cuadros B., *La Paz*, 93; Salmón, *La Paz en Su Cuarto Centenario*, 45; "Distritos de La Paz 1917 Ordenanza," in *Anuario de leyes y disposiciones suprema 1917* (La Paz: Imprenta Nacional, 1918), 1123.
21 Imagine the Plaza Murillo surrounded by a three-square-block area. This is the central district. In the period 1900–30, the elite considered the area outside this small central district as *extramuro* despite the fact that San Francisco, San Pedro, and Santa Barbara were legally urban districts.
22 For a detailed discussion of indigenous urban settlements and the efforts of Spaniards to settle in the New World, see Arq. Ramón Gutiérrez, *Pueblo de indios: Otro urbanismo en la región Andina* (Quito: Biblioteca Ayba-yala, 1993), 8–47.
23 *Tambos* are a combination of warehouse and inn. They were collection points for specific agricultural products brought to the city. *Tambos* predate Spanish colonization and remained important to urban markets well into the twentieth century.
24 Cuadros B., *La Paz*, 112.
25 Cuadros B., *La Paz*, 134.
26 "Obreros Visitan a La Reforma," *El Hombre Libre*, November 16, 1920.
27 Cuadros B., *La Paz*, 134.
28 Herbert S. Klein, *Parties and Political Change in Bolivia, 1880–1952* (London: Cambridge University Press, 1969), 120.
29 The similarities with Augusto B. Leguía in Peru are uncanny. Both Leguía and Saavedra used populist discourses, promulgated social reforms, and persecuted their enemies. Leguía seems to have been much more successful in his efforts to control national politics. For an overview of the Peruvian case, see Thomas E. Skidmore and Peter H. Smith, *Modern Latin America*, 5th ed. (New York: Oxford University Press, 2001), 192–202.
30 The military socialists were a political group of junior military officers who had served in the Chaco War in various capacities on both the front lines and the military high command.
31 Klein, *Parties and Political Change in Bolivia*, 133.
32 In the countryside, the Jesús de Machaca uprising of 1921 and the subsequent repression of participants challenged the Saavedra government's commitment to "pro-indigenous" policies. In the mines, the miners' strike at Uncía in Oruro

province in 1923 and its subsequent repression also called into question Saavedra's commitment to Bolivia's "laboring classes." Esteban Ticona Alejo and Xavier Albó, *Jesús de Machaca en el tiempo* (La Paz: Fundación Diálogo, 1998); Herbert S. Klein, *A Concise History of Bolivia* (Cambridge: Cambridge University Press, 2003), 158.

33 "La Doctrina Radical del Doctor Saavedra," *El Hombre Libre*, November 12, 1920; Klein, *Parties and Political Change in Bolivia*, 76.
34 *El Hombre Libre*, October 20, 1920.
35 "Nota Policiaria," *La Reforma*, March 18, 1921.
36 Gotkowitz, *A Revolution for Our Rights*.
37 "Nota Policiaria," *La Reforma*, March 18, 1921.

Chapter 1

1 Some of the material in this chapter is based on L. M. Sierra, "Colonial Specters: The Extramuro, History, Memory, and Urbanization in La Paz, Bolivia, 1900-1947," *Journal of Urban History* 45, no. 6 (2019): 1131–52. https://doi.org/10.1177/0096144218791269.
2 *El Figaro*, May 8, 1918. The extramuro—literally, outside the walls—was the region of La Paz where indigenous Aymara inhabitants lived before and during the colonial era. The wall itself served as a defensive barrier between the Spanish city and its indigenous suburbs during the pan-Andean rebellion of the late eighteenth century.
3 "Informes," *Boletín Municipal de La Paz*, May 1933, 21.
4 "Informes," *Boletín Municipal de La Paz*, July 1935, 98.
5 Ximena Soruco Sologuren, *La ciudad de los cholos: mestizaje y colonialidad en Bolivia, siglos XIX y XX* (Lima: Instituto Francés de Estudios Andinos, 2011). See also Rossana Barragán, "Entre polleras, lliqllas y ñañacas. Los mestizos y la emergencia de la tercera república," in *Etnicidad, economía y simbolismo en los Andes: II congreso internacional de etnohistoria* (Lima: Institut français d'études andines, 1992).
6 These neighborhoods were Gran Poder, San Francisco Locería, 14th of September, and San Sebastián; *Boletín Municipal de La Paz*, November 1943, 43.
7 "Informe del Alcalde de La Paz," *Boletín Municipal de La Paz*, August 1946, 2–4.
8 Dress traditionally associated with the countryside and indigenous peoples in Bolivia. The vicuña is a wild camelid related to the alpaca whose wool has been used to make winter ponchos and shawls. *Calzon rajado* are short pants made of a rough-spun cotton cloth. They are typically associated with the countryside and with indigenous peoples in Bolivia. Taller de Historia Oral Andina, *Los constructores de la ciudad: Tradiciones de lucha y de trabajo del sindicato central de constructores y albañiles de Bolivia* (La Paz: UMSA, 1986), 28.

9 Taller de Historia Oral Andina, *Los constructores de la ciudad.*
10 Soruco Sologuren, Ximena, Institut français d'études andines, and Programa de Investigación Estratégica en Bolivia, *La Ciudad De Los Cholos: Mestizaje Y Colonialidad En Bolivia, Siglos Xix Y Xx*, Colección "travaux De L'institut Français D'études Andines," T. 283 (Lima: Instituto Francés de Estudios Andinos, 2011).
11 Rossana Barragán, "Entre polleras, lliqllas y ñañacas: Los mestizos y la emergencia de la tercera república," in *Etnicidad, economía y simbolismo en los Andes: II congreso internacional de etnohistoria. Coroicoi*, edited by Silvia Arze et al., new online edition (Lima: Institut français d'études andines, 1992), accessed November 6, 2019, http://books.openedition.org/ifea/2274.
12 Complicating the simple story of elite versus popular harassment, President Bautista Saavedra (1921–25) was nicknamed *"el cholo Saavedra."* This highlights a curious element of the stories of many political elites in Latin America: many of them refer to their indigenous and mixed-race antecedents. Thus, questioning a politician's origins became a common insult that brought the reality of mixed-race origins and a lack of "pure" whiteness to the fore. For example, Benito Juárez and Porforio Díaz, who were both from the Oaxacan Sierra, came from humble and indigenous origins. Other examples could be Tomas Guardia and Jose Figueres Ferrer in Costa Rica. Stories also circulated about the origins of Rafael Trujillo and Anastasio Somoza. Thus, it is unsurprising that Saavedra's origins served as fodder for such insults. Barragán, "Entre polleras, lliqllas y ñañacas." See also Luis M. Sierra, "Union Activism in La Paz Before and after the Chaco War, 1920–1947," in *The Chaco War: Environment, Ethnicity, and Nationalism*, edited by Bridget Maria Chesterton (London: Bloomsbury Press, 2016), 43–66.
13 Taller de Historia Oral Andina, *Los constructores de la ciudad;* Laura Gotkowitz, *A Revolution for Our Rights* (Durham, NC: Duke University Press, 2008); Brooke Larson, "Forging the Unlettered Indian: The Pedagogy of Race in the Bolivian Andes," in *Histories of Race and Racism: The Andes and Mesoamerica from Colonial Times to the Present*, edited by Laura Gotkowitz (Durham, NC: Duke University Press, 2012), 134–57; Waskar Ari Chachaki, "Race and Subaltern Nationalism: AMP Activist-Intellectuals in Bolivia, 1921–1964" (PhD diss., Georgetown University, 2004); and Seemin Quayum, "Indian Ruins, National Origins," in *Histories of Race and Racism: The Andes and Mesoamerica from Colonial Times to the Present*, edited by Laura Gotkowitz (Durham, NC: Duke University Press, 2012).
14 I first encountered the term *extramuro* in a letter in the Archivo Historico de La Paz in 2006. I was intrigued to see that this letter mentioned the *extramuro* and the people living there as the cause of disorder, drunkenness, and noise. ("Correspondencia Prefectural," Febrero 14, 1919, Archivo de La Paz/ Honorable Consejo Municipal.) In 2009, after a fine Bolivian lunch and while playing cards, my hosts—older women in their sixties who were supporters of the Movimiento

Nacionalista Revolucionario—asked me about my research. After I explained the overall idea of my project, one of them asked if my work focused only on the *extramuro*. The fact that a fine, upstanding middle-class Bolivian woman maintained a mental map of La Paz that included a notion of the *extramuro* further piqued my interest given that the wall had not existed for over 200 years in La Paz. The story that emerged from this conversation was one of segregation and then transformation after the 1952 Revolution. In a discussion with the eminent architect Emilio Villanueva's grandson, I discussed the *extramuro* and the origins of the prohibition. He highlighted the idea that it was a racist state that enacted a prohibition against Indians in the city. As a foreigner and student, I was able to ask people what the term meant to them. These two notions of racial targeting and a mental map of segregated spaces were common themes.

15   The lore surrounding the prohibition remains an intriguing question. Scholars argue that the government prohibited indigenous peoples from entering the Plaza Murillo. One would think that such a prohibition would have made its way into national or municipal ordinances, police regulations, or newspaper notices, but I could not find such a prohibition anywhere. I asked several prominent Bolivian scholars for leads about the prohibition. In a private email exchange, Brooke Larson pointed me to Xavier Albó, Laura Gotkowitz, and Rossana Barragán who might have had better leads. In the Archivo de La Paz and the Archivo Municipal, I approached other scholars including Laura Gotkowitz, Pilar Mendieta, Liz Shesko, and E. Gabrielle Kuenzli. I have asked other scholars of La Paz, including Carlos Villagómez, Álvaro Caudros, Luis Antezanas, and the director of the municipal archive, Ivica Tadic. I also interviewed the director of the Archivo del Congreso. Many of these scholars pointed to the abolition of the prohibition. Gotkowitz's *A Revolution for Our Rights* and Taller de Historia Oral Andina, *Los Constructores De La Ciudad*, mention the abolition of the prohibition but do not cite the law itself. In an email exchange, Liz Shesko pointed out that the abolition of the prohibition appeared in newspapers in 1935, and Waskar Ari Chachaki cites the abolition in *Race and Subaltern Nationalism: AMP Activist-Intellectuals in Bolivia, 1921–1964*. This led to an extensive search in the municipal archives and the congressional archives in La Paz. I found a reference in a newspaper from 1925 that printed a 1904 municipal ordinance that was redeployed during the centennial celebrations. The language prohibited the "indigenous outfit" and marked the boundaries the police should patrol to ensure that no one wearing the outfit entered the city center. However, it did not explicitly prohibit indigenous peoples from entering the Plaza Murillo in different clothing—an important distinction in terms of the biopolitics of race.

16   Alain Corbin, "Commercial Sexuality in Nineteenth-Century France: A System of Images and Regulations," *Representations* 14, no. 1 (1986): 209–19.

17 Judith R. Walkowitz, *City of Dreadful Delight: Narratives of Sexual Danger in Late-Victorian London* (Chicago: University of Chicago Press, 1992).
18 Jacob A. Riis and Luc Sante, *How the Other Half Lives: Studies Among the Tenements of New York* (New York: Penguin Books, 1997); Charles E. Rosenberg, *The Cholera Years: The United States in 1832, 1849, and 1866* (Chicago: University of Chicago Press, 1987).
19 Isabel Wilkerson, *The Warmth of Other Suns: The Epic Story of America's Great Migration* (New York: Vintage Press, 2011).
20 Sarah Chambers, *From Subjects to Citizens: Honor, Gender, and Politics in Arequipa, Peru, 1780–1854* (University Park: Pennsylvania State University Press, 1999).
21 Marisol de la Cadena, *Indigenous Mestizos: The Politics of Race and Culture in Cuzco, Peru, 1919-1991* (Durham, NC: Duke University Press, 2000).
22 My sources—which voice the view of elites who attempted to enforce racial division from above—see race as nearly insurmountable partly because the indelibility of race conveniently preserves the position of elites at the top. Chambers's sources lead to a different view, the optimistic hope of subalterns that race divisions are malleable. Although race was a malleable category even for elites, that was not the case in my source base.
23 Ernesto Capello, *City at the Center of the World: Space, History, and Modernity in Quito* (Pittsburgh, PA: University of Pittsburgh Press, 2012).
24 Guadalupe Garcia, *Beyond the Walled City: Colonial Exclusion in Havana* (Oakland: University of California Press, 2016).
25 Michel Foucault, *The History of Sexuality, Vol. 1: An Introduction* (New York: Vintage, 1990), 140.
26 Foucault, *The History of Sexuality*, 145.
27 Richard Rothstein, *The Color of Law: A Forgotten History of How Our Government Segregated America* (New York: W. W. Norton, 2017).
28 Ann Stoler, *Race and the Education of Desire: Foucault's History of Sexuality and the Colonial Order of Things* (Durham, NC: Duke University Press, 1995), Chapter 1.
29 This topic is the focus of my research. I analyze how migration and settlement in these neighborhoods transformed the morphology of the city and the politics of La Paz in the context of massive political and social transformations at the national level in the period before the 1952 Revolution. See Luis M. Sierra, "Indigenous Neighborhood Residents in the Urbanization of La Paz, Bolivia, 1910–1950" (PhD thesis, State University of New York at Binghamton, 2013). See also Luis Sierra, "The Indigenous Neighborhoods of La Paz: Urbanization, Migration, and Political Activism in La Paz, 1920–1947," *Journal of Global South Studies* (Fall 2018): 213–41.
30 The *tambo* has pre-Columbian origins. The social and religious leaders of *ayllus* originally controlled the *tambos*. In the colonial era and in the nineteenth century, *tambos* were collection points for agricultural products and livestock and served as

inns for agricultural producers. *Tambos* usually specialized in particular products and livestock.

31 For a brilliant and concise explanation of *ayllus*, indigenous labels, and contrasting processes in Cochabamba and other highland regions, see Tristan Platt, "The Andean Experience of Bolivian Liberalism, 1825–1900: Roots of Rebellion in 19th-Century Chayanta (Potosí)," in *Resistance, Rebellion, and Consciousness in the Andean Peasant World, 18th to 20th Centuries*, edited by Steve J. Stern (Madison: University of Wisconsin Press, 1987), 280–323. An *ayllu* is a unit of governance and social identity. For basic background, see Herbert S. Klein, *A Concise History of Bolivia* (Cambridge: Cambridge University Press, 2003). For the importance of *ayllus* to the state as a source of revenue and a political unit in the colonial period, see Tristan Platt, *Estado Boliviano y Ayllu Andino: Tierra y Tributo en el Norte de Potosí* (Lima: Centro de Investigaciones Sociales de la Vicepresidencia mayo de 2016, 1982). See also Brooke Larson, *Cochabamba, 1550–1900: Colonialism and Agrarian Transformation in Bolivia* (Durham, NC: Duke University Press, 1998); Sergio Serulnikov, *Subverting Colonial Authority: Challenges to Spanish Rule in Eighteenth-Century Southern Andes* (Durham, NC: Duke University Press, 2003); and Sinclair Thomson, *We Alone Will Rule: Native Andean Politics in the Age of Insurgency* (Madison: University of Wisconsin Press, 2002). For the importance of *ayllus* in the national era, see Brooke Larson, *Trials of Nation Making: Liberalism, Race, and Ethnicity in the Andes, 1810–1910* (Cambridge: Cambridge University Press, 2008).

32 For the importance of changes in land tenure patterns for *ayllus* in La Paz province, see Rossana Barragán and Dora Cajías, eds., *El Siglo XIX: Bolivia y América Latina* (La Paz: Muela del Diablo Editores, 1997). For a study of communal land fragmentation, the development of wheat as a commodity, and the importance of Cochabamba's production in the regional economy, see Larson, *Cochabamba*. All of these factors influenced how effective *ayllus* were as social, political, and economic institutions in the nineteenth century. The Aymara, like many indigenous peoples after conquest, were homogenized under the rubric of Indian. The Aymara label refers primarily to linguistic commonality. Even though Spaniards homogenized the Aymara, distinctions between *ayllus* and regions continue to exist. For instance, the Aymara dialect spoken in La Paz province is considered to be different from the dialect spoken in the Oruro province. The survival of local ayllu identities is one reason for local distinctions. The alienation of communal lands under the 1874 Leyes de Ex-Vinculación, which privatized indigenous *ayllu* communal landholding, was the rallying point for the Cacique Apoderado movement, whose members used their indigenous identity to organize. See Leandro Condori Chura and Esteban Ticona Alejo, *El escribano de los caciques apoderados* (La Paz: Hisbol, 1992), 61; and Platt, *Estado Boliviano y ayllu Andino*. After independence,

indigenous rights and privileges came under assault. In the republican era, the colonial category of *indio* lost its salience as a social and fiscal category. Elites began to use the term *indígena* to remove the connection between *indios'* obligations and their rights and privileges under the Spanish colonial regime. For a discussion of the laws and processes of defining indigenous people, see Erwin P. Grieshaber, "Survival of Indian Communities in Nineteenth-Century Bolivia: A Regional Comparison," *Journal of Latin American Studies* 12, no. 2 (November 1980): 223–69. See also Erwin P. Grieshaber, "Fluctuaciones en la definifición del indio: Comparación de los censos de 1900 y 1950," *Historia Boliviana* 5, nos. 1–2 (1985): 45–65.

As Laura Gotkowitz has argued, in the specific context of early twentieth-century Bolivia, "elite politicians and intellectuals further imbued the term 'Indian' with notions of poverty, ignorance, or savagery and . . . intrinsic inferiority," in *A Revolution for Our Rights: Indigenous Struggles for Land and Justice in Bolivia, 1880–1952* (Durham, NC: Duke University Press, 2007), 13. Gotkowitz also shows how the same people were simultaneously labeled *colonos, comunarios, indígena, raza indígena,* and *campesinos.*

33 Serulnikov, *Subverting Colonial Authority*; Thomson, *We Alone Will Rule.*
34 Historian Brooke Larson argues that the city was the bastion of elite culture and knowledge; see "Forging the Unlettered Indian." In the colonial period, La Paz was the regional nucleus of Spanish colonial administration and power. In the nineteenth century, La Paz and the other Bolivian cities represented the *criollo* face of Bolivia and its elites. Elites looked toward the knowledge, technology, architecture, art, economy, and governmental structures of Europe and North America for inspiration in ruling Bolivia and in creating differences from the large indigenous populations of Bolivia's rural areas.
35 While the outer, higher-up neighborhoods of Pura, Achachicala, and El Alto de La Paz experienced some growth in this period, they did not truly urbanize until the 1960s and 1970s.
36 Álvaro Cuadros B., *La Paz* (La Paz: Facultad de Arquitectura, Urbanismo y Artes, Universidad Mayor de San Andrés, 2002), 122.
37 *Garitas* were colonial road connection points. Several in La Paz mark colonial-era trade routes. The Garitas de Potosí and de Lima continue to serve as important landmarks. In the colonial era, the Garita de Lima was an enforced stopping point for all trade caravans headed in and out of La Paz toward Potosí, Oruro, and Lima. Several *tambos* were located in and around the area. In the nineteenth and twentieth centuries, the Garita de Lima was located between two railway terminals and continued to play an important role as a major distribution point. Today, it is located at the heart of the Gran Poder celebrations as participants weave down from the steep streets toward the city center.

38 Cuadros B., *La Paz*, 134.
39 "Censo de la ciudad de La Paz—Distribución por distritos," *Boletín Municipal de La Paz*, November 1943, 28–35.
40 Antonio Carvajal and Armando Quispe, Injurias (Slander), 1944, Caja 65, Corte Superior de Distrito, Archivo de La Paz.
41 Seemin Quayum, María Luisa Soux, and Rossana Barragán, *De terratenientes a amas de casa: mujeres de la élite de La Paz en la primera mitad del siglo XX* (La Paz: Ministerio de Desarrollo Humano, Secretaría de Asuntos Étnicos, de Género y Generacionales, Subsecretaría de Asuntos de Género, 1997), 50.
42 E. Gabrielle Kuenzli, *Acting Inca: National Belonging in Early Twentieth Century Bolivia* (Pittsburgh: Pittsburgh University Press, 2013); Larson, *Trials of Nation Making*.
43 Ramiro Condarco Morales, *Zárate, el "temible" Willka: historia de la rebelión indígena de 1899 en la República de Bolivia* (La Paz: 1983); Pilar Mendieta, *Entre la alianza y la confrontación: Pablo Zárrate Willka y la rebelión indígena de 1899 en Bolivia* (Lima: Instituto Francés de Estudios Andinos, UMIFRE 17, CNRS-MAEE, 2010); Larson, *Trials of Nation Making*; and Kuenzli, *Acting Inca*.
44 These laws sought to parcel out indigenous communal lands to individuals in order to privatize the land and thus force indigenous people to join the market economy.
45 The idea of race war emerged as one of prosecutors' main theories during the trials political Aymara leaders faced for the supposed atrocities they committed during the war. Historian E. Gabrielle Kuenzli suggests that the Aymara participants saw themselves as liberals and full participants in the 1899 Civil War and that for them this was never a race war. See Kuenzli, *Acting Inca*; and Brooke Larson, *Trials of Nation-Making* for a basic narrative of the war and its importance.
46 Kuenzli, *Acting Inca*, 49.
47 E. Gabrielle Kuenzli, "Acting Inca: The Parameters of National Belonging in Early Twentieth-Century Bolivia," *Hispanic American Historical Review* 90, no. 2 (2010): 247–81.
48 *Boletín Municipal de La Paz*, January 1921, 8; *Boletín Municipal de La Paz*, August 1923, 12–15.
49 "Patentes," January 10, *Anuario de Leyes y Disposiciones 1918* (La Paz: Imp. Oficial, 1919), 102. The tax could be cost prohibitive for most of the people living in the indigenous neighborhoods because anyone organizing an event would have to pay hundreds of bolivianos up front, an impossibility for most working people.
50 "Clasificación de vagos," December 15, *Anuario de Leyes y Disposiciones 1932* (La Paz: Imp. Oficial, 1933), 1949–51.
51 Ineke Dibbits, *Agitadoras de Buen Gusto: Historia del Sindicato de Culinarias (1935–1958)*, Serie Mujer Y Participación, 1 (La Paz: TAHIPAMU, 1989), 56; *Boletín Municipal de La Paz*, May 1945, 68.

52 *Boletín Municipal de La Paz*, March 1929, 39.
53 *Boletín Municipal de La Paz*, November 1923, 35–42.
54 E. Gabrielle Kuenzli asserts that a discourse that used the indigenous past made indigenous peoples central to the Bolivian nation-building project. The discussion here centers on elite efforts to deal with and manage the living population of Aymaras in and around the city. Kuenzli, *Acting Inca*, 49.
55 Larson, *Trials of Nation Making*, 17.
56 Dirección General de Estadística, "Censo de La Paz," in *Demografía: 1929* (La Paz: Oficina Nacional de Estadistica, 1929), 34.
57 Cuadros, *La Paz*, 142; "Junta de Almonedas," *Boletín Municipal de La Paz*, December 1926, 39; "Informe," Dirección Nacional de Estadística, *Actas y Estadísticas* (La Paz: Oficina Nacional de Estadistica, 1929), 14.
58 Comité Pro Cuarto Centenario de la Fundación de La Paz and Eloy Salmón, *La Paz en su IV centenario, 1548–1948*, Tomo IV ([La Paz]: Comité Pro IV Centenario de la Fundación de la Paz, 1948), 76; Cuadros B., *La Paz*, 160; Correspondencia Honorable Consejo Municipal, Enero 1917, Archivo de La Paz/Prefectura.
59 *Boletín Municipal de La Paz*, October 1923, 39; *Boletín Municipal de La Paz*, December 1926, 30; Dirección Nacional de Estadística, "Cerco urbano," in *Acta y Estadísticas* 1929, 26; *Boletín Municipal de La Paz*, May 1934, 11; Cuadros B., *La Paz*, 134–8.
60 For relevant information on urban crime, see Thomas H. Holloway, *Policing Rio de Janeiro: Repression and Resistance in a 19th-Century City* (Stanford, CA: Stanford University Press, 1993); and Pablo Piccato, *City of Suspects: Crime in Mexico City, 1900–1931* (Durham, NC: Duke University Press, 2001). For the Andean context and the policing of market women, see Mary Weismantel, *Cholas and Pishtacos: Stories of Race and Sex in the Andes* (Chicago: University of Chicago Press, 2001). For staking claims on public space, see Setha M. Low, *On the Plaza: The Politics of Public Space and Culture* (Austin: University of Texas Press, 2000). See also Laura Gotkowitz, "Trading Insults: Honor, Violence, and the Gendered Culture of Commerce in Cochabamba, Bolivia, 1870s–1950s," *Hispanic American Historical Review* 83, no. 1 (2003): 83–118.
61 "Actas," *Boletín Municipal de La Paz*, August 1923, 76. For the links between public transportation and urban identities in Mexico, see John Lear, *Workers, Neighbors, and Citizens: The Revolution in Mexico City* (Lincoln: University of Nebraska Press, 2001); and Piccato, *City of Suspects*.

The idea that a person's whiteness and wealth meant that they could not spread disease is an example of how science was used to justify and support systems of hierarchy and domination. See Nancy Leys Stepan, *The Hour of Eugenics: Race, Gender, and Nation in Latin America* (Ithaca, NY: Cornell University Press, 1991); Nancy Leys Stepan, *Picturing Tropical Nature* (London: Reaktion Books, 2001);

Nancy P. Appelbaum, Anne S. Macpherson, and Karin Alejandra Rosemblatt, "Introduction," in *Race and Nation in Modern Latin America*, edited by Nancy P. Appelbaum, Anne S. Macpherson, and Karin Alejandra Rosemblatt (Chapel Hill: University of North Carolina, 2003), 1–31; Katherine Elaine Bliss, *Compromised Positions: Prostitution, Public Health, and Gender Politics in Revolutionary Mexico City* (University Park: Pennsylvania State University Press, 2001); and Sidney Chalhoub, "The Politics of Disease Control: Yellow Fever and Race in Nineteenth-Century Rio de Janeiro," *Journal of Latin American Studies* 25, no. 3 (1993): 441–63.

62 *Boletín Municipal de La Paz*, September 1926, 11–17.
63 *Boletín Municipal de La Paz*, October 1923, 39; *Boletín Municipal de La Paz*, December 1926, 30; Dirección Nacional de Estadística, "Cerco urbano," 26.
64 Holloway, *Policing Rio de Janeiro*.
65 Piccato, *City of Suspects*.
66 Low, *On the Plaza*.
67 Weismantel, *Cholas and Pishtacos*.
68 "Informe," *Boletín Municipal de La Paz*, September 1926, 61.
69 Alcaldía Municipal de La Paz, "Informe casas de tolerancia," in *Memorias 1909* (La Paz: Imp. Oficial, 1910), 21; "Las casas de tolerancia," *El Hombre Libre*, January 12, 1918; "Casa de tolerancia: prohibidas en toda la República," *Anuario Leyes, Decretos, y Resoluciones*, April 5, 1923 (La Paz: Imprenta Oficial, 1924), 76.
70 *Boletín Municipal de La Paz*, August 1923, 9; "La famosísima cloaca de illampu," *El Hombre Libre*, January 1918; "Un Foco de Infección," *El Hombre Libre*, May 12, 1918; "Eso canales," *El Hombre Libre*, June 6, 1918.
71 "Fiebre exemática," *La Reforma*, December 18, 1920.
72 *Boletín Municipal de La Paz*, March 1921, 5; *Boletín Municipal de La Paz*, November 1923, 16.
73 *Boletín Municipal de La Paz*, May 1933, 16.
74 *Boletín Municipal de La Paz*, July 1935, 15.
75 "Correspondencia Prefectural," Febrero 14, 1919, Honorable Consejo Municipal, Correspondencia, Archivo de La Paz.
76 Carlos Villagómez, *La Paz ha muerto: arte, arquitectura, ciudad* (La Paz, Bolivia: Plural Editores, 2004); Cuadros B., *La Paz*, 156.
77 *Boletín Municipal de La Paz*, January 1921; Thomas Alan Abercrombie, *Pathways of Memory and Power: Ethnography and History Among an Andean People* (Madison: University of Wisconsin Press, 1998).
78 "Circular nacional," in *Anuario de Leyes y Disposiciones* (La Paz: Imprenta Nacional, 1918), 114–16.
79 "La civilización de las razas quechua y aymara," *La Reforma*, March 18, 1921. In addition, Ann Laura Stoler's edited volume includes some excellent work on comparative empire, colonialism, and the construction of racial categories; see

Haunted by Empire: Geographies of Intimacy in North American History (Durham, NC: Duke University Press, 2006).
80 "El problema educacional indígena," *La Reforma*, March 19, 1921.
81 *Boletín Municipal de La Paz*, August 1923, 21–4.
82 "La cuestión agraria y el indio," *La Reforma*, March 23, 1921. The Jesús de Machaca rebellion took place on March 12, 1921, in La Paz Department in the Ingavi Province. The government violently repressed an indigenous rebellion against a hated local official and massacred several indigenous people.
83 "Carnaval de 1925," *La República*, February 15, 1925; "Tallares de sastería," *Anuario de Leyes y Disposiciones 1924* (La Paz: Imprenta Nacional, 1925); "Carros funebres," *Anuario de Leyes y Disposiciones 1917* (La Paz: Imprenta Nacional, 1918).
84 Quoted in Rolando Costa Ardúz, *La Paz: sus rostros en el tiempo*, vol. 2 (La Paz: Honorable Alcaldía de La Paz, 1993), 119.
85 "Aviso Municipal," *La República*, April 25, 1925.
86 "Catastro urbano," *Boletín Municipal de La Paz*, September 1926, 3.
87 These sources are never clear about which elements made a person indigenous. At times, it was dress, behavior, diet, or appearance.
88 "Aviso Municipal," *La Republica*, April 25, 1925, cites a municipal ordinance from 1899.
89 Appelbaum, Macpherson, and Karin Alejandra Rosemblatt, "Introduction," in *Race and Nation in Modern Latin America*, edited by Nancy P. Appelbaum, Anne S. Macpherson, and Karin Alejandra Rosemblatt (Chapel Hill: University of North Carolina, 2003), 1–31.
90 Quayum, Soux, and Barragán, *De terratenientes a amas de casa*; Gotkowitz, *A Revolution for Our Rights*.

Chapter 2

1 Today Bolivia recognizes several dozen indigenous groups.
2 William Roseberry, "Hegemony and the Language of Contention," in *Everyday Forms of State Formation: Revolution and the Negotiation of Rule in Modern Mexico*, edited by Gilbert M. Joseph and Daniel Nugent (Durham, NC: Duke University Press, 1994), 355–66. Roseberry argues that elites tried to control the language and rules of engagement in the field of contention by discounting certain narratives. In Bolivia, although the language of contention made it difficult for indigenous peoples to participate because the racial discourses argued that they were not coherent political actors, the indigenous identity remained central to all of the nation-building projects of the twentieth century.
3 In the nineteenth and early twentieth centuries, the Bolivian national government passed laws that privatized land, thus making it possible for nonindigenous

people to purchase communal lands indigenous people had occupied for many generations. These laws erased the special status indigenous people had enjoyed throughout the colonial era. The Caciques Apoderados fought for the return of communal lands they had lost as a result of these laws.

4 Daniel Sanchez Bustamante, "Estudio Preliminar," in J. Ricardo Alarcón A., *Bolivia en el primer centenario de su independencia* (New York: University Society, 1925), x.

5 Bustamante, "Estudio Preliminar," xi–xii.

6 For parallels with colonial discourses in other post-emancipation societies, see Constantino Tancara Quispe, *La promesa de Warisata* (La Paz: Inst. Internacional de Integración del Convenio Andrés Bello, 2011); Martin Brienen, "Warisata y la renovación de la educación rural indigenal boliviana, 1931–1948," in *Campesinos y escolares: la construcción de la escuela en el campo latinoamericano, siglos XIX y XX*, edited by Alicia Civera, Juan Alfonseca G., and Carlos Escalante Fernández (Zinacantepec, Estado de México: Colegio Mexiquense, 2011), Chapter 10. For debates about public and private reforms, see Brooke Larson, "Capturing Indian Bodies, Hearths, and Minds: 'El hogar campesino' and Rural School Reform in Bolivia, 1920s–1940s," in *Proclaiming Revolution: Bolivia in Comparative Perspective*, edited by Merilee Serrill Grindle and Pilar Domingo (London: Institute of Latin American Studies, 2003), Chapter 8.

7 Bustamante, "Estudio Preliminar," xi–xii.

8 "Circular 17 Enero," in *Ministro de Agricultura y Instrucción* (La Paz: Imprenta Nacional, 1918), 715.

9 "Circular 17 Enero," 715.

10 Tristan Platt, "The Andean Experience of Bolivian Liberalism, 1825–1900: Roots of Rebellion in 19th-Century Chayanta (Potosí)," in *Resistance, Rebellion, and Consciousness in the Andean Peasant World, 18th to 20th Centuries*, edited by Steve J. Stern (Madison: University of Wisconsin Press, 1987), 280–323. *Hacendados* were owners of large rural properties.

11 E. Gabrielle Kuenzli, *Acting Inca: National Belonging in Early Twentieth Century Bolivia* (Pittsburgh: Pittsburgh University Press, 2013).

12 See Brooke Larson, "Forging the Unlettered Indian: The Pedagogy of Race in the Bolivian Andes," in *Histories of Race and Racism*, edited by Laura Gotkowitz (Durham, NC: Duke University Press, 2011), 134–59; Kuenzli, *Acting Inca*; Laura Gotkowitz, *A Revolution for Our Rights: Indigenous Struggles for Land and Justice in Bolivia, 1880–1952* (Durham, NC: Duke University Press, 2007); Rossana Barragán, *Indios, mujeres y ciudadanos: legislación y ejercicio de la ciudadanía en Bolivia (siglo XIX)* (La Paz: Fundación Diálogo, 1999); William E. Carter and Mauricio Mamani, *Irpa chico: individuo y comunidad en la cultura aymara* (La Paz: Librería Editorial Juventud, 1983); and Brooke Larson, "Redeemed Indians,

Barbarized Cholos," in *Political Cultures in the Andes, 1750–1950*, edited by Nils Jacobsen and Cristóbal Aljovín de Losada (Durham, NC: Duke University Press, 2005), 230–52.

13 "Festividad religiosa," *Boletín Municipal de La Paz,* February 1921, 26–35; M. Rigoberto Paredes, "Altiplanicie, el habitante y la población," *Boletín de la Sociedad Geográfica de La Paz* 33–35 (1925): 130–45; Vicente Donoso Torres, *El estado actual de la educación indigenal en el país* (La Paz: Renacimiento, 1940); and Luis Terán Gómez, "El Indio ante la realidad," *Boletín de la Sociedad Geográfica de La Paz* 52, no. 63 (1941): 80–90. Voting rights were not extended to women or indigenous peoples until the passage of universal suffrage after the 1952 Revolution. While indigenous peoples were citizens, they were excluded from voting and from most positions of authority.

14 Carlos Bravo and Daniel Bustamante founded the Geographic Society in 1889. J. Ricardo Alarcón A., *Bolivia en el primer centenario de su independencia* (New York: University Society, 1925), 733.

15 Sarah Chambers, "Little Middle Ground: The Instability of a Mestizo Identity in the Andes, Eighteenth and Nineteenth Centuries," in *Race and Nation in Modern Latin America*, edited by Nancy Appelbaum, Anne S. Macpherson, and Karin A. Rosemblatt (Chapel Hill: University of North Carolina Press, 2003), 32–56; Gerardo Renique, "Race, Region, and Nation: Sonora's Anti-Chinese Racism and Mexico's Post-Revolutionary Nationalism, 1920s–1930s," in *Race and Nation in Modern Latin America*, edited by Nancy P. Appelbaum, Anne S. Macpherson, and Karin Alejandra Rosemblatt (Chapel Hill: University of North Carolina Press, 2003), 211–36; Barbara Weinstein, "Racializing Regional Difference: Sao Paulo versus Brazil, 1932," in *Race and Nation in Modern Latin America*, edited by Nancy P. Appelbaum, Anne S. Macpherson, and Karin Alejandra Rosemblatt (Chapel Hill: University of North Carolina Press, 2003), 237–62; Brooke Larson, *Trials of Nation Making: Liberalism, Race, and Ethnicity in the Andes, 1810–1910* (Cambridge: Cambridge University Press, 2004); Marisol de la Cadena, "From Race to Class: Insurgent Intellectuals *de Provincia* in Peru, 1910–1970," in *Shining and Other Paths: War and Society in Peru, 1980–1995*, edited by Steve J. Stern (Durham, NC: Duke University Press, 1998), 22–59; Marisol de la Cadena, *Indigenous Mestizos: The Politics of Race and Culture in Cuzco, Peru, 1919–1991* (Durham, NC: Duke University Press, 2000).

16 For Paredes's participation in the liberal nation-building project, see Kuenzli, *Acting Inca*.

17 The Paredes family were Aymara caciques who came from the altiplano. This personal history helps situate his reservations about the capacities of the mixed-race peoples of Bolivia. He presents a fascinating case study of the complicated relationship between class, race, and the liberal nation-building project in the early twentieth century. See Kuenzli, *Acting Inca*.

18 Kuenzli, *Acting Inca*. Daniel Sanchez Bustamante was a Bolivian politician and intellectual. Luis Terán Gómez was a politician. Vicente Donoso Torres was a politician, intellectual, and theorist. Gómez and Torres argued for separate and unequal integration.

19 Kuenzli argues that because indigenous identity remained central to all Bolivian nation-building efforts, an acceptable non-Aymara indigenous identity had to be constructed. This identity was the Inca alternative that was imagined as somewhere between nonindigenous and not white but also (importantly) as not Aymara. See *Acting Inca*, chapter 2.

20 I discuss this phenomenon in more detail in Chapter 5.

21 M. Rigoberto Paredes, "Altiplanicie, El Habitante y La Población," in Ricardo Alarcón, *Bolivia en el primer centenario de su independencia* (New York: University Society, 1925), 19–45.

22 Paredes, "Altiplanicie, El Habitante y La Población," J. Ricardo Alarcón A., *Bolivia en el primer centenario de su independencia* (New York: University Society, 1925), 19–22.

23 Each of these uprisings had different origins and causes, but they were all rural rebellions that responded to abuses by political elites. The 1917 rebellion was centered on the labor indigenous Aymaras were meant to provide to local *hacendados*. The indigenous community members argued that the *hacendados* were abusing their authority and demanding too much time and labor from the indigenous peasants. The 1921 Jesús de Machaca rebellion began as a protest against a hated *corregidor* and his partisans. In the Chayanta rebellion of 1927, nearly 10,000 indigenous Bolivians fought against the expansion of hacienda lands and fought to regain communal lands they had lost in the previous fifty years to a process of consolidation by elites.

24 Iturralde was an important politician, a city councilor, and a member of the Bautista Saavedra's Republican Party. He opposed indigenous dancing, processions, and religious celebrations within the old colonial boundaries of La Paz.

25 "Festividad religiosa," *Boletín Municipal de La Paz*, January 1921, 26–35.

26 "El problema educacional indígena," *La Reforma*, March 19, 1921.

27 "La cuestión agraria y el indio," *La Reforma*, March 23, 1921.

28 "Festividad religiosa," *Boletín Municipal de La Paz*, January 1921, 9; "Radio Urbano," *Boletín Municipal de La Paz*, March 1929, 54.

29 Quoted in Rolando Costa Ardúz, *La Paz: sus rostros en el tiempo*, vol. 2 (La Paz: Honorable Alcaldía de La Paz, 1993), 119.

30 "Aviso Municipal," *La República*, April 25, 1925.

31 *Boletín Municipal de La Paz*, January 1921, 25–36; *Boletín Municipal de La Paz*, June 1923, 11. By the mid-1930s, Tamayo had become a principal leader of the Socialist Party. See Guillermo Lora, *Historia del movimiento obrero boliviano*, vol. 2 (La Paz, Cochabamba: Editorial Los Amigos del Libro, 1967), especially chapter 2.

32 Gotkowitz, *A Revolution for Our Rights*, chapter 3; "Patentes," in *Anuario de leyes, decretos y resoluciones supremas 1921* (La Paz: Imprentas Unidas, 1922), 1162.
33 "Los Obreros de Santa Cruz por Bautista Saavedra," *La Reforma*, January 16, 1921; "La Sociedad Obrera de La Paz," *El Fígaro*, October 20, 1920. In reply to a letter from the Sociedad that backed his candidacy, Bautista Saavedra argued that the coup was about maintaining the public order. See "Los Matarifes en Huelga: El Pueblo de La Paz Próximo en Morir de Hambre," *El Hombre Libre*, January 27, 1920; and Klein, *Parties and Political Change in Bolivia*, especially chapter 6.
34 It bears repeating that the policies proposed by the intellectual elite and Bolivia's leading politicians and policy makers overlapped. These policies reflected the ideas of intellectuals, which were integral to the political elite's nation-building efforts. Manuel Ballivián, the longtime president of the Geographic Society of La Paz, was involved in several government institutions in the liberal period. His father was a man of letters, considered by some to be the father of the Bolivian novel. The younger Ballivián was educated in Europe. In 1875, he worked as President Tomás Frías's secretary. In the late nineteenth century, he served as director of the nation's Immigration, Statistics, and Propaganda Department and helped direct the 1902 La Paz census with historian and La Paz scholar Luis S. Crespo. Ballivián was also minister of agriculture from 1905 to 1908. He published over seventy titles, including pamphlets, articles, and books. Ballivián was president of the society until his death in 1921. The Geographic Society published tracts on human geography, Bolivia's natural resources, and the expeditions that explored and settled in Bolivia's lowland regions. Ballivián published regularly in the *Boletín de la Sociedad Geográfica de La Paz*.
35 Daniel Sanchez Bustamante, "Estudio Preliminar," x.
36 Paredes, "Altiplanicie, el habitante y la población," 19–22.
37 Xavier Albó, "From MNRista to Katarista," in Silvia Rivera Cusicanqui, *Oppressed but Not Defeated: Peasant Struggles among the Aymara and Qhechwa in Bolivia, 1900–1980* (Geneva: United Nations Research Institute for Social Development, 1987), 379–419; Esteban Ticona Alejo, *Saberes, conocimientos y prácticas anticoloniales del pueblo aymara-quechua en Bolivia* (La Paz: AGRUCO, UMSS-FCAyP/COSUDE, 2010); Esteban Ticona Alejo, *Bolivia en el inicio del "Pachakuti": La larga lucha anticolonial de los pueblos aimara y quechua* (Madrid: Akal, 2011); Carlos Mamani Condori, *Taracú: 1866–1935: Masacre, guerra y "renovación" en la biografía de Eduardo L. Nina Qhispi* (La Paz Ediciones Aruwiyiri, 1991). For an example of the contemporary difficulty in defining identity, see Robert Albro, "Confounding Cultural Citizenship and Constitutional Reform in Bolivia," *Latin American Perspectives* 37, no. 3 (2010): 71–90.
38 Paredes, "Altiplanicie, el habitante y la población," 25–6.
39 Paredes, "Altiplanicie, el habitante y la población," 28–30.

40 Paredes, "Altiplanicie, el habitante y la población," 31.
41 Paredes, "Altiplanicie, el habitante y la población," 31.
42 Paredes, "Altiplanicie, el habitante y la población," 32.
43 Paredes, "Altiplanicie, el habitante y la población," 32.
44 Paredes, "Altiplanicie, el habitante y la población," 37.
45 Paredes, "Altiplancie, el habitante y la población," 37, 41.
46 For the argument that moral codes also helped support cultural racism, see de la Cadena, *Indigenous Mestizos*.
47 Paredes, "Altiplancie, el habitante y la población," 43.
48 Larson, "Forging the Unlettered Indian." Larson argues that Paredes's ideas about mestizos and *cholos* created and maintained the privileges of white urbanites.
49 Paredes, "Altiplanicie, el habitante y la población," 44.
50 Paredes, "Altiplanicie, el habitante y la población," 45.
51 See, for example, Larson, "Forging the Unlettered Indian."
52 Kuenzli, *Acting Inca*.
53 The Bolivian national government violently put down the Uncía miners' strike in western Bolivia on behalf of Simon I. Patiño, one of the richest and most influential men in the nation. The several hundred miners who struck for better working conditions and pay did not anticipate the ferocity of the government's response. Klein, *Parties and Political Change in Bolivia*.
54 The Jesús de Machaca rebellion began as a protest against a hated local official and turned violent when he and his family were murdered. Thousands of indigenous Bolivians joined to protest land dispossession and abuses by other local authorities.
55 See Esteban Ticona Alejo and Xavier Albó, *Jesús de Machaca en el tiempo* (La Paz: Fundación Diálogo, 1998).
56 Urban and national census takers continued to define "mestizo" and "white" as separate categories. See Alarcón A., *Bolivia en el primer centenario de su independencia*, 13.
57 "October 15," in *Anuario de leyes, decretos y resoluciones supremas 1927* (La Paz: Imprentas Unidas, 1929), 1775–80.
58 "Clasificación de Vagos," December15, in *Anuario de Leyes y Disposiciones 1932*, 1949–51.
59 Dibbits, *Agitadoras de buen gusto*, 56; *Boletín Municipal de La Paz*, May 1945, 68.
60 *Boletín Municipal de La Paz*, March 1929, 39.
61 Larson argues that Andean "writers and politicians preferred idioms of race, region, and culture to reinforce class inequalities and to position its indigenous peoples at the margins of nation and modernity." At the same time, indigenous peoples "increasingly turned to issues and identities of class and citizenship, Andean people evolved new discourses and practices of ethnic self-empowerment, which eventually worked their way into the core national political struggle over culture, power, and identity." Larson, *Trials of Nation Making*, 17–18.

62 In fact, Saavedra was one of the defense attorneys for the Aymara leaders accused of treason in the 1899 Civil War.
63 Luis Antezana Ergueta, *Historia Secreta del Movimiento Nacionalista Revolucionario* (La Paz: Librería Editorial "Juventud," 1984), 3:456; Herbert S. Klein, *A Concise History of Bolivia* (Cambridge: Cambridge University Press, 2003), 150.
64 Several leftist groups, including a Bolivian Socialist Party, Grupo Túpac Amaru, Izquierda Bolivia, Kollosuyo, and Exiliados, were politically active before the war but usually only from exile. Their memberships were limited to students, intellectuals, and radical elements of the middle class. They united during the war to help create the Partido Obrero Revolucionario (POR). Marxist parties did not gain strength and legitimacy in Bolivia until after the Chaco War.
65 Klein, *Parties and Political Change in Bolivia, 1880–1952* (London: Cambridge University Press, 1969, 197); Luis Antezana Ergueta, interview with the author, June 2009; and Carlos Montenegro, *Nacionalismo y coloniaje* (Buenos Aires: Ediciones Pleamar, 1967). The people who founded the Movimiento Nacionalista Revolucionario (MNR) in 1942 illustrate some of the continuities in politics before and after the war. For example, journalist Carlos Montenegro, who fought in the war, helped found the MNR. His influential work *Nacionalismo y Coloniaje* (1939) promoted the idea of unifying excluded groups under the banner of a nationalist movement. The book also formed one of the intellectual foundations of the nationalist movement and Montenegro became one of the preeminent intellectuals of the MNR. Víctor Paz Estenssoro, another founder of the MNR, had supported Hernando Siles and the Nationalist Party in the 1920s. Paz Estenssoro worked for Siles in the National Statistics Office and served in the Chaco War as a common soldier. After the war, he served as a senator, a congressional deputy, and economics minister for the Peñaranda government, and as finance minister in the Villarroel government. He ran for president in 1947 and 1951 and served as president of Bolivia four times after the 1952 Revolution. He also wrote for several newspapers and met Montenegro while writing in La Paz in the 1920s. As journalists and politicians after the war, these leftists and future MNR leaders helped bring about the realignments of the postwar period. They participated in the military socialist experiment (1936–39) and the Villarroel government (1943–46).
66 Klein, *Parties and Political Change in Bolivia*; "El socialismo de las masas," *La Calle*, May 1, 1938; "Colonos de una hacienda desencadenan una gran lucha Obrera," *La Calle*, May 3, 1938.
67 "Adolfo Paco cariaga un obrero ejemplar," *La Calle*, May 8, 1938.
68 "Comité Pro Cuarto Centenario de la Fundación de La Paz," *La Paz en su IV centenario, 1548–1948*, Tomo III, *Monografías literaria, científica, artística, religiosa y folklórica* (La Paz: Comité Pro IV Centenario de la Fundación de la Paz, 1948),

273. See also David M. Guss, "The Gran Poder and the Reconquest of La Paz," *Journal of Latin American Anthropology* 11, no. 2 (2006): 294–328.
69 Marcia Stephenson, *Gender and Modernity in Andean Bolivia* (Austin: University of Texas Press, 1999).
70 I cover the growth of the unions and neighborhood associations in Chapter 5.
71 *Anuario de leyes, decretos y resoluciones supremas 1941* (La Paz: Imprentas Unidas, 1942), 267–8, 534, and 876. General Peñaranda of the Concordancia issued several states of siege decrees in rural La Paz provinces.
72 Gotkowitz has shown how several of the *cacique apoderados* labored as porters in the city while doing community business. See Gotkowitz, *A Revolution for Our Rights*. Waskar Ari has found similar connections, see Waskar Ari, "Race and Subaltern Nationalism: AMP Activist-Intellectuals in Bolivia, 1921-1964" (PhD diss., Georgetown University, 2004).
73 "Decreto Supremo," in *Anuario de leyes, decretos y resoluciones supremas 1943* (La Paz: Imprentas Unidas, 1944), 245.
74 Klein, *Parties and Political Change in Bolivia*, 375. I will develop the relation between the municipal government, national government, the MNR, and La Paz unions in Chapter 4.
75 Gotkowitz, *A Revolution for Our Rights*, 219; Jorge Dandler and Juan Torrico A., "From the National Indigenous Congress to the Ayopaya Rebellion: Bolivia, 1945–1947," in *Resistance, Rebellion, and Consciousness in the Andean Peasant World, 18th to 20th Centuries*, edited by Steve J. Stern (Madison: University of Wisconsin Press, 1987), 334–78.
76 Gómez, "El Indio ante la realidad," 80–90.
77 Gómez, "El Indio ante la realidad," 81–5. This theory is based on social Darwinism and the eugenics of the pre–Second World War racial sciences. Gómez seems to have subscribed to a racial science that argued that genetic components and the environment could be manipulated through education and improvements in the social environment that could reverse what he saw as "degeneracy."
78 Gómez, "El Indio ante la realidad," 81–5.
79 Gómez, "El Indio ante la realidad," 86.
80 Gómez, "El Indio ante la realidad," 86. For a discussion of how morality shapes racial distinctions, see De la Cadena, *Indigenous Mestizos*.
81 Gómez, "El Indio ante la realidad," 86.
82 Gómez, "El Indio ante la realidad," 88–90.
83 *Anuario de leyes, decretos y resoluciones supremas 1939* (La Paz: Imprentas Unidas, 1940), 1180–1, 1193–5.
84 De la Cadena, *Indigenous Mestizos*.
85 For discussions of anthropometry and cranial measurements, see Stephen Jay Gould, *The Mismeasure of Man* (New York: Norton, 1981); Seemin Quayum, "Indian Ruins, National Origins: Tiwanaku and Indigenismo in La Paz, 1897–

1933," in *Histories of Race and Racism*, edited by Laura Gotkowitz (Durham, NC: Duke University Press, 2011), 159-178; and Alexandra Minna Stern, "From Mestizophilia to Biotypology: Racialization and Science in Mexico, 1920–1960," in *Race and Nation in Modern Latin America*, edited by Nancy P. Appelbaum, Anne S. Macpherson, and Karin Alejandra Rosemblatt (Chapel Hill: University of North Carolina Press, 2003), 187–210.

86 Thomas C. Holt, *The Problem of Race in the Twenty-First Century* (Cambridge, MA: Harvard University Press, 2000).

87 Arturo Posnansky, "Crítica de las Críticas," *Boletín de la Sociedad Geográfica de La Paz* 68 (December 1945): 191–9.

88 Torres, *El estado actual de la educación indigenal en el país*; Vicente Donoso Torres, *Filosofía de la educación boliviana* (Buenos Aires: Editorial Atlántida, 1946); Vicente Donoso Torres, *El proceso histórico de Bolivia* (La Paz: Editorial Letras, 1963); Vicente Donoso Torres, *Lecciones de didáctica general* (Buenos Aires: Matera, 1964).

89 Vicente Donoso Torres, "El factor humano en la geografía nacional," *Boletín de la Sociedad Geográfica de La Paz* 68 (December 1945): 7.

90 Torres, "El factor humano en la geografía nacional," 11.

91 Torres, "El factor humano en la geografía nacional," 12.

92 Torres, "El factor humano en la geografía nacional," 14.

93 Torres, "El factor humano en la geografía nacional," 14.

94 Torres, "El factor humano en la geografía nacional," 13.

95 Torres, "El factor humano en la geografía nacional," 13.

96 Torres, "El factor humano en la geografía nacional," 13.

97 Torres, "El factor humano en la geografía nacional," 14.

98 Torres, "El factor humano en la geografía nacional," 14.

99 Torres, "El factor humano en la geografía nacional," 14.

100 Torres, "El factor humano en la geografía nacional," 15.

101 Torres, "El factor humano en la geografía nacional," 16.

102 Torres, "El factor humano en la geografía nacional," 16.

103 Although liberal ideology sought to strip all markers of difference and instill equality before the law, Brooke Larson shows how liberals actually helped reinscribe difference. See Larson, "Forging the Unlettered Indian."

104 Torres, "El factor humano en la geografía nacional," 17.

105 Alan Knight, "Racism, Revolution, and Indigenismo, 1910–1940," in *The Idea of Race in Latin America, 1870–1940*, edited by Richard Graham (Austin: University of Texas Press, 1990), 71–113.

106 In La Paz, whites and elites believed that they were the only arbiters of morality and the morality of *mestizos* and *cholos* was suspect. See de la Cadena, *Indigenous Mestizos*.

107 This discourse had the effect of permitting *indígenas* to participate in politics, but it also disempowered them on the ground of their indigeneity if they were too politically active. See Gotkowitz, *A Revolution for Our Rights*; and de la Cadena, *Indigenous Mestizos*.

108 Larson, "Forging the Unlettered Indian."

Chapter 3

1 Much of the material in this chapter draws on Luis M. Sierra, "Union Activism in La Paz Before and After the Chaco War, 1920–1947," in *The Chaco War: Environment, Ethnicity, and Nationalism*, edited by Bridget Maria Chesterton (London: Bloomsbury Press, 2016), 43–66.

2 Herbert S. Klein, *Parties and Political Change in Bolivia, 1880–1952* (London: Cambridge University Press, 1969), 133.

3 In the countryside, the 1921 Jesús de Machaca uprising and repression challenged the Saavedra government's "pro-indigenous" policies. In the mines, the government's repression of the 1923 Uncía miners' strike in Oruro province also called into question Saavedra's commitment to Bolivia's "laboring classes."

4 Klein, *Parties and Political Change in Bolivia*, 76.

5 Álvaro Cuadros, *La Paz* (La Paz: Facultad de Arquitectura, Urbanismo y Artes, Universidad Mayor de San Andrés, 2002), 156.

6 Klein, *Parties and Political Change in Bolivia*; Taller de Historia Oral Andina, *Los constructores de ciudad*; Trifonio Delgado González and Guillermo Delgado, *100 años de lucha obrera en Bolivia* (La Paz: Ediciones ISLA, 1984); "La Huelga de Telegrafistas del Estado," *El Hombre Libre*, June 17, 1920.

7 "El sufragio de maestro artesanos," in Bolivia, *Anuario de leyes, resoluciones legislativas, decretos, resoluciones supremas y circulares, 1926*, 1530.

8 Klein, *Parties and Political Change in Bolivia*.

9 "La respuesta del Doctor Saavedra al pliego de la Federación Obrera," *La República*, April 28, 1925.

10 Klein, *Parties and Political Change in Bolivia*, 143.

11 Klein, *Parties and Political Change in Bolivia*.

12 The editor of *La Reforma*, Vicente Mendoza, appeared on the rolls of the Radical Party. "Directorio," *El Hombre Libre*, January 13, 1918. See also J. Ricardo Alarcón A., *Bolivia en el primer centenario de su independencia, 1825–1925* (New York: University Society, 1925), 96.

13 "Los Obreros de La Paz por Bautista Saavedra," *La Reforma*, January 6, 1921.

14 Klein, *Parties and Political Change in Bolivia*, 76.

15 "Los Obreros de Santa Cruz por Bautista Saavedra."

16 "La Sociedad Obrera de La Paz," *El Fígaro*, October 20, 1920. In Bautista Saavedra's reply to a letter from the *sociedad* backing his candidacy, he argued that the July coup was about maintaining public order. "Saavedra Responde a La Sociedad Obrera de La Paz," *El Fígaro*, October 22, 1920.
17 "El concepto moderno de la política," *La Reforma*, January 8, 1921.
18 "El Partido Republicano y el pueblo trabajador," *La República*, March 28, 1921.
19 "Los matarifes en huelga: El pueblo de La Paz próximo en morir de hambre," *El Hombre Libre*, January 27, 1920; "El Partido Republicano y el pueblo trabajador," *La República*, March 28, 1921.
20 "El Partido Republicano y el pueblo trabajador," *La República*, March 28, 1921.
21 "La respuesta del Doctor Saavedra al pliego de la Federación Obrera," *El Hombre Libre*, October 20, 1920.
22 "El registro de ciudadanos," *El Hombre Libre*, January 22, 1920.
23 "De la policía de garantía personal de la calificación de vagos y mal entretenidos," in *Ley reglamentaria de Policía de Seguridad La Paz* (La Paz: Imprenta "El Nacional," 1886), Capitulo 5, Sección 4, Articulo 32.
24 *Ley reglamentaria de Policía de Seguridad La Paz*. This was a reference to people involved in prostitution.
25 *Ley reglamentaria de Policía de Seguridad La Paz*; "Al jefe de seccion," Correspondencia, February 5, 1913, Administracion de Policia, 1913–1919, Archivo de La Paz; "Asilo de San Ramon," *Boletín Municipal de La Paz*, April 1934, 45.
26 Most of the tin mines of Bolivia are located in two provinces, La Paz and Potosí The mines in La Paz province are maybe two hours from the city by bus. The Potosí mines are more than six hours from the city by bus.
27 The *pollera* is a petticoat skirt imported from Europe and that mixed-race women in La Paz and other Andean regions adopted. This skirt is a marker of race and social position for women in the city. See Rossana Barragán, "Entre Polleras, ñañacas y lliqllas: los mestizos y cholas en la conformación de la tercera república," in *Tradición y modernidad en los Andes*, edited by Henrique Urbano (Cusco: Centro Bartolomé de las Casas, 1993), 43–74; Mary Weismantel, *Cholas and Pishtacos: Stories of Race and Sex in the Andes* (Chicago: University of Chicago Press, 2001); and Linda J. Seligmann, *Peruvian Street Lives: Culture, Power, and Economy among the Market Women of Cuzco* (Urbana: University of Illinois Press, 2004).
28 Taller de Historia Oral Andina, *Los constructores de la ciudad: Tradiciones de lucha y de trabajo del sindicato central de constructores y albañiles de Bolivia* (La Paz: UMSA, 1986), 36.
29 "A la clase obrera," *La República*, April 26, 1925; Taller de Historia Oral Andina, *Los constructores de la ciudad*, 36.
30 Ana Cecilia Wadsworth and Ineke Dibbits, *Agitadoras de buen gusto: historia del Sindicato de Culinarias (1935–1958)* ([La Paz]: Hisbol, 1989), 32.

31 Wadsworth and Dibbits, *Agitadoras de buen gusto*, 43.
32 Taller de Historia Oral Andina, *Los constructores de la ciudad*, 38.
33 Wadsworth and Dibbits, *Agitadoras de buen gusto*.
34 Wadsworth and Dibbits, *Agitadoras de buen gusto*, 39. Patón proposed structural solutions to this kind of discrimination that included public cafeterias and childcare facilities for working women.
35 Marcia Stephenson, *Gender and Modernity in Andean Bolivia* (Austin: University of Texas Press, 1999).
36 *Pongueaje* was a type of traditional rotating labor arrangement whereby tenants on rural haciendas provided goods and labor to the landowner as part of their payment for access to land. The *culinarias* union argued that maids and male servants were not interested in unionization. These employees were often indigenous people who lived or worked in elite haciendas in the countryside and were brought to the city through the *pongueaje* labor practices. These employees, who were often monolingual Aymara speakers, were beholden to the hacienda owner.
37 Wadsworth and Dibbits, *Agitadoras de buen gusto*; Seemin Quayum, María Luisa Soux, and Rossana Barragán, *De terratenientes a amas de casa: mujeres de la élite de La Paz en la primera mitad del siglo XX* (La Paz: Ministerio de Desarrollo Humano, Secretaría de Asuntos Étnicos, de Género y Generacionales, Subsecretaría de Asuntos de Género, 1997).
38 Wadsworth and Dibbits, *Agitadoras de buen gusto*, 62.
39 Wadsworth and Dibbits, *Agitadoras de buen gusto*, 56.
40 Wadsworth and Dibbits, *Agitadoras de buen gusto*, 62.
41 Godofredo Sandoval and Xavier Albó, *Ojje por encima de todo: historia de un centro de residentes ex-campesinos en La Paz* (La Paz: Centro de Investigación y Promoción del Campesinado, 1978); William E. Carter and Mauricio Mamani, *Irpa Chico: individuo y comunidad en la cultura aymara* (La Paz: Librería-Editorial Juventud, 1983); Quayum et al., *De terratenientes a amas de casa*. For Cochabamba, see Daniel M. Goldstein, *The Spectacular City: Violence and Performance in Urban Bolivia* (Durham, NC: Duke University Press, 2005).
42 Literacy tests limited the electorate to a small proportion of the population. About 10 percent of the eligible population actually had voting rights; see Klein, *Parties and Political Change in Bolivia*, 161, 404–6.
43 Taller de Historia Oral Andina, *Los constructores de la ciudad*, 6.
44 Alarcón A., *Bolivia en el primer centenario de su independencia*, 567; Bolivia, *Anuario de leyes, resoluciones legislativas, decretos, resoluciones supremas y circulares, 1926* (La Paz: [s.n.]), 1395–6.
45 One member of the *sindicato* referred to this as "[our] way of speaking and our appearance." Wadsworth and Dibbits, *Agitadoras de buen gusto*, 62.

46 The union was formed in 1916 and lasted until 1947, when a repressive national government forced the union members to cease operations or face a prison term. Taller de Historia Oral Andina, *Los constructores de la ciudad*.
47 Wadsworth and Dibbits, *Agitadoras de buen gusto*; Taller de Historia Oral Andina, *Los constructores de la ciudad*, 8. These are typically considered "indigenous" and *mestizo* ways of dressing. Taller de Historia Oral Andina, *Los constructores de la ciudad*, 8.
48 THOA, *Los constructores de la ciudad*, 6.
49 Taller de Historia Oral Andina, *Los constructores de la ciudad*, 6.
50 Taller de Historia Oral Andina, *Los constructores de la ciudad*, 10.
51 THOA, *Los constructores de la ciudad*, 10–12.
52 Several authors have provided full accounts of the Chaco War. See, for example, Klein, *Parties and Political Change in Bolivia*; Herbert S. Klein, *A Concise History of Bolivia* (Cambridge: Cambridge University Press, 2003); David Zook, *The Conduct of the Chaco War* (New York: Bookman Associates, 1960); Bruce W. Farcau, *The Chaco War: Bolivia and Paraguay, 1932–1935* (Westport, CT: Greenwood Publishing Group, 1996); and Adrian J. English, *The Green Hell: A Concise History of the Chaco War between Bolivia and Paraguay, 1932–35,* Spellmount Military Studies (New York: Spellmount Limited Publishers, 2008).
53 Víctor Paz Esstensoro was punished for his political transgressions in the city and was forced to serve in a fighting unit. Other men of his rank and status did not fight or serve in front line units at all. Luis Antezana Ergueta, *Historia secreta del Movimiento Nacionalista Revolucionario*, Tomos 1–8 (La Paz: Librería-Editorial "Juventud," 1984–92).
54 Klein, *Parties and Political Change in Bolivia*, 142.
55 "La civilización de las clases trabajadoras," *La Reforma*, March 18, 1921; Comité Pro Cuarto Centenario de la Fundación de La Paz and Eloy Salmón, *La Paz en su IV centenario, 1548–1948*, Tomo 2, *Monografía histórica* ([La Paz]: Comité Pro IV Centenario de la Fundación de la Paz, 1948), 232, 302–3.
56 Agustín Barcelli S., *Medio siglo de luchas sindicales revolucionarias en Bolivia, 1905–1955* (N.p.: N.p., 1957); Magdalena Cajías de la Vega, "El discurso anarquista en el discurso minero del pre-52," *Estudios Bolivianos 12: La Cultura del Pre-52* (2004): 15–79. Cajías de la Vega argues that links between the countryside, miners, and urban labor leaders began in the late 1920s and shaped the radicalization of all three sectors.
57 "Para la unificacion de la nacion Boliviana no habran juicios politicos," in *Anuario de leyes, decretos y resoluciones supremas 1936* (La Paz: Imprentas Unidas, 1938), 1086A.
58 "Amnestia a los soldados del Chaco," in *Anuario de Leyes, Decretos y Disposiciones 1936* (La Paz: Imprentas Unidas, 1938), 1452–3, 1086.

59 "Estado de Sitio," in *Anuario de leyes, decretos y resoluciones supremas 1936* (La Paz: Imprentas Unidas, 1938), 1315–8.
60 Ineke Dibbits, *Polleras libertarias: Federación Obrera Femenina, 1927–1965* (La Paz: TAHIPAMU/HISBOL, 1989), 4.
61 Wadsworth and Dibbits, *Agitadoras de buen gusto*, 121.
62 Wadsworth and Dibbits, *Agitadoras de buen gusto*, 34.
63 Wadsworth and Dibbits, *Agitadoras de buen gusto*, 67.
64 "Casas de Tolerancia," *Boletín Municipal Acta y Estadísticas*, April 1929, 13.
65 Ann Zulawski, *Unequal Cures: Public Health and Political Change in Bolivia, 1900–1950* (Durham, NC: Duke University Press, 2007).
66 Wadsworth and Dibbits, *Agitadoras de buen gusto*, 114.
67 "Sucesos," *La Calle*, October 16, 1936.
68 "Sucesos," *La Calle*, October 16, 1936.
69 Wadsworth and Dibbits, *Agitadoras de buen gusto*.
70 Stephenson, *Gender and Modernity in Andean Bolivia*.
71 Dibbits, *Polleras libertarias*, 9.
72 The city government's efforts to force *culinarias*, market vendors, and food vendors to purchase identity cards and pay fees for market stalls motivated other unions to organize. Members of market vendor unions repeatedly refused to submit to testing and pay the market fees. Dibbits, *Polleras libertarias*, 11; Wadsworth and Dibbits, *Agitadoras de buen gusto*, 156.
73 Dibbits, *Polleras libertarias*, 15.
74 Dibbits, *Polleras libertarias*, 16.
75 Dibbits, *Polleras libertarias*, 12.
76 *La Calle*, October 8, 1938. *La Calle* was closely tied to the reformist politicians and parties of the post–Chaco War era.
77 I believe that the context of neoliberalism and the revalorization of indigenous contributions to Bolivian society shape these memories.
78 Dibbits, *Polleras libertarias*, 6–7.
79 Dibbits, *Polleras libertarias*. Despite these recollections, intraclass and interethnic tensions were also part of daily life. Many participants in the oral history project also recalled conflicts between unions and insults among indigenous neighborhood residents. See Denise Y. Arnold, Rossana Barragán R., David Llanos, Carmen B. Loza, and Carmen Solíz, *¿Indígenas u obreros? la construcción política de identidades en el Altiplano boliviano* (La Paz: UNIR, 2009); and Rossana Barragán, "Mas allá de lo mestizo, mas allá de lo aymara: organización y representaciones de clase y etnicidad en La Paz," *América Latina Hoy: Revista De Ciencias Sociales* 43 (2006): 107–30.
80 Dibbits, *Polleras libertarias*; Taller de Historia Oral Andina, *Los constructores de ciudad*.

81 Klein, *Parties and Political Change in Bolivia*, 326.
82 Klein, *Parties and Political Change in Bolivia*, 326.
83 Several markets opened in the late 1930s and the 1940s, including the Riosinho and Sopocachi markets in 1939 and the Rodríguez, Miraflores, and Calama markets in 1943. Comité Pro Cuarto Centenario de la Fundación de La Paz and Eloy Salmón, *La Paz en su IV centenario*.
84 Taller de Historia Oral Andina, *Los constructores de la ciudad*, 43.
85 Dibbits, *Polleras libertarias*, 21.
86 "Productos de Primaria Necesidad," *Boletín Municipal de La Paz*, August 1942, 43; "Precios de la Canasta Basica," *Boletín Municipal de La Paz*, November 1942; "Aumenta Precio de la Carne," *Boletín Municipal de La Paz*, September 1943; Dibbits, *Polleras libertarias*.
87 "Informe: Al Consejo Municipal," Correspondencia, Honorable Consejo Municipal, 1920–45, Archivo de La Paz.
88 Dibbits, *Polleras libertarias*, 13.
89 The city government ultimately did this in the period from 1943 to 1948; see "Informe Inspeccion de Mercados," *Boletín Municipal de La Paz*, June 1949, 41.
90 "Sistema central de precios se establece en la ciudad," *La Calle*, September 20, 1939.
91 Wadsworth and Dibbits, *Agitadoras de buen gusto*, 115.
92 Wadsworth and Dibbits, *Agitadoras de buen gusto*, 117.
93 Michael L. Conniff, *Populism in Latin America* (Tuscaloosa: University of Alabama Press, 1999); Michael L. Conniff, *Urban Politics in Brazil: The Rise of Populism, 1925–1945* (Pittsburgh, PA: University of Pittsburgh Press, 1981); Jeffrey L. Gould, "'For an Organized Nicaragua': Somoza and the Labour Movement, 1944–1948," *Journal of Latin American Studies* 19, no. 2 (1987): 353–87; Danny James, *Doña María's Story: Life History, Memory, and Political Identity* (Durham, NC: Duke University Press, 2000); John D. French, *The Brazilian Workers' ABC: Class Conflict and Alliances in Modern São Paulo* (Chapel Hill: University of North Carolina Press, 1992); Amelia M. Kiddle and María L. O. Muñoz, *Populism in Twentieth Century Mexico: The Presidencies of Lázaro Cárdenas and Luis Echeverría* (Tucson: University of Arizona Press, 2010); Joel Wolfe, *Working Women, Working Men: São Paulo and the Rise of Brazil's Industrial Working Class, 1900–1955* (Durham, NC: Duke University Press, 1993).
94 Klein, *Parties and Political Change in Bolivia*; Porfirio Díaz Machicao, *Toro, Busch, Quintanilla, 1936–1940* (La Paz: Editorial "Juventud," 1957).
95 For a detailed account of this national socialist-inspired unionization drive and government representation efforts, see Klein, *Parties and Political Change in Bolivia*; and Carlos Montenegro, *Frente al derecho del estado el oro de la Standard Oil* (La Paz: Editorial Trabajo, 1938).

Chapter 4

1. Some of the material in this chapter comes from Luis Sierra, "The Indigenous Neighborhoods of La Paz: Urbanization, Migration, and Political Activism in La Paz, 1920–1947," *Journal of Global South Studies* (Fall 2018), 213–41.
2. Luis M. Sierra, "Union Activism in La Paz before and after the Chaco War, 1920–1947," in *The Chaco War: Environment, Ethnicity, and Nationalism*, edited by Bridget María Chesterton (London: Bloomsbury Press, 2016), 43–66; Rossana Barragán, *Indios, mujeres y ciudadanos: legislación y ejercicio de la ciudadanía en Bolivia (siglo XIX)* (La Paz: Fundación Diálogo, 1999); James Dunkerley, *Bolivia: Revolution and the Power of History in the Present: Essays* (London: Institute for the Study of the Americas, 2007).
3. In thinking about this internal building, I go back to a beautiful line I once heard from film director Danny Boyle about Dharavi, a slum of two million people in India: "They don't have enough resources. There isn't enough sanitation. There isn't running water or not sufficiently enough running water. The electricity is intermittent and slightly dangerous. But those things are not their fault. The things that they have responsibility for, they organize amazingly well. And the thing works. And it works so well that it can absorb a film crew no problem, you know, and let us not only get on with the film but benefit from their help in making the movie, you know." It is an outsider's view, but it helps capture that dreaded word "agency."
4. I do not use the term "barrio" in this chapter because in translation it usually means "neighborhood" or "marginal or working-class neighborhood." The term lacks precision and in this case is not an accurate translation of the term used in La Paz's *zona indígena*, or indigenous zone. I use the term "indigenous neighborhoods" in an attempt to maintain some precision in geographic space while also recognizing the mixed racial and class dynamics found in several of the indigenous neighborhoods. Census data on indigenous neighborhoods is sketchy before the late 1940s and early 1950s. Most did not break down the city's population by race. For sources on census data, see Álvaro Cuadros Bustos, *La Paz* (La Paz: Facultad de Arquitectura, Urbanismo y Artes, Universidad Mayor de San Andrés, 2002); and Comité Pro Cuarto Centenario de la Fundación de La Paz and Eloy Salmón, *La Paz en su IV centenario, 1548–1948* ([La Paz]: Comité Pro Cuarto Centenario de la Fundación de la Paz, 1948). Curiously, primary sources and scholarship rarely mention neighborhood associations; they focus on indigenous people's participation in various social and religious celebrations. See Xavier Albó and Josep M. Barnadas, *La cara india y campesina de nuestra historia* (La Paz: UNITAS, 1990); David M. Guss, "The Gran Poder and the Reconquest of La Paz," *Journal of Latin American Anthropology* 11, no. 2 (2006); Arze and Barragán, *La Paz, Chuquiago*; and Rossana Barragán and Cleverth Cárdenas Plaza, *Gran Poder: la morenada* (La Paz: Instituto de Estudios Bolivianos, 2009).

5 Most elites lived near the Plaza Murillo, on the Alameda, lower Sopocachi, San Jorge, and Obrajes, all of which were south of the city center. All of the second district neighborhoods, with the exception of Sopocachi, which extended south, are north and west of the city center in the hills surrounding the Choqueyapu River. The city and prefecture nominally imposed a grid pattern on certain sectors of these neighborhoods, like Challapampa, where the central railway station and customs house were located, but the preexisting patterns dominated by two major arteries extending out toward El Alto from the Garita de Lima conditioned settlement between the city and the altiplano. The region is hilly and climbs southeast to northwest toward the lip of the canyon, la ceja de El Alto, the "eyebrow" of highland plain toward El Alto. The elevation in this part of La Paz, perhaps a three-mile extension, rises from about 9000 to 12,000 feet at the rim of the canyon. The roads and alleys before 1945 were principally dirt roads, or laid with stone; the only paved road was the old road to El Alto which still functions as a route for public transportation. The rest were small unpaved paths, trails, and alleyways. Cuadros Bustos, *La Paz*, 124; Taller de Historia Oral Andina, *Los constructores de la ciudad: tradiciones de lucha y de trabajo del Sindicato Central de Constructores y Albañiles de Bolivia, 1908–1980* (La Paz: Universidad Mayor de San Andrés, 1986); Guss, "The Gran Poder and the Reconquest of La Paz," 294–328; Silvia Arze and Rossana Barragán, *La Paz, Chuquiago: El escenario de la vida de la ciudad* ([La Paz]: Alcaldía Municipal de La Paz, Oficialía Mayor de Cultura, 1988); Comité Pro Cuarto Centenario de la Fundación de La Paz and Eloy Salmón, *La Paz en su IV centenario*; and *Boletín del H. Ayuntamiento Municipal de La Paz*, August 1945.
6 "Alcalde y Vecinos Dedican Lineas de Agua Potable," *Boletín del H. Ayuntamiento Municipal de La Paz*, December 1945, 1.
7 "Alcalde y Vecinos Dedican Lineas de Agua Potable."
8 Daniel M. Goldstein, *The Spectacular City: Violence and Performance in Urban Bolivia* (Durham, NC: Duke University Press, 2005); Sarah Hines, "La construccion historica de los usos y costumbres del agua en Cochabamba," in *Construcción de la Agenda Departamental del Agua de Cochabamba*, edited by the Gobierno Autónomo (Cochabamba: Gobierno Departamental, 2013), 17–47; Sian Lazar, *El Alto, Rebel City: Self and Citizenship in Andean Bolivia* (Durham, NC: Duke University Press, 2008).
9 For examples, see Porfirio Díaz Machicao, *Toro, Busch, Quintanilla, 1936–1940* (La Paz: Editorial Juventud, 1957); James Malloy, *Bolivia: The Uncompleted Revolution* (Pittsburgh: University of Pittsburgh Press, 1970); Luis Antezana Ergueta, *Historia secreta del Movimiento Nacionalista Revolucionario*, Tomo 7, *La revolución del MNR del 9 de abril 1952* (La Paz: Librería Editorial Juventud, 1988); and Jacobo Libermann Z., *Bolivia: 10 años de revolución [1952–1962]* (N.p., 1962).
10 In 1937, a congress of La Paz's neighborhood associations founded and organized FEDJUVE to vie for the rights of all associations and to mediate

with the city government. FEDJUVE was formed in response to decrees of the military socialists that required all civil society groups to create corporate bodies. The original purpose of FEDJUVE was to negotiate with the national and city governments on behalf of all the individual associations. The executive boards of the neighborhood associations constituted the pool of candidates for FEDJUVE's board, and they also elected that board. Díaz Machicao, *Toro, Busch, Quintanilla*.

11 Other groups that emerged after the war included a lawyers' guild, a machinists' federation, a federation of small retailers, and a federation of shoe shiners. See Taller de Historia Oral Andina, *Los constructores de la ciudad*; Comité Pro Cuarto Centenario de la Fundación de la Paz and Eloy Salmón, *La Paz en su IV centenario*; and *Boletín del H. Ayuntamiento Municipal de La Paz*, March 1936.

12 "Una concepción biológica del problema municipal," *La Calle*, June 23, 1938.

13 *Boletín Municipal de La Paz*, May 1945, 35. Several of the department heads and the head of the urbanism department were in their jobs from the late 1930s through to the revolution in 1952. In contrast to earlier administrations, these department heads were often experts in their respective field or a related one. In previous administrations, department heads may have been educated in the law or letters, but those who held posts between the late 1930s and 1952 were accountants, architects, and medical doctors. The city government's change in policy and comprehensive approach contrasted with earlier urban policies.

14 James Mahoney, *The Legacies of Liberalism: Path Dependence and Political Regimes in Central America* (Baltimore, MD: Johns Hopkins University Press, 2001), Chapter 5.

15 Michael C. Meyer, William L. Sherman, and Susan M. Deeds, *The Course of Mexican History* (New York: Oxford University Press, 1999).

16 E. Gabrielle Kuenzli, *Acting Inca: National Belonging in Early Twentieth-Century Bolivia* (Pittsburgh: Pittsburgh University Press, 2013), esp. chapter 1; Barragán, *Indios, mujeres y ciudadanos*.

17 Carlos Montenegro, *Nacionalismo y coloniaje, su expresión histórica en la prensa de Bolivia* ([La Paz]: Ediciones Autonomía, 1943); Antezana Ergueta, *Historia secreta del Movimiento Nacionalista Revolucionario*, Tomo 1, *Del derrocamiento de Siles a la muerte de Busch 1929-1938* (La Paz: Editorial Juventud, 1984), 54; Libermann Z., *Bolivia*; Herbert Klein, *Parties and Political Change in Bolivia, 1880–1952* (London: Cambridge University Press, 1969).

18 Some government officials in the post-Chaco period (1936–52) were traditional political elites and some leaders of the MNR were related to traditional political elites. Other government officials came from a professional class of lawyers, engineers, architects.

19 Díaz Machicao, *Toro, Busch, Quintanilla*.

20 Malloy, *Bolivia*; Dunkerley, *Bolivia*; Jerry W. Knudson, *Bolivia: Press and Revolution, 1932-1964* (Lanham, MD: University Press of America, 1986); Gregory J. Papp, "The Bolivian MNR: Aspects of Nationalism" (MA thesis, University of Akron, 1973); Robert J. Alexander and Eldon M. Parker, *A History of Organized Labor in Bolivia* (Westport, CT: Praeger, 2005).

21 John Lear, *Workers, Neighbors, and Citizens: The Revolution in Mexico City* (Lincoln: University of Nebraska Press, 2001); Katherine Elaine Bliss, *Compromised Positions: Prostitution, Public Health, and Gender Politics in Revolutionary Mexico City* (University Park: Pennsylvania State University Press, 2001); Ernesto Capello, *City at the Center of the World: Space, History and Modernity* (Pittsburgh, PA: University of Pittsburgh Press, 2012); Guadalupe Garcia, *Beyond the Walled City: Colonial Exclusion in Havana* (Berkeley: University of California Press, 2016).

22 John Lear, "Mexico City: Space and Class in the Porfirian Capital, 1884-1910," *Journal of Urban History* 22, no. 4 (1996): 454–92.

23 Pablo Piccato, *City of Suspects: Crime in Mexico City, 1900–1931* (Durham: Duke University Press, 2001).

24 *Boletín Municipal de La Paz*, August 1935.

25 A prefecture is a form of government that fits between a city and a provincial government. The term is often translated as county, but not all counties are prefectures. Some prefectures provide a full range of services (including public transportation, water, and electricity) in a metropolitan area that often includes an area that is not incorporated by a municipality.

26 The scholarship on the discourse of urbanization and modernity is extensive. For La Paz elites, "modernity" meant postindustrial infrastructure, the loss of "backward" indigenous customs and costumes, and an orderly city. For more on the discourse of modernity in urban studies, see Marshall Berman, *All That Is Solid Melts into Air: The Experience of Modernity* (New York: Simon and Schuster, 1982); David Harvey, *Paris: Capital of Modernity* (New York: Routledge, 2003); and Manuel Castells, *The City and the Grassroots: A Cross-Cultural Theory of Urban Social Movements* (Berkeley: University of California Press, 1983). See also Brodwyn Fischer, "Quase Pretos De Tão Pobres? Race and Social Discrimination in Rio De Janeiro's Twentieth-Century Criminal Courts," *Latin American Research Review* 39, no. 1 (2004): 31–59.

27 Romulo Costa Mattos, "Shantytown Dwellers' Resistance in Brazil's First Republic (1890–1930): Fighting for the Right to Reside in the City of Rio de Janeiro," *International Labor and Working Class History* 83 (Spring 2013): 55–69. In La Paz, cases of eviction and government destruction of property were framed in terms of progress and modernity. The power the post–Chaco War governments wielded made resistance difficult. However, court cases related to housing demonstrate resistance to eviction and the destruction of "irregular" dwellings. Habeas Corpus,

Pascual de Alarcón vs. Juez de Vivienda, Caja 80 y 81, Corte Superior de Distrito Juzgado (1948–56), Archivo de La Paz, 4 and 4v; "Informe Dirreccion General de Urbanismo," *Boletín Municipal de La Paz*, March 1946, 40.

28 Harvey, *Paris, Capital of Modernity*; Judith R. Walkowitz, *City of Dreadful Delight: Narratives of Sexual Danger in Late-Victorian London* (Chicago: University of Chicago Press, 1992); Charles E. Rosenberg, *The Cholera Years: The United States in 1832, 1849, and 1866* (Chicago: University of Chicago Press, 1987).

29 Ronald T. Takaki, *Strangers from a Different Shore: A History of Asian Americans*, updated and rev. ed. (Boston: Little, Brown, 1998).

30 Marisol de la Cadena, *Indigenous Mestizos: The Politics of Race and Culture in Cuzco, Peru, 1919–1991* (Durham, NC: Duke University Press, 2000).

31 José Vasconcelos, *La raza cósmica: Misión de la raza iberoamericana, Argentina y Brazil* (México: Espasa-Calpe Mexicana, 1966); José Vasconcelos and Didier T. Jaén, *The Cosmic Race: A Bilingual Edition* (Baltimore, MD: Johns Hopkins University Press, 1997).

32 For a more detailed discussion of modernity, identity, and space, see Luis M. Sierra, "Colonial Specters: The Extramuro, History, Memory, and Urbanization in La Paz, Bolivia, 1900–1947," *Journal of Urban History* (Fall 2018): 1131–52.

33 Díaz Machicao, *Toro, Busch, Quintanilla*.

34 *Boletín del H. Ayuntamiento Municipal de La Paz*, August 1945.

35 *Boletín del H. Ayuntamiento Municipal de La Paz*, July 1932. Neighborhood associations did not always provide laborers. The city government could also hire its own laborers for work. The city government completed its own construction projects using a variety of laborers. Some came from the San Pedro Prison, which housed a cross-section of Paceño society: skilled and unskilled laborers, *indígenas*, those without residence or honorable occupation, and men of means. Prisoners provided labor for various projects, including paving streets, digging trenches, and doing masonry work for some of the city's plazas. Prisoners who were more well off had the influence to avoid labor of that kind; they could also purchase food of higher quality during their incarceration. The city's reliance on inexpensive prison labor also provided opportunities to those with few resources to exchange their labor for goods and services while in prison. *Nacif vs. Zaiduni*, Asesinato (Murder), 1945, Caja 73 y 74, Corte Superior de Distrito (1948) Archivo de La Paz; *Moreno vs. Renteria*, Asesinato (Murder), 1945, Caja 75, Corte Superior de Distrito (1948) Archivo de La Paz; *Luis Castillo vs. Rosendo Lopez*, Robo (Theft), Caja 80 y 81, Corte Superior de Distrito Juzgado (1948), Archivo de La Paz.

36 *Boletín del H. Ayuntamiento Municipal de La Paz*, November 1942.

37 The neighborhood associations could petition for dissolution and reconstitution with new board members, and in at least one instance dissolution became the punishment for neighbors who had not legally constituted their association.

This led to conflicts within the neighborhood and disagreement about whether an association was legitimate. The power to approve or reject neighborhood associations became a tool FEDJUVE used to manage and control the associations. "Se constituye nueva mesa directiva," *Boletín del H. Ayuntamiento Municipal de La Paz*, August 1945, 54.

38 Comité Pro Cuarto Centenario de la Fundación de la Paz and Eloy Salmón, *La Paz en su IV centenario*.
39 *Boletín del H. Ayuntamiento Municipal de La Paz*, September 1945.
40 *Boletín del H. Ayuntamiento Municipal de La Paz*, October 1945.
41 *Boletín del H. Ayuntamiento Municipal de La Paz*, December 1945, 27.
42 *Boletín del H. Ayuntamiento Municipal de La Paz*, December 1945, 27.
43 "Mesas Directivas," *Boletín del H. Ayuntamiento Municipal de La Paz*, April 1945, 120.
44 June C. Nash, *We Eat the Mines and the Mines Eat Us: Dependency and Exploitation in Bolivian Tin Mines* (New York: Columbia University Press, 1979); Thomas Abercrombie, *Pathways of Memory and Power* (Madison: University of Wisconsin Press, 1998), chapter 1. The rotating leadership structure of the *cargo* system provided continuity and protected seniority within lay brotherhoods and neighborhood associations. The brotherhoods elected their own representatives and established social hierarchies and ladders based on years of service. Abercrombie, *Pathways of Memory and Power*, 65; *Boletín del H. Ayuntamiento Municipal de La Paz*, November 1942. In the Challapata parish and neighborhood, the lay brotherhood celebrated the Day of the Virgin of the Salvation. Taller de Historia Oral Andina, *Los constructores de la ciudad*, 36.
45 The Sopocachi brotherhood, for example, was inactive for part of the year and geared up only in the months before and immediately after the festival for the Virgin of Sopocachi, *Boletín del H. Ayuntamiento Municipal de La Paz*, February 1921.
46 *Boletín del H. Ayuntamiento Municipal de La Paz*, July 1935; *Boletín del H. Ayuntamiento Municipal de La Paz*, May 1945.
47 Taller de Historia Oral Andina, *Los constructores de la ciudad*.
48 Taller de Historia Oral Andina, *Los constructores de la ciudad*, 56.
49 *Boletín del H. Ayuntamiento Municipal de La Paz*, November 1942. In 1925, the Los Andes lay brotherhood wrote to the council to request the city government's help in installing electricity in that neighborhood; *Boletín del H. Ayuntamiento Municipal de La Paz*, March 1925. In 1927, a lay brotherhood from Churubamba attended several city council meetings to request a new market; *Boletín del H. Ayuntamiento Municipal de La Paz*, September 1927. In the Challapampa area, the president of a lay brotherhood petitioned the city council in 1929 for more police presence and better roads between the city center and Challapampa; *Boletín del H. Ayuntamiento Municipal de La Paz*, January 1929.

50 "Informe Casas de Tolerancia," *Boletín del H. Ayuntamiento Municipal de La Paz*, April 1934, 56.
51 *Boletín del H. Ayuntamiento Municipal de La Paz*, March 1946.
52 The city government appointed experts and professionals such as architects, accountants, and doctors to head its departments. Successive city administrations in the 1930s and 1940s laid out clear rules for construction bids, helped improve the tax code, modernized markets, and attempted housing reforms. One of the major aims of tax code reform was to improve the accuracy of property appraisals and the collection of property and sales taxes. *Boletín Municipal de La Paz*, April 1936.
53 Laura Gotkowitz, *A Revolution for Our Rights: Indigenous Struggles for Land and Justice, 1880–1952* (Durham, NC: Duke University Press, 2007); Esteban Ticona Alejo, *El escribano de los caciques apoderados* Platt, *Estado Boliviano y Ayllu Andino;* Waskar Ari Chachaki, "Race and Subaltern Nationalism: AMP Activist-Intellectuals in Bolivia, 1921–1964" (PhD diss., Georgetown University, 2004). The Cacique Apoderado movement, for instance, fought to regain lost lands and successfully pressured the Bolivian government to hold its First Indigenous Congress in 1945. The national government also recognized indigenous peoples' individual rights and guarantees (*amaparo y garantias*) as well as the formal abolition of *pongueaje*. Indigenous people's strategy of submitting the same or similar petitions to competing government and religious authorities has a long history in Latin America.
54 Gotkowitz, *A Revolution for Our Rights*.
55 *Boletín del H. Ayuntamiento Municipal de La Paz*, August 1945, 65. Although the prefecture had no power over the city council or the FEDJUVE, these residents appealed to a competing authority in their effort to protect themselves and their rights against the other neighborhood association.
56 *Boletín del H. Ayuntamiento Municipal de La Paz*, December 1945, 25.
57 Vecinos de Chijini, "Señor Prefecto del Departamento de La Paz," Junio 23, 1945, Correspondencia, Caja 1, Archivo de La Prefectura de La Paz.
58 "Señor Prefecto del Departamento de La Paz."
59 In *A Revolution for Our Rights*, Laura Gotkowitz shows how as elected caciques (indigenous authorities), rural indigenous activists used the rights of *amparo* and *garantías* (constitutionally protected individual rights and guarantees) to pressure the Bolivian state and regional and local authorities to protect communal lands. Using powers of attorney (*poderes*), these caciques pressured authorities on behalf of communities in the period from 1880 to 1920. After 1920, repression forced the caciques to use new tactics to demand protection and guarantees, but always, Gotkowitz stresses, with the interests of the majority of the community at the core of their efforts. The activism of caciques forced Gualberto Villarroel to consider land reform and that ultimately forced his government to institute the indigenous labor decrees of 1945 and abolish the "traditional" labor service (*pongueaje*) due to landowners.

60 *Boletín del H. Ayuntamiento Municipal de La Paz*, June 1945.
61 "Señor Prefecto del Departamento de La Paz."
62 *Boletín del H. Ayuntamiento Municipal de La Paz*, April 1946.
63 *Boletín del H. Ayuntamiento Municipal de La Paz*, August 1945 and March 1948; "Señor Prefecto del Departamento de La Paz."
64 *Boletín del H. Ayuntamiento Municipal de La Paz*, March 1946, 107–8. People with the surname Velasco served on all three boards.
65 *Boletín del H. Ayuntamiento Municipal de La Paz*, March 1936.
66 *Boletín del H. Ayuntamiento Municipal de La Paz*, March 1936, 25.
67 Cuadros Bustos, *La Paz*, 124; Taller de Historia Oral Andina, *Los constructores de la ciudad*; Guss, "The Gran Poder and the Reconquest of La Paz"; Arze and Barragán, *La Paz, Chuquiago*; Comité Pro Cuarto Centenario de la Fundación de la Paz and Eloy Salmón, *La Paz en su IV centenario*; and *Boletín del H. Ayuntamiento Municipal de La Paz*, August 1945
68 The La Paz city government and the national government benefited from the stirrings of a global economic recovery especially regarding mining. The municipality during the military socialist period developed rules and regulations for handling construction projects and bids. In addition, the national and local governments made use of bonds to fund construction project. See Klein, *Parties and Political Change in Bolivia*. See also Taller de Historia Oral Andina, *Los constructores de la ciudad*; Ana Cecilia Wadsworth and Ineke Dibbits, *Agitadoras de buen gusto: historia del Sindicato de Culinarias (1935–1958)* ([La Paz]: TAHIPAMU, 1989); and Sierra, "Union Activism in La Paz before and after the Chaco War."
69 *Boletín del H. Ayuntamiento Municipal de La Paz*, April 1941.
70 "Informe Dirección Vivienda," 1936, Caja 1, Archivo de la Prefectura de La Paz, Archivo de La Paz; "Al Señor Alcalde," September 9, 1943, Caja 1: Correspondencia Alcaldía, Archivo de la Prefectura de La Paz, Archivo de La Paz.
71 Similar to the concepts of race and class, "modernity" and "hygiene" were social constructs inflected with racial and socioeconomic markers. These markers helped create a definition of modernity that measured Bolivia's progress as a modern nation used the progress of the industrialized nations of the world. In areas such as infrastructure, wages, urban planning, and health indicators, Bolivian elites felt that their failure to attain modernity was partly attributable to the fact that the population included indigenous and mixed-race poor people. Hygiene has similar implications and embedded ideas. It was clearly related to infrastructure, industrialization, and perceptions of modernity, but it could also have gendered and racial components. As Charles Rosenberg argues, disease is a social construction that "in some ways ... does not exist until we have agreed that it does, by perceiving, naming, and responding to it"; *Framing Disease: Studies in Cultural History* (New Brunswick, NJ: Rutgers University Press, 1992), xiii. The same could be said for hygiene.

72 One might assume that these improvements to urban infrastructure would have come about without pressure from neighborhood associations. However, neighborhood activism was an important factor in the types of investment national and local governments made in indigenous neighborhoods. In the mid-1920s, for example, the city abandoned a worker housing project in midstream. It purchased a plot of land for the housing project but backed out when the cost of construction became clear. The city even took the seller to court to try to get a refund. "Al Inspector Municipal," Correspondencia, Administración, 1927, Archivo de la prefectura de La Paz, Archivo de La Paz. Eventually, the land became the site of the Mercado Uruguay. In another example from the 1920s, the city abandoned a market construction project on the site of a Concebidas convent. After years of neglect, this site eventually became the Palacio Consistorial (municipal building), which was modeled on Paris's Hôtel de Ville. See Cuadros Bustos, *La Paz*; José de Mesa, Teresa Gisbert, and Carlos D. Mesa, *Historia de Bolivia* (La Paz: Editorial Gisbert, 1998); and G. C. Mesa and Jaime Sáenz, *Emilio Villanueva: Hacia Una Arquitectura Nacional, Con 111 Ilustraciones* (La Paz, Bolivia: Escuela Don Bosco, 1984). In contrast, in the period from 1937 to 1945, the city completed sectional markets in Lanza, Camacho, Caja de Agua, Sopocachi, and Miraflores, and Rodríguez Market. Several of these were located in the indigenous neighborhoods. This was not a coincidence. Officials had not invested in indigenous neighborhoods before this and needed to be convinced to do so. Before the 1930s, they were reluctant to fund expensive and relatively invisible projects (water, electricity) in indigenous neighborhoods; see "Inspección a Domicilio," Caja 252, Correspondencia/1917–37, Archivo de la Prefectura de La Paz, Archivo de La Paz. In one case the city council noted that it was the neighbors who had "helped the city improve [the neighborhood's] lot": *Boletín Municipal de La Paz*, April 1934, 39. The military socialists created a committee that focused on completing worker housing; see Bolivia, *Anuario de leyes, decretos y resoluciones supremas 1936* (La Paz: Imprentas Unidas, 1938), 1452–3. By 1943, city housing inspectors recognized that workers in indigenous neighborhoods needed better housing and proposed that the city expropriate the *tambos* (inns that provided temporary housing) so it could build permanent housing on those sites; see *Boletín Municipal de La Paz*, May 1943. In 1956, the MNR government expropriated twenty-seven properties and began construction on 1,100 homes and had plans to build more housing.

Chapter 5

1 *Endara v. Loza*, 1936, Injurias [Insults], Caja 67, Corte Superior de Distrito, Archivo de La Paz, 6–11.

2 *Chinahuanca v. Choquehuanca*, 1942–1948, 118, Asesinato [Murder], Caja 77, Corte Superior de Distrito, Archivo de La Paz, 118.
3 *Chinahuanca v. Choquehuanca*, 2–12. Women who had lost husbands, brothers, and fathers in the war also faced limited opportunities in the countryside and moved to the city. See Ineke Dibbits, *Polleras Libertarias: Federación Obrera Femenina, 1927–1964* (La Paz: Taller de Historia y Participación de la Mujer, 1986); and Taller de Historia Oral Andina, *Los Constructores de la Ciudad: Tradiciones de Lucha y de Trabajo del Sindicato Central de Constructores y Albañiles de La Paz, 1908–1980* (La Paz: THOA, 1986).
4 The second district of the superior court included all of the northern and western neighborhoods, which were indigenous neighborhoods. These were the most densely populated neighborhoods in the city. According to census data published just after the Chaco War, nearly 40 percent of the city's 150,000 people lived in Gran Poder, San Pedro, and San Sebastián. By early 1942, nearly 60 percent of the city's 250,000 residents lived in indigenous neighborhoods. By 1950, the city's population had reached 350,000 people and the majority of the people in indigenous neighborhoods were mixed race and Aymara. This population boom made transformations of space and conflicts inevitable. Housing, infrastructure, work, and society all had to realign to the new larger urban population.

Throughout the twentieth century, housing in indigenous neighborhoods included large two-story houses with internal patios, rented rooms, small homes, and rooms in *tambos*. Most homes on the periphery—in Chijini, San Pedro Alto, and Sopocachi Alto—were the single-story thatched-roof homes made of adobe that were typical of the countryside. In the urbanized regions—Gran Poder, Sopocachi, San Pedro, and San Sebastián—two-story homes made of adobe and brick were more common. Many property owners saw the opportunity the influx of people represented and converted large houses into apartments and rooms for rent. Few of these houses had indoor plumbing and in those that had access to running water, all of the residents shared a common spigot. In some cases, the front entrance might lead to an internal patio that the owner and the owner's family might use, and an adjacent patio surrounded by apartments would house several tenants. Paceños and other Latin Americans commonly refer to this type of housing as the *conventillo*. Tenants and owners alike prized the street-level rooms because they could convert these into small businesses. In the peripheral areas of indigenous neighborhoods, housing closely resembled rural residential structures with small, enclosed patios surrounding modest thatched-roof homes. For the precariously employed or temporary visitors, the city's *tambos* provided housing. No matter where they lived, honest work was a way for residents to assert claims to honor.
5 Julian Alfred Pitt-Rivers, *The People of the Sierra* (Chicago, IL: University of Chicago Press, 1974), 21; Pablo Piccato, *The Tyranny of Opinion: Honor in the*

Construction of the Mexican Public Sphere (Durham, NC: Duke University Press, 2010), 12.
6   Piccato, *The Tyranny of Opinion*, 15.
7   The Bolivian state's dependence on taxes indigenous communities paid helped maintain a collective identity for Aymara and Quechua populations. Tristan Platt highlights how indigenous identities and communal landholding could have conceivably remained viable into the late nineteenth century. Brooke Larson echoes this in her discussion of indigenous communal landholding and the Willka Zarate Rebellion. See Tristan Platt, "The Andean Experience of Bolivian Liberalism, 1825–1900s: Roots of Rebellion in 19th-Century Chayanta (Potosí)," in *Resistance, Rebellion, and Consciousness in the Andean Peasant World, 18th to 20th Centuries*, edited by Steve J. Stern (Madison: University of Wisconsin Press, 1987); and Brooke Larson, *Trials of Nation Making: Liberalism, Race, and Ethnicity in the Andes, 1810–1910* (Cambridge: Cambridge University Press, 2004).
8   Herbert Klein highlights how the military socialist governments at the municipal and national level insisted on taking over several recordkeeping functions. For example, after 1939, the municipality of La Paz kept far more complete records of deaths and burials in the municipal cemetery. In addition, the city and national governments added several new technocratic divisions to government portfolios, such as architectural and structural codes for construction projects, expanded or revived hygiene and sanitation departments, efforts to improve public health and safety, greater efforts to centralize recordkeeping, new rules for handling food, new worker safety regulations, and new "scientific" taxation schemes to improve revenue. In addition, the national government changed the rules for construction bids and government contracts in an effort to create transparency in regulations. See Herbert S. Klein, *A Concise History of Bolivia* (Cambridge: Cambridge University Press, 2003).
9   The judicial system provided public defenders for any defendant in need of a lawyer. According to reports from the San Pedro penitentiary in La Paz, public defenders held office hours at the prison once a week and usually arranged to accompany defendants to court. In several cases, the defendant provided a statement to the police, the lawyer filed legal papers on his behalf, and the defendant testified in court. All of these documents composed part of the record. Sometimes the defendant and the plaintiff could pose questions to witnesses during hearings. It is extremely difficult to parse whose language or with what "voice" the defendants spoke. Arrest records probably record the least mediated voice of the persons involved, but often defendants were not forthcoming with the police. Police reports were designed to meet a minimum standard for arresting a person. For a discussion of who might be speaking in police reports, see James Sanders, *Contentious Republicans: Popular Politics, Race, and Class in Nineteenth-Century Colombia*

(Durham, NC: Duke University Press, 2004); James Scott, *Domination and the Arts of Resistance: Hidden Transcripts* (New Haven, CT: Yale University Press, 1990); E. Gabrielle Kuenzli, *Acting Inca: National Belonging in Early Twentieth Century Bolivia* (Pittsburgh: Pittsburgh University Press, 2013); Laura Gotkowitz, "Trading Insults: Honor, Violence, and the Gendered Culture of Commerce in Cochabamba, Bolivia, 1870s–1950s," *Hispanic American Historical Review* 83, no. 1 (2003): 83–118; and Laura Gotkowitz, "Commemorating the Heroínas: Gender and Civic Ritual in Early-Twentieth-Century Bolivia," in *Hidden Histories of Gender and the State in Latin America*, edited by Elizabeth Dore and Maxine Molyneux (Durham, NC: Duke University Press, 2000).

10 Brooke Larson, "Redeemed Indians, Barbarized Cholos," in *Political Cultures in the Andes, 1750–1950*, edited by Nils Jacobsen and Cristóbal Aljovín de Losada (Durham, NC: Duke University Press, 2005). See also Marisol de la Cadena, *Indigenous Mestizos: The Politics of Race and Culture in Cuzco Peru, 1919–1991* (Durham, NC: Duke University Press, 2000); David M. Guss, "The Gran Poder and the Reconquest of La Paz," *Journal of Latin American Anthropology* 11, no. 2 (2006): 294–328; Mary Weismantel, *Cholas and Pishtacos: Stories of Race and Sex in the Andes* (Chicago: University of Chicago Press, 2001); and Benjamin S. Orlove, "Down to Earth: Race and Substance in the Andes," *Bulletin of Latin American Research* 17, no. 2 (1998): 207–27.

11 The myth of racial democracy helped combat the hard eugenics that gave short shrift to the idea of education as a means to acquiring the things designed to make one "civilized," hardworking, and intelligent. Northern Europeans tended to subscribe to hard eugenics, which posited that a person's environment played little role in changing their essential character because it was an instinctual drive. For those who subscribed to eugenic science, skin color gradations related to class and played a fundamental role in determining occupation and innate character. Gender was seamlessly woven into this grammar of race and class. For the history and historiography of race in Latin America, see Nancy P. Appelbaum, Anne S. Macpherson, and Karin Alejandra Rosemblatt, "Introduction: Racial Nations," in *Race and Nation in Modern Latin America*, edited by Nancy P. Appelbaum, Anne S. Macpherson, and Karin Alejandra Rosemblatt (Chapel Hill: University of North Carolina Press, 2003). For a discussion of race in the Andes, see Laura Gotkowitz, "Introduction," in *Histories of Race and Racism: The Andes and Mesoamerica from Colonial Times to the Present,* edited by Laura Gotkowitz (Durham. NC: Duke University Press, 2012), 1–39. For a concise discussion of racial science and racial ideology in modern Europe, see Neil MacMaster, *Racism in Europe, 1870–2000* (Hampshire: Palgrave, 2000).

12 Brodwyn Fischer, "Quase Pretos De Tão Pobres? Race and Social Discrimination in Rio De Janeiro's Twentieth-Century Criminal Courts," *Latin American Research Review* 39 no. 1 (2004): 31–59.

13 *Méndez v. Monje*, 42, 1939, Asesinato [Murder], Caja 178, Corte Superior de Distrito, Archivo de La Paz.
14 Sueann Caulfield, "Interracial Courtship in the Río de Janeiro Courts, 1918–1940," in *Race and Nation in Modern Latin America*, edited by Nancy P. Appelbaum, Anne S. Macpherson, and Karin Alejandra Rosemblatt (Chapel Hill: University of North Carolina Press, 2003), 163–87.
15 Gotkowitz, "Trading Insults."
16 Gotkowitz, "Trading Insults."
17 *Méndez v. Monje*.
18 *Méndez v. Monje*, 42.
19 Gotkowitz, "Trading Insults."
20 In most cases, it was difficult to determine a person's age because the court required only that a witness be an adult. Litigants sometimes submitted birth or marriage certificates, which include birth dates and age. I have examined 171 cases from 1906 to 1956. These cases all came from the Second District Superior Court in La Paz, which included the indigenous neighborhoods of San Pedro, San Pedro Alto, Locería, San Francisco, Gran Poder, Los Andes, Cemetery District, Villa Victoria, Achachicala, and Sopocachi.
21 The La Paz Superior District Court was divided into Instrucciones and Partidos and each Instruccion and Partido had Penal and Civil divisions. I thank the archive staff, especially Claudia Riberos at the Archivo De La Paz, for explaining this and for explaining which areas of La Paz belonged to the Second District Superior Court. The number of the back of a page of a court document was usually denoted with a "v" for *vuelta*. The names that usually appear here follow the names in the cases that were filed in the Superior Court and the names the Archivo de La Paz used to archive them for scholarly use.
22 Herbert S. Klein, *Parties and Political Change in Bolivia, 1880–1952* (London: Cambridge University Press, 1969); Luis Antezana Ergueta, *Historia Secreta del Movimiento Nacionalista Revolucionario*, Tomo 2 (La Paz: Librería Editorial "Juventud," 1984); Carlos Montenegro, *Nacionalismo y coloniaje, su expresión histórica en la prensa de Bolivia* (La Paz: Ediciones Autonomía, 1943); Jacobo Libermann Z., *Bolivia: 10 años de revolución [1952-1962]* (N.p., 1962); Jerry W. Knudson, *Bolivia: Press and Revolution, 1932–1964* (Lanham, MD: University Press of America, 1986).
23 *Álvarez v. Ríos*, 1936, Abusos (Rape) Caja 156, Corte Superior de Distrito, Archivo de La Paz, 21; *Moreno v. Rentería*, 1938, Asesinato [Murder], Caja 56, Corte Superior de Distrito Archivo de La Paz; *Pardo v. Rodríguez*, Asesinato [Murder], 1943, Caja 170, Corte Superior de Distrito, Archivo de La Paz, 19–21v; *Nacif v. Safadi*, Asesinato [Murder], 1945, Caja 156, Corte Superior de Distrito Archivo de La Paz, 52, 55; *Rómulo Guzmán v. Julio Ramos Quispe*, 1939 Robo [Theft], Caja 65, Corte Superior de Distrito Archivo de La Paz.

24 Pablo Piccato, *City of Suspects: Crime in Mexico City, 1900–1931* (Durham, NC: Duke University Press, 2001), 80–3.
25 Arturo Posnansky made these claims. See Instituto Tihuanacu De Antropología, Etnografía, y Prehistoria (La Paz) and Arthur Posnansky, *Antropología y sociología de las razas interandinas y de las regiones adyacentes* (La Paz: Editorial "Renacimiento," 1937); and Carlos Ponce Sanjinés, *Arthur Posnansky: Biografía intelectual de un pionero* (La Paz: Producciones CIMA, 1994). Historians have shown how such discourses were functions of larger debates over national belonging. See Kuenzli, *Acting Inca*; Laura Gotkowitz, *A Revolution for Our Rights: Indigenous Struggles for Land and Justice in Bolivia, 1880–1952* (Durham, NC: Duke University Press, 2007); Larson, *Trials of Nation Making*; and de la Cadena, *Indigenous Mestizos*.
26 *Chinahuanca v. Choquehuanca*, 108.
27 *Chinahuanca v. Choquehuanca*, 243v.
28 *Méndez v. Monje*, 24.
29 *Méndez v. Monje*, 31.
30 *Méndez v. Monje*, 40.
31 *Méndez v. Monje*, 80.
32 *Méndez v. Monje*, 120.
33 *Méndez v. Monje*, 80, 120, and 123.
34 *Méndez v. Monje*, 13.
35 *Méndez v. Monje*, 43.
36 *Méndez v. Monje*, 121. Sabelia Monje's honor was questioned because she willingly "entered into a sexual relationship" with Méndez, who was married.
37 Gotkowitz, "Trading Insults"; Caulfield, "Interracial Courtship in the Río de Janeiro Courts, 1918–1940"; Marcia Stephenson, *Gender and Modernity in Andean Bolivia* (Austin: University of Texas Press, 1999).
38 Gotkowitz, "Trading Insults."
39 *Chinahuanca v. Choquehuanca*, 208, 254.
40 *Abraham v. Castro*, 1938, 2v, Robo [Theft], Caja 56, Corte Superior de Distrito; *Ministerio v. Luna*, 1945, Asesinato [Murder], Caja 96, Corte Superior de Distrito; *Moreno v. Rentería* Asesinato [Murder], 1938, Caja 56, Corte Superior de Distrito. All in Archivo de La Paz.
41 Bolivia and Ramón Salinas Mariaca, *Códigos bolivianos: compilación especial por Ramón Salinas Mariaca. Contiene: Código civil, Código penal, Código mercantil, Código de minería, Código del trabajo y un apéndice con las pricipales leyes y decretos supremos modificatorio* (La Paz: Gisbert, 1955), Art. 521–41, 244–8.
42 *Álvarez v. Ríos*, 1936, Abusos (Rape) Caja 156, Corte Superior de Distrito, Archivo de La Paz, 43.
43 *Viuda de Pardo v. Rodríguez Suárez*, 1938, Asesinato [Murder], Caja 56, Corte Superior de Distrito, Archivo de La Paz, 45.

44 Dibbits, *Polleras Libertarias*.
45 *Viuda de Croc v. Mendoza*, 1948, Robo [Theft], 5, Caja 87, Corte Superior de Distrito, Archivo de La Paz.
46 *Chinahuanca v. Choquehuanca*, 135.
47 *Chinahuanca v. Choquehuanca*, 137–9.
48 Some elites saw *cholos* as citified *indígenas*.
49 *Monje v. Méndez*, 134.
50 *Moreno v. Rentería*, 76 Asesinato [Murder], Caja 56, Corte Superior de Distrito, Archivo de La Paz.
51 *Viuda de Croc v. Mendoza*, 34; *Endara v. Loza*, 1-2v.
52 Ríos had a long history of conflict with women. According to several complaints against him, he had faced charges for threatening his mother-in-law while they argued in her patio. In the patio of his own home, he had slandered Hortencia de Villanueva, the owner of the house where he lived. She requested the court's guarantees (*garantías*) that he would not hurt her. On another occasion, Ríos punched Celestina Illanes in the presence of two other women. In another incident, he struck Fermina Rosas, a seamstress, outside his shop. Bonifasia Rodríguez, who rented a room in his mother-in-law's house, stated that Ríos was frequently drunk. *Álvarez v. Ríos*, 65.
53 "Houses, Lodging, and Tambos," *Boletín Municipal de La Paz*, December 1945.
54 *Rómulo Guzmán v. Julio Ramos Quispe*, 1936, Injurias (Slander) Caja 156, Corte Superior de Distrito, Archivo de La Paz, 34.
55 *Rómulo Guzmán v. Julio Ramos Quispe*, 31.
56 *Álvarez v. Ríos*, 18–23.
57 Another witness, a cobbler, stated that he was working in his own guild-approved workshop when he heard someone hitting the door that led to the street. The cobbler testified that he found broken windows in the front of the house and damage to the front door. *Álvarez v. Ríos*, 15.
58 *Álvarez v. Ríos*, 56, 57v–58v.
59 *Álvarez v. Ríos*, 59.
60 *Álvarez v. Ríos*, 13.
61 *Álvarez v. Ríos*, 42.
62 *Álvarez v. Ríos*, 34.
63 *Álvarez v. Ríos*, 45.
64 *Álvarez v. Ríos*, 127–130v.
65 *Ministerio Público v. Domingo Luna*, 91.
66 *Ministerio Público v. Domingo Luna*, 2, 43, 75v, 91.
67 *Ministerio Público v. Domingo Luna*, 91.
68 *Ministerio Público v. Domingo Luna*, 7–8.
69 *Ministerio Público v. Domingo Luna*, 24.

70 *Ministerio Público v. Domingo Luna*, 10v.
71 Neighbors grew suspicious when Domingo claimed that he did not know where Félix was and reported Domingo to the police when one of them saw an article in the paper about the body of a young boy in the river. *Ministerio Público v. Domingo Luna*, 43v.
72 Police reports often stated that indigenous actors maintained "precarious residence" in the city. For three cases where this language was used to describe indigenous actors and witnesses, see *Bernandino Espinoza v. Bacilio Casas*, 1939, Perjurio [Perjury], Caja 80, Corte Superior de Distrito, Archivo de La Paz; *Bedregal v. Quisbert*, 1950, Robo [Theft], Caja 143, Corte Superior de Distrito, Archivo de La Paz; and *Ministerio Público v. Domingo Luna*.
73 Larson, *Trials of Nation Making*; Gotkowitz, *A Revolution for Our Rights*.
74 Larson, *Trials of Nation Making*, esp. chapter 5; Larson, *Cochabamaba 1550-1900: Colonialism and Agarian Transformation*, esp. chapter 9; Gotkowitz, *A Revolution for Our Rights*.
75 Rossana Barragán, "The 'Spirit' of Bolivian Laws: Citizenship, Patriarchy, and 'Infamy,'" in *Honor, Status, and Law in Modern Latin America*, edited by Sueann Caulfield, Sarah C. Chambers, and Lara Putnam (Durham, NC: Duke University Press, 2005).
76 *Blanco v. Conde and Cesárea de Conde*, Caluminas [Libel], 1944, Caja 77, Corte Superior de Distrito, Archivo de La Paz.
77 *Amurrio v. Gonzáles*, 1947, Corte Superior De Distrito Juzgado 80 Corte Superior de Distrito, Archivo de La Paz; *Rosenda de Alba v. Munguía*, 1945, Caluminas [Slander], Caja 81 Corte Superior de Distrito, Archivo de La Paz; *Pascual de Alarcón v. Policia de Seguridad*, 1936, Habeus Corpus, Caja 67, Corte Superior de Distrito, Archivo de La Paz.
78 Dibbits, *Polleras Libertarias*.
79 *Francisca Loza v. Agustín Callejos*, 1947 Heridas [Assault], Cajas 78 y 79, Corte Superior de Distrito, Archivo de La Paz; *Juan Jáuregui v. Antonio Vargas*, Robo [Theft], 1944, Cajas 70 y 71, Corte Superior De Distrito, Archivo de La Paz; *Quiroga Baldivieso v. Unknown*, Heridas [Injuries], 1947, Cajas 78, Corte Superior De Distrito, Archivo de La Paz; *Callasaya v. Callasaya*, Heridas, 1944, Cajas 79, Corte Superior De Distrito, Archivo de La Paz; *Álvarez v. Alarcón*, Heridas, 1948, Cajas 98, Corte Superior De Distrito, Archivo de La Paz.
80 *Apaza v. Callejos*, 1935, Injurias [Slander], Cajas 23, Corte Superior de Distrito Juzgado Archivo de La Paz; *Miranda v. Quispe*, 1946, Injurias [Slander], Cajas 92, Corte Superior de Distrito Juzgado Archivo de La Paz; *Quiroga Baldivieso v. Unknown*, 1935, Robo [Theft] Cajas 41, Corte Superior de Distrito Juzgado Archivo de La Paz; *Moreno v. Renteria*; *Pastor Loza v. Francisco Endara*; *Carmen de Chusi v. Quispe*, 1948, Asesinato [Murder], Cajas 23, Corte Superior de Distrito Juzgado Archivo de La Paz.

81 *Chinahuanca v. Choquehuanca*, 183–183v.
82 Through an analysis of over 500 cases, Brodwyn Fischer demonstrates how racial and social categories overlapped and the courts did not explicitly use race as a valid category for determining outcomes, but race was clearly tied to class markers. See Fischer, "Quase Pretos De Tão Pobres? Race and Social Discrimination in Rio De Janeiro's Twentieth-Century Criminal Courts," 31–59.

Chapter 6

1 *La Calle*, October 8, 1938, quoted in Ana Cecilia Wadsworth and Ineke Dibbits, *Agitadoras de buen gusto: historia del Sindicato de Culinarias (1935–1958)* ([La Paz]: TAHIPAMU, 1989). The editors of *La Calle* had close ties with reformist politicians and the reform parties of the post–Chaco War era.
2 The context of neoliberalism and the revalorization of the indigenous contributions to Bolivian society shaped these memories.
3 Herbert S. Klein, *Parties and Political Change in Bolivia, 1880–1952* (London: Cambridge University Press, 1969).
4 At most, a few hundred men were artisans in the city since the law stipulated that only those who owned their shops were eligible.
5 Pilar Mendieta Parada, "Memorias de la Revolucion del 52," *Historia* 37 (August 2016): 11–42.
6 Herbert S. Klein, *A Concise History of Bolivia* (Cambridge: Cambridge University Press, 2003); Porfirio Díaz Machicao, *Toro, Busch, Quintanilla, 1936–1940* (La Paz: Editorial "Juventud," 1957).
7 For a scathing analysis of the historiography in relation to this period and the mythology of the MNR, see Mario Murillo, *La bala no mata sino el destino: Una crónica de la insurrección popular de 1952 en Bolivia* (La Paz: Plural, 2012).
8 Antezana Ergueta, *Historia secreta del Movimiento Nacionalista Revolucionario*, Tomo 2 (La Paz: Librería Editorial "Juventud," 1988); Klein, *A Concise History of Bolivia*; Edwin A. Möller, *El dios desnudo de mi conciencia revolucionaria: autobiografía y revolución nacional* (La Paz: Plural Editores, 2001).
9 Larson, *Trials of Nation Making*; Silvia Rivera Cusicanqui, *Oppressed but Not Defeated: Peasant Struggles among the Aymara and Qhechwa in Bolivia, 1900–1980* (Geneva: United Nations Research Institute for Social Development, 1987); Gotkowitz, *A Revolution for Our Rights*; David M. Guss, "The Gran Poder and the Reconquest of La Paz," *Journal of Latin American Anthropology* 11, no. 2 (2006): 298; Brooke Larson, "'Forging the Unlettered Indian': The Pedagogy of Race in the Bolivian Andes," in *Histories of Race and Racism*, edited by Laura Gotkowitz (Durham, NC: Duke University Press, 2011), 134–56; Laura Gotkowitz,

"Introduction," in *Histories of Race and Racism: The Andes and Mesoamerica from Colonial Times to the Present*, edited by Laura Gotkowitz (Durham, NC: Duke University Press, 2011), 1–39. https://www.dukeupress.edu/histories-of-race-and-racism; Rossana Barragán, "The Census and the Making of a Social 'Order' in Nineteenth-Century Bolivia," in *Histories of Race and Racism: The Andes and Mesoamerica from Colonial Times to the Present*, edited by Laura Gotkowitz (Durham, NC: Duke University Press, 2011), 113–33.

10 For example, Laura Gotkowitz argues that a long rural revolution preceded the 1952 revolution and that indigenous corporate identity shaped the battles over land expropriations and justice. She shows that as early as the 1910s and 1920s, *caciques apoderados* traveled among rural communities and to the national and regional archives as part of a long-standing political practice and that these leaders used and manipulated the legal system and political context to pursue land claims and seek justice. Gotkowitz, *A Revolution for Our Rights*.

11 Pilar Mendieta highlights this tension, arguing that there is much validity to the Kataristas' approach to history and the recovery of the subaltern voices. But she rightly points out that the conclusions that some of these scholars reach are too reductionist and totalizing. See Parada, "Memorias de la Revolucion del 52."

12 Xavier Albó, for example, argues that class and race in the Aymara regions were co-constitutive categories and that the lived experiences of activists informed their efforts to organize politically. See Xavier Albó, "From MNRista to Katarista to Katari," in *Resistance, Rebellion, and Consciousness in the Andean Peasant World, 18th to 20th Centuries*, edited by Steve J. Stern (Madison: University of Wisconsin Press, 1987), 379–419.

13 Cusicanqui, *Oppressed but Not Defeated*, 12–18.

14 Leandro Condori Chura and Esteban Ticona Alejo, *El escribano de los caciques apoderados = Kasikinakan purirarunakan qillqiripa* (La Paz: Hisbol, 1992). In his role as a scribe, Condori bridged the rural and urban divide. Condori was an Aymara who had migrated to La Paz and who also wrote in and spoke Spanish.

15 This scholarship includes such works as Cusicanqui, *Oppressed but Not Defeated*; Esteban Ticona Alejo, *Saberes, conocimientos y prácticas anticoloniales del pueblo aymara-quechua en Bolivia* (La Paz: AGRUCO, UMSS-FCAyP/COSUDE, 2010); Esteban Ticona Alejo, *Bolivia en el inicio del "Pachakuti": La larga lucha anticolonial de los pueblos aimara y quechua* (Madrid: Akal, 2011); and Carlos Mamani Condori, *Taraqu: 1866–1935: Masacre, guerra y "renovación" en la biografía de Eduardo L. Nina Qhispi* (La Paz: Ediciones Aruwiyiri, 1991).

16 Ergueta, *Historia secreta del Movimiento Nacionalista Revolucionario*, Tomo 2; Klein, *A Concise History of Bolivia*; Möller, *El dios desnudo de mi conciencia revolucionaria*.

17 Guss, "The Gran Poder and the Reconquest of La Paz," 298.

18 Ergueta, *Historia secreta del Movimiento Nacionalista Revolucionario*, Tomo 2; Klein, *A Concise History of Bolivia*.
19 Silvia Arze and Rossana Barragán, *El centro urbano durante los siglos XIX y XX* (La Paz: Alcaldía Municipal de La Paz, 1988).
20 "Censo de la ciudad de La Paz—Distribución por distritos," *Boletín Municipal de La Paz*, November 1943, 28–35.
21 Larson, *Trials of Nation Making*.
22 Stephen Jay Gould, *The Mismeasure of Man* (New York: Norton, 1981).
23 Larson, "Forging the Unlettered Indian"; Barragán, "The Census and the Making of a Social 'Order' in Nineteenth-Century Bolivia"; and Seemin Quayum, "Indian Ruins, National Origins: Tiwanaku and Indigenismo in La Paz, 1897–1933," in *Histories of Race and Racism*, edited by Laura Gotkowitz (Durham, NC: Duke University Press, 2011), 159–78.
24 See Erwin P. Grieshaber, "Survival of Indian Communities in Nineteenth-Century Bolivia: A Regional Comparison," *Journal of Latin American Studies* 12, no. 2 (1980): 223–69.
25 Grieshaber, "Survival of Indian Communities in Nineteenth-Century Bolivia."
26 Gotkowitz, *A Revolution for Our Rights*, 13.
27 Gotkowitz, *A Revolution for Our Rights*, 14.
28 Nancy P. Appelbaum, Anne S. Macpherson, and Karin Alejandro Rosemblatt, "Introduction," in *Race and Nation in Modern Latin America*, edited by Nancy P. Appelbaum, Anne S. Macpherson, and Karin Alejandro Rosemblatt (Chapel Hill: University of North Carolina Press, 2003), 1–31.
29 Vicente Donoso Torres, *El estado actual de la educación indigenal en el país* (La Paz: Renacimiento, 1940).
30 Antonio Carvajal and Armando Quispe, 1937, Injurias (Slander), Caja 68, Corte Superior de Distrito, Archivo de La Paz; *Blanco vs. Fermín y Conde*, May 4 1944, Injurias (Slander), Caja 77, Corte Superior de Distrito, Archivo de La Paz; *Viuda de Croc vs. Mendoza*, 1936, Robo (Theft), Caja 71, Corte Superior de Distrito, Archivo de La Paz; *Carmen de Chusi vs. Quispe*, September 1936, Asesinato (Attempted Murder), Caja 71, Corte Superior de Distrito, Archivo de La Paz; *Chinahuanca vs. Choquehuanca*, 1936, Murder, Caja 72, Corte Superior de Distrito, Archivo de La Paz.
31 "Inspeccion de sanidad en vias publicas," *Boletín Municipal Acta y Estadísticas*, August 1929, 12–15.
32 "Distribucion de Alimentos," *Boletín Municipal de La Paz*, September 1945, 21–3.
33 "Distribucion de Alimentos," *Boletín Municipal de La Paz*, September 1945, 19.
34 "Informe Seccion de Mercados," *Boletín Municipal de La Paz*, May 1943, 24.
35 "Informe Seccion deMercados," *Boletín Municipa de La Paz*, May 1943, 24.
36 "Informe Seccion de Urbanismo," *Boletín Municipa de La Paz*, March 1946, 25.

37 "Informe Seccion de Urbanismo," *Boletín Municipal de La Paz*, March 1946, 40.
38 Álvaro Cuadros B., *La Paz* (La Paz: Facultad de Arquitectura, Urbanismo y Artes, Universidad Mayor de San Andrés, 2002), 122.
39 Cuadros B., *La Paz*, 93; Eloy Salmón, *La Paz en su IV centenario, 1548–1948* (La Paz: Comité Pro IV Centenario de la Fundación de la Paz, 1948), 45; "Distritos de La Paz 1917 Ordenanza," in *Anuario de leyes y disposiciones suprema 1917* (La Paz: Imprenta Nacional, 1918), 1123. A *tambo* is a combination of warehouse and inn. *Tambos* were collection points for specific agricultural products brought to the city. They predate Spanish colonization and remained important to urban markets well into the twentieth century.
40 Imagine the Plaza Murillo surrounded by a three-square-block area. This is the central district. In the period between 1900 and 1930, the elite considered the area outside this small central district as *extramuro* despite the fact that San Francisco, San Pedro, and Santa Barbara were legally urban districts.
41 For a detailed discussion of indigenous urban settlements and the efforts of Spaniards to settle in the New World, see Arq. Ramón Gutiérrez, *Pueblo de indios: Otro urbanismo en la región Andina* (Quito: Biblioteca Ayba-yala, 1993), 8–47.
42 Cuadros B., *La Paz*, 112.
43 Cuadros B., *La Paz*, 134.
44 "Obreros Visitan a La Reforma," *El Hombre Libre*, November 16, 1920.
45 Cuadros B., *La Paz*, 134.
46 Klein, *Parties and Political Change in Bolivia*, 120.
47 The similarities to Augusto B. Leguía in Peru are uncanny. Both Leguía and Saavedra used populist discourses, promulgated social reforms, and persecuted their enemies. Leguía seems to have been much more successful in his efforts to control national politics. For an overview of the Peruvian case, see Thomas E. Skidmore and Peter H. Smith, *Modern Latin America*, 5th ed. (New York: Oxford University Press, 2001), 192–202.
48 The military socialists were a political group of junior military officers who had served in the Chaco War in various capacities on both the front lines and in the military high command.
49 Klein, *Parties and Political Change in Bolivia*, 133.
50 In the countryside, the Jesús de Machaca uprising of 1921 and the subsequent repression of participants challenged the Saavedra government's commitment to "pro-indigenous" policies. The miners' strike at Uncía in Oruro province in 1923 and its subsequent repression also called into question Saavedra's commitment to Bolivia's "laboring classes." Esteban Ticona Alejo and Xavier Albó, *Jesús de Machaca en el tiempo* (La Paz: Fundación Diálogo, 1998); Klein, *A Concise History of Bolivia*, 158.
51 "La Doctrina Radical del Doctor Saavedra," *El Hombre Libre*, November 12, 1920; Klein, *Parties and Political Change in Bolivia*, 76.

52 *El Hombre Libre*, October 20, 1920.
53 The city council and the national government repeatedly tried to impose strict measures to end "speculation" in the market for basic necessities. Black market activity was a constant issue that politicians of all political persuasions sought to end. "Informe Al Concejo Muncipal," 1917–1937, Caja 256, Correspondencia, Archivo de La Paz; "Informe: Al Consejo Municipal," 1920–45, Correspondencia, Honorable Consejo Municipal, Archivo de La Paz; Bolivia, "Articulos de Primera Necesidad," in *Anuario de leyes, decretos y resoluciones supremas 1939* (La Paz: Imprentas Unidas, 1940), 1582–83; "Sistema central de precios se establece en la ciudad," *La Calle*, September 20, 1939; "Precios de Mercados," *Boletín Municipal*, August 1942, 43; "Informe Seccion Mercados," *Boletín Municipal*, November 1942; "Articulos de Primera Necesidad," *Boletín Municipal*, September 1943; Ineke Dibbits, *Polleras libertarias: Federación obrera femenina, 1927–1964* (La Paz: Taller de Historia y Participación de la Mujer, 1986), 13; "Especulacion en La Paz," *Boletín Municipal de La Paz*, September 1945, 19; "La Federación de Juntas Vecinales Sugiere la Atención de Los Barrios Populares," *Ultima Hora*, February 16, 1951; "Campaña contra la especulación," *En Marcha*, July 21, 1952; "Se pondran a la venta al consumidor harina de trigo y azúcar decomisadas," *En Marcha*, July 21, 1952; "Para establecer la libreta familiar hubo reuniones en el Ministerio de Economía," *En Marcha*, September 29, 1953.
54 From 1935 to 1947, among the most influential mayors of La Paz were Luis Nardín Rivas, Juan Luis Gutiérrez Granier, and Humberto Muñoz Cornejo. They oversaw a reorganization of the municipal departments under the military socialists that created a stable cadre of experts in executive positions throughout 1936 to 1950. This made it possible for the city to enact a series of reforms under the guidance of a stable municipal regime. "Informe Alcaldia," *Boletín Municipal de La Paz*, August 1934, 87; "Señor Alcalde," *Boletín Municipal de La Paz*, November 1942, 56; Bolivia, "Decreto Supremo: Expropriacion de Terrenos," *Anuario de leyes, decretos y resoluciones supremas 1936* (La Paz: Imprentas Unidas, 1938), 683; Decreto Supremo, "Reglamentacion de Contratos," in Bolivia, *Anuario de leyes, decretos y resoluciones supremas 1940* (La Paz: Imprentas Unidas, 1941), 480; Salmón, *La Paz en su IV centenario*.
55 Klein, *Parties and Political Change in Bolivia*.
56 Klein, *Parties and Political Change in Bolivia*, 226–7.
57 Klein, *Parties and Political Change in Bolivia*, 225.
58 Michael L. Conniff, *Populism in Latin America* (Tuscaloosa: University of Alabama Press, 1999); Michael L. Conniff, *Urban Politics in Brazil: The Rise of Populism, 1925–1945* (Pittsburgh: University of Pittsburgh Press, 1981); Jeffrey L. Gould, "'For an Organized Nicaragua': Somoza and the Labour Movement, 1944–1948," *Journal of Latin American Studies* 19, no. 2 (1987): 353–87; Danny James, *Doña María's*

Story: Life History, Memory, and Political Identity (Durham, NC: Duke University Press, 2000); Amelia M. Kiddle and María L. O. Muñoz, *Populism in Twentieth Century Mexico: The Presidencies of Lázaro Cárdenas and Luis Echeverría* (Tucson: University of Arizona Press, 2010); John D. French, *The Brazilian Workers' ABC: Class Conflict and Alliances in Modern São Paulo* (Chapel Hill: University of North Carolina Press, 1992); Joel Wolfe, *Working Women, Working Men: São Paulo and the Rise of Brazil's Industrial Working Class, 1900–1955* (Durham: Duke University Press, 1993).

59 Machicao, *Toro, Busch, Quintanilla*.
60 Klein, *Parties and Political Change in Bolivia*; Machicao, *Toro, Busch, Quintanilla*.
61 For a detailed account of this national socialist-inspired unionization drive and government experimentation with fascist-inspired corporatism, see Carlos Montenegro, *Frente al derecho del Estado el oro de la Standard Oil* (La Paz: Editorial Trabajo, 1938).

Chapter 7

1 This account is taken from "La Juventud del MNR en accion," *La Nacion*, April 9, 1955.
2 "La Juventud del MNR en accion," *La Nacion*, April 9, 1955.
3 "La Juventud del MNR en accion," *La Nacion*, April 9, 1955.
4 "La Juventud del MNR en accion," *La Nacion*, April 9, 1955.
5 "La Juventud del MNR en accion," *La Nacion*, April 9, 1955.
6 "La Juventud del MNR en accion," *La Nacion*, April 9, 1955. The Estado Mayor is the Bolivian Army's general staff headquarters in the Miraflores section of La Paz.
7 Luis Antezana Ergueta, *Historia secreta del Movimiento Nacionalista Revolucionario*, Tomo 7, *La revolución del MNR del 9 de abril* (La Paz: Librería Editorial "Juventud," 1988). Mario Murillo, *La bala no mata sino el destino: Una crónica de la insurreción popular de 1952 en Bolivia* (La Paz: Plural, 2012); Pilar Mendieta Parada, "Memorias de la Revolucion del 52," *Historia*, 37 (agosto 2016): 11–42. ISSN 2519-025. Antezana and Carlos Mesa are primary proponents of the myth-making about the MNR. Antezana's nine-volume *Historia secreta del MNR* is required reading for any historian who wants to understand the MNR. However, it sometimes portrays things that are not clear with certainty and it portrays events where little or no documentation exists as facts. Perhaps Antezana's close association with the MNR leadership and his eyewitness testimony enable him to make these claims. Mendieta's oral history shows how the MNR triumph meant very little to some rural residents and how some elites portrayed a much more coherent narrative that made connections way back to the Chaco War and sometimes farther back

than that. Murillo also uses oral history, but the relation to the larger context and traditional historiography is largely absent from his informants' accounts. He takes the traditional historiography to task, especially in chapter 1, for its role in making the MNR's mythology possible.

8 This account is taken from "La Juventud del MNR en accion," *La Nacion*, April 9, 1955. Another classic account that engages in a teleological explanation of the MNR revolution is Luis Antezana Ergueta, *Historia secreta del Movimiento Nacionalista Revolucionario*, Tomo 7.

9 For a scathing analysis of "nationalist" historiography in relation to the mythology of the MNR, see Murillo, *La bala no mata sino el destino*.

10 For examples of this historiography, see Luis Antezana Ergueta, *Historia secreta del Movimiento Nacionalista Revolucionario:* Tomo 1–9 (La Paz: Librería Editorial "Juventud," 1984); Herbert S. Klein, *A Concise History of Bolivia* (Cambridge: Cambridge University Press, 2003); and Edwin A. Möller, *El dios desnudo de mi conciencia revolucionaria: autobiografía y revolución nacional* (La Paz: Plural Editores, 2001).

11 Herbert S. Klein, *Parties and Political Change in Bolivia, 1880–1952* (London: Cambridge University Press, 1969), 375.

12 Bolivia, "Decreto Supremo," *Anuario de leyes, decretos y resoluciones supremas 1943* (La Paz: Imprentas Unidas, 1944), 245.

13 Bolivia, "Decreto Supremo," 245.

14 Laura Gotkowitz, *A Revolution for Our Rights: Indigenous Struggles for Land and Justice in Bolivia, 1880–1952* (Durham, NC: Duke University Press, 2007), 219; Jorge Dandler and Juan Torrico A., "From the National Indigenous Congress to the Ayopaya Rebellion: Bolivia, 1945–1947," in *Resistance, Rebellion, and Consciousness in the Andean Peasant World, 18th to 20th Centuries*, edited by Steve J. Stern (Madison: University of Wisconsin Press, 1987), 334–78.

15 The murder of several political opponents was among the heinous acts of the government. José de Mesa, Teresa Gisbert, and Carlos D. Mesa Gisbert, *Historia de Bolivia*, novena edición, actualizada y aumentada (La Paz, Bolivia: Editorial Gisbert, 2016).

16 The July 21, 1952, edition of *En Marcha* was dedicated to the assassination of Villarroel. Over the next several issues, *En Marcha* published various images of the events of 1946 and articles that attempted to discern who had participated in the assassination and desecrated the body.

17 Hertzog ostensibly stepped down due to declining health, but contemporary accounts suggest that he stepped down due to his inability to manage a declining economy and because of agitation in the countryside and cities. Hertzog was seen as much more conciliatory and willing to negotiate. Urriolagotía apparently had few qualms about using government forces to quell unrest. "Sembrando Vientos," *Ultima Hora*, January 23, 1951.

18 "La represions de campesinado durante el sexenio," *La Nación*, October 13, 1952; "El Tragico Simbolo de la Represion Rosca Comunista," *En Marcha*, July 22, 1952.
19 *Ultima Hora*, January 9, 1951.
20 *Ultima Hora*, January 9, 1951.
21 "A los propietarios y vecinos de Villa Dolores," *Ultima Hora*, March 26, 1949; "Pasando sobre las leyes abusa una dueña de casa," "Campaña contra la especulación," "Escasez de inmuebles," "Paro en el Banco," "Proyectos de Construccion," "Pliego de los vecinos de Villa Potosi," *En Marcha*, July 21, 1952; "Proyectos en Tembladerani," "Barrio Ferroviario," *Boletin Municipal* Abril 1953 No. 1036.
22 "No aceptan un desalojo varios inquilinos," *Ultima Hora*, March 5, 1949.
23 "Sembrando Vientos," *Ultima Hora*, January 23, 1951.
24 "Sembrando Vientos," *Ultima Hora*, January 23, 1951.
25 "La Federación Obrera Sindical amenaza promover mitines de protesta," *Ultima Hora*, March 24, 1949.
26 "A.M.I.G. en huelga de hambre," *Ultima Hora*, April 26, 1949.
27 "MNR revuelve al campesinado," *Ultima Hora*, March 7, 1949. See also Pilar Mendieta Parada, "De la Revolución del 52 a Evo Morales: El recorrido político del sindicalismo campesino en Bolivia," *Tinkazos* 18, no. 37 (2015): 35–47.
28 "Federación de Juntas Vecinales vista Ultima Hora," *Ultima Hora*, June 29, 1949.
29 "Cuerpo directivo de la Federación de Juntas Vecinales," *Ultima Hora*, July 15, 1949.
30 "Trabajadores en Huelga por problemas en las fabricas Soligno, Said," *Ultima Hora*, August 25, 1949.
31 "120 detenidos en La Paz por actividades subversivas en Oruro, Santa Cruz, y Tarija," *Ultima Hora*, August 27, 1949.
32 "La autoridad moral de un gobierno," *Ultima Hora*, January 22, 1951.
33 "Escase de Agua en Villa Pabon," *Ultima Hora* January 27, 1951.
34 "Con escala especial, piden aumento de salarios los mineros de Milluni," *Ultima Hora*, January 25, 1951; "En su primer tramite, los pliegos de aumento de sueldos y salarios de varias organizaciones obreras," *Ultima Hora*, January 27, 1951; "Sorprendio a inquilinos y propietarios la supresión de la oficina de vivienda," *Ultima Hora*, January 27, 1951.
35 "La autoridad moral de un gobierno," *Ultima Hora*, January 22, 1951.
36 "El jefe del Partido Liberal es Tomas Manuel Elio su reunion tuvo lugar en el Club de La Paz," *Ultima Hora*, January 20, 1951
37 "El jefe del Partido Liberal es Tomas Manuel Elio su reunion tuvo lugar en el Club de La Paz," *Ultima Hora*, January 20, 1951.
38 "FSB apoya la candidature de Rioja Bilboa-Flores," *Ultima Hora*, April 14, 1951. The Falange Socialista Boliviana was a far-right political party.
39 "Notas Marginales: Garantias a los Partidos," *Ultima Hora*, April 12, 1951.

40 "Periodista de Ultima Hora Arrestado," *Ultima Hora*, April 14, 1951.
41 On April 16, 1951, the MNR plot was foiled. The party denied any violent activity or subversive plots, "Aumentan las denuncias por procedimientos ilegales en la campaña electoral," *Ultima Hora*, April 17, 1951.
42 "La huelga proclaman estudiantes, obreros, y MNR," *Ultima Hora*, April 20, 1951; "Madres y esposas de detenidos del MNR se declaran en huelga de Hambre," *Ultima Hora*.
43 "El ejemplar disciplina de la clase trabajadora," *En Marcha*, May 1951.
44 "El ejemplar disciplina de la clase trabajadora," *En Marcha*, May 1951.
45 "El ejemplar disciplina de la clase trabajadora," *En Marcha*, May 1951.
46 "El jefe felicita al partido," *En Marcha*, May 1951.
47 "El jefe felicita al partido," *En Marcha*, May 1951.
48 "El General Bilbao Rioja denuncia a la junta de gobierno," *Ultima Hora*, April 14, 1951.
49 "El General Bilbao Rioja denuncia a la junta de gobierno," *Ultima Hora*, April 14, 1951.
50 "El jefe felicita al partido," *En Marcha*, May 1951.
51 "El jefe felicita al partido," *En Marcha*, May 1951.
52 "La Junta de Gobierno se dirige a la nacion," *Ultima Hora*, May 17, 1951.
53 "La juventud del MNR en accion," *La Nacion*, April 9, 1955.
54 Elizabeth Shesko, *Conscript Nation: Coercion and Consent in the Bolivian Barracks* (Pittsburgh: University of Pittsburgh Press, forthcoming).
55 This is not to say that well-placed snipers or well-defended machine guns would not have been able to hold a defensive position, but the MNR made no mention of using these tactics.
56 "La juventud del MNR en accion," *La Nacion*, April 9, 1955.
57 Donato Millán had been involved in persecuting the political opposition to the military junta that had ruled Bolivia since May 16, 1951. However, it is unclear whether Millán was a supporter of the MNR; he worked to repress all forms of political opposition in the period before April 1952. According to General Seleme, Millán's superior, Millán followed orders to mobilize the police and distribute weapons to the MNR. Ergueta, *Historia secreta del MNR*, Tomo 7; Víctor Silva, "La noche de Seleme," *La Razón*, April 25, 2018.
58 Shesko, *Conscript Nation*.
59 Many rank-and-file police and junior officers supported the MNR.
60 Silva, "La noche de Seleme."
61 The Falange Socialista Boliviano (FSB), a far-right party, was founded in 1937 by several Bolivian exiles residing in Chile. Its members drew inspiration from fascism. Like the members of the MNR, they advocated reforms designed to erode the power of Bolivia's oligarchs. It was a minor party in the 1940s but gained a

broader following after the revolution, especially among well-to-do university students and disaffected elites. James Malloy, *Bolivia: The Uncompleted Revolution* (Pittsburgh: University of Pittsburgh Press, 1970).
62 Silva, "La noche de Seleme."
63 The MNR's histories omit the significant roles residents of indigenous neighborhoods played in taking the arsenal and garrison in Villa Victoria and stopping the military's counterattacks on La Paz. The numbers of MNR militants were simply not large enough to make the plan work, as Mario Murillo notes in his oral history of the revolution. Murillo, *La bala no mata sino el destino*.
64 "La juventud del MNR en accion," *La Nacion*, April 9, 1955.
65 "La juventud del MNR en accion," *La Nacion*, April 9, 1955.
66 "La juventud del MNR en accion," *La Nacion*, April 9, 1955.
67 "La juventud del MNR en accion," *La Nacion*, April 9, 1955.
68 "La juventud del MNR en accion," *La Nacion*, April 9, 1955.
69 "La juventud del MNR en accion," *La Nacion*, April 9, 1955.
70 Murillo, *La bala no mata sino el destino*.
71 Murillo, *La bala no mata sino el destino*, 92.
72 Murillo, *La bala no mata sino el destino*, 92.
73 Murillo, *La bala no mata sino el destino*, 92.
74 Murillo, *La bala no mata sino el destino*, 95.
75 Murillo, *La bala no mata sino el destino*, 95.
76 Murillo, *La bala no mata sino el destino*, 95.
77 "Nueva filiación de los militantes del MNR: el comando departamental de Movimiento Nacionalista Revolucionario," *La Nacion*, May 3, 1953. In a speech commemorating Bolivian independence in 1809, Juan Luis Gutiérrez Granier argued that the MNR needed to carefully vet all applicants for party membership. He said, "The Pedro Domingo Murillo cell of the [MNR] Party has received 300 applications for membership and only 20 have been accepted. We must safeguard the revolution by careful examination of those who seek to enter into its ranks. The Party must exclude opportunists who are not committed to the national revolution and everything it implies." *Boletín Municipal de La Paz*, June 1953, 1.
78 In the 1947 elections, the MNR candidate for president garnered only 8 percent of the vote. Official results for the 1951 elections show that the MNR candidate garnered a plurality of votes for the presidency, but unsurprisingly, official numbers for congressional elections were never released. http://www.oep.org.bo/centro_doc/cuadernos_tra/cuaderno_tra2_sistemas.pdf.
79 The Barzolas became a leading pressure group in the city after 1946. The MNR gave the Barzolas, the FSTMB, and other allied unions financial support in exchange for their support, their work to mobilize union members, and their coordination of action among the various workers' organizations. The *culinarias* criticized these

organizations, arguing that they sought members in order to collect mandatory dues, not to help workers.

These political alliances and the diversity of the organizations (MNR, POR, socialist, communist, and anarchist) point to the vitality, origins, aims, and flexibility of the workers' movement. For unions and labor federations, organization from below was as important as the broader opening that occurred in the post-Chaco period. The activism of the labor organizations was not tied to one party, one union, one political ideology, or even one urban space.

80 Klein, *Parties and Political Change in Bolivia*; Ineke Dibbits, *Polleras libertarias: Federación Obrera Femenina, 1927–1965* (La Paz: TAHIPAMU/HISBOL, 1989); Ana Cecilia Wadsworth and Ineke Dibbits, *Agitadoras de buen gusto: historia del Sindicato de Culinarias (1935–1958)* ([La Paz]: Hisbol, 1989).

81 "Comando Zonal de Sopocachi," *Boletín Municipal de La Paz*, June 1953, 12.

82 "Pasando sobre las leyes abusa una dueña de casa," *En Marcha*, July 21, 1952; Campaña contra la especulación," *En Marcha*, July 21, 1952; "Escasez de inmuebles," *En Marcha*, July 21, 1952; "Paro en el banco," *En Marcha*, July 21, 1952; "Projection of Our Building Plans," *En Marcha*, July 21, 1952; "Petition for the Neighbors of Villa Potosi," *En Marcha*, July 21, 1952; "Proyectos en Tembladerani," *Boletín Municipal de La Paz*, April 1953, 41; "Barrio Ferroviario," *Boletín Municipal de La Paz*, April 1953, 34.

83 "Se adquirira un inmueble para trabajadores mineros," *En Marcha*, July 21, 1952; "Peticion a favor de los vecinos de Villa Potosi," *En Marcha*, July 21, 1954.

84 Elizabeth Shesko presents a concise description of the period before the MNR revolution and the importance of the Chaco War to the success of the belligerents in 1952 in *Conscript Nation*.

Conclusion

1 Before 1952, the franchise excluded women and indigenous peoples indirectly by including property requirements and literacy tests in voting laws; Laura Gotkowitz, *A Revolution for Our Rights: Indigenous Struggles for Land and Justice in Bolivia, 1880–1952* (Durham, NC: Duke University Press, 2007). Master artisans gained the right to vote in 1926; Herbert Klein, *Parties and Political Change in Bolivia, 1880–1952* (London: Cambridge University Press, 1969). After 1952, indigenous peoples and women gained the right to vote with no property restrictions.

2 For other Latin American nations, see Sarah Chambers, "Little Middle Ground: The Instability of a *Mestizo* Identity in the Andes, Eighteenth and Nineteenth Centuries," in *Race and Nation in Modern Latin America*, edited by Nancy P. Appelbaum, Anne S. Macpherson, and Karin Alejandro Rosemblatt (Chapel Hill: University of North

Carolina Press, 2003), 32–55; Gerardo Renique, "Race, Region, and Nation: Sonora's Anti-Chinese Racism and Mexico's Post-Revolutionary Nationalism, 1920s–1930s," in *Race and Nation in Modern Latin America*, edited by Nancy P. Appelbaum, Anne S. Macpherson, and Karin Alejandra Rosemblatt (Chapel Hill: University of North Carolina Press, 2003); and Barbara Weinstein, "Racializing Regional Difference: Sao Paulo versus Brazil, 1932," in *Race and Nation in Modern Latin America*, edited by Nancy P. Appelbaum, Anne S. Macpherson, and Karin Alejandra Rosemblatt (Chapel Hill: University of North Carolina Press, 2003). All in *Race and Nation in Modern Latin America*, edited by Nancy P. Appelbaum, Anne S. Macpherson, and Karin Alejandra Rosemblatt (Chapel Hill: University of North Carolina Press, 2003).

3 Thomas Alan Abercrombie, *Pathways of Memory and Power: Ethnography and History among an Andean People* (Madison: University of Wisconsin Press, 1998), 145. See also Brooke Larson, "'Forging the Unlettered Indian': The Pedagogy of Race in the Bolivian Andes," in *Histories of Race and Racism*, edited by Laura Gotkowitz (Durham, NC: Duke University Press, 2011).

4 The best comparisons in Latin America are Guatemala or Peru—like Bolivia, countries with large, non-Spanish-speaking highland Indian populations. See Marisol de la Cadena, *Indigenous Mestizos: The Politics of Race and Culture in Cuzco, Peru, 1919-1991* (Durham, NC: Duke University Press, 2000); Chambers, "Little Middle Ground"; Mary Weismantel, *Cholas and Pishtacos: Stories of Race and Sex in the Andes* (Chicago: University of Chicago Press, 2001); Benjamin S. Orlove, "Down to Earth: Race and Substance in the Andes," *Bulletin of Latin American Research* 17, no. 2 (1998); Linda J. Seligmann, *Peruvian Street Lives: Culture, Power, and Economy Among Market Women of Cuzco* (Urbana, IL: University of Illinois Press, 2004); Greg Grandin, *The Blood of Guatemala: A History of Race and Nation* (Durham, NC: Duke University Press, 2000); and Ernesto Capello, *City at the Center of the World: Space, History, and Modernity in Quito* (Pittsburgh, PA: University of Pittsburgh Press, 2011).

5 Quoted in Rolando Costa Ardúz, *La Paz: Sus rostros en el tiempo*, Volume I (La Paz: Honorable Alcaldía de La Paz, 1993), 119.

6 "Critica de las Críticas," *Boletín de la Sociedad Geográfica de La Paz* 68 (December 1945): 191–9.

7 R. Matthew Gildner, "Andean Atlantis: Race, Science and the Nazi Occult in Bolivia," *The Appendix* 1, no. 2 (2013), http://theappendix.net/issues/2013/4/andean-atlantis-race-science-and-the-nazi-occult-in-bolivia.

8 Vicente Donoso Torres, "El factor humano en la geografía nacional," *Boletín de la Sociedad Geográfica de La Paz* 68 (December 1945): 13.

9 "Informe," *Boletín Municipal de La Paz*, April 1945, 26; "Informe," *Boletín Municipal de La Paz*, June 1953, 16.

10. "De la Policía de garantía personal de la calificación de vagos y mal entretenidos," in *Ley reglamentaria de Policía de Seguridad La Paz* (La Paz: Imprenta "El Nacional," 1886), Capítulo 5, Sección 4, Artículo 32.
11. Ana Cecilia Wadsworth and Ineke Dibbits, *Agitadoras de buen gusto: Historia del Sindicato de Culinarias (1935–1958)* ([La Paz]: TAHIPAMU, 1989), 114.
12. "Informe," *Boletín Municipal de La Paz*, April 1945, 26.
13. *Carmen de Chusi vs. Quispe*, 48, Asesinato (Attempted Murder), September 1936, Caja 71, Corte Superior de Distrito, Juzgado 2, Archivo de La Paz.
14. Elizabeth Shesko presents a concise description of the period before the MNR revolution and the importance of the Chaco War to the success of the belligerents in 1952 in Chapter 7 of *Conscript Nation: Coercion and Consent in the Bolivian Barracks* (Pittsburgh: University of Pittsburgh Press, forthcoming).
15. "Alcalde y Vecinos Dedican Lineas de Agua Potable," *Boletín del H. Ayuntamiento Municipal de La Paz*, December 1945.

Bibliography

Newspapers

El Comercio (La Paz)
El Estado (La Paz)
El Fígaro (La Paz)
El Hombre Libre (La Paz)
En Marcha (La Paz)
La Calle (La Paz)
La Nación (La Paz)
La Patria (La Paz)
La Paz (La Paz)
La Razón (La Paz)
La Reforma (La Paz)
La República (La Paz)
Ultima Hora (La Paz)

Journals

Boletín Municipal de La Paz.
Boletín de la Sociedad Geográfica de La Paz, 1899–1948.
Etnología: boletín del Museo Nacional de Etnografía y Folklore, 1900–95.

Manuscript Sources

Archivo de la Paz

Álvaro Villa Personal Papers, 1880–1900, Archivo de La Paz
Correspondencia, 1913–52, Prefectura de La Paz, Archivo de La Paz
Corte Superior de Distrito, 1910–56, Archivo de La Paz
Departamento de Sanidad, 1908–39, Administración, Archivo de La Paz
Mapas y Planos, 1880–1930, Prefectura de La Paz, Archivo de La Paz
Obras Públicas, 1900–33, Prefectura de La Paz, Archivo de La Paz
Pedidos y Expedientes, 1880–1956, Prefectura de La Paz, Archivo de La Paz
Sociedad Geográfica Papers, 1891–1918, Archivo de La Paz

Archivo del Congreso de la Nación

Ordenanzas Municipales 1901-14

Published Primary Sources

Acosta, Nicolás. *Guía del viajero en la Paz; noticias estadísticas, históricas, locales, religiosas, templos, hoteles, edificios, antigüedades, etc.* La Paz: Impr. de la Unión Americana, 1880.

Bolivia. *Anuario Administrativo de Ministerio de Gobierno y Justicia, 1899-1937.* La Paz: Litografías e imprentas unidas.

Bolivia. *Anuario de Leyes y Disposiciones 1918.* La Paz: Imp. Oficial, 1919.

Bolivia. *Anuario de leyes, decretos y resoluciones supremas 1921.* La Paz: Imprentas Unidas, 1922.

Bolivia. *Anuario de Leyes y Disposiciones 1924.* La Paz: Imprenta Nacional, 1925.

Bolivia. *Anuario de leyes, resoluciones legislativas, decretos, resoluciones supremas y circulares, 1926.* La Paz: Imprentas Unidas, 1927.

Bolivia. *Anuario de leyes, decretos y resoluciones supremas 1927.* La Paz: Imprentas Unidas, 1929.

Bolivia. *Anuario de Leyes y Disposiciones 1932.* La Paz: Imprenta Nacional, 1933.

Bolivia. *Anuario de leyes, decretos y resoluciones supremas 1936.* La Paz: Imprentas Unidas, 1938.

Bolivia. *Anuario de leyes, decretos y resoluciones supremas 1939.* La Paz: Imprentas Unidas, 1940.

Bolivia. *Anuario de leyes, decretos y resoluciones supremas 1940.* La Paz: Imprentas Unidas, 1941.

Bolivia. *Anuario de leyes, decretos y resoluciones supremas 1941.* La Paz: Imprentas Unidas, 1942.

Bolivia. *Anuario de leyes, decretos y resoluciones supremas 1943.* La Paz: Imprentas Unidas, 1944.

Bolivia. *Anuario de leyes y disposiciones suprema 1917.* La Paz: Imprenta Nacional, 1918.

Bolivia. *Anuario de leyes, resoluciones legislativas, decretos, resoluciones supremas y circulares, 1926.* La Paz: [s.n.]

Bolivia, and Ramón Salinas Mariaca. *Códigos bolivianos; compilación especial por el Dr. Ramón Salinas Mariaca: Contiene: código civil, Código penal, Código mercantil, Código de minería, Código del trabajo y un apéndice con las principales leyes y decretos supremos modificatorios.* La Paz, Bolivia: Imp. y editorial "Artística" de Calderón & Otero, 1946.

Bolivia, and Ramón Salinas Mariaca. *Códigos bolivianos; compilación especial por Ramón Salinas Mariaca. Contiene: Código civil, Código penal, Código mercantil, Código de minería, Código del trabajo y un apéndice con las principales leyes y decretos supremos modificatorios.* La Paz: Gisbert, 1955.

Donoso Torres, Vicente. "El factor humano en la geografía nacional." *Boletín de la Sociedad Geográfica de La Paz* 68 (December 1945): 13.
Donoso Torres, Vicente. *El estado actual de la educación indigenal en el país*. La Paz: Renacimiento, 1940.
Donoso Torres, Vicente. *El proceso histórico de Bolivia*. La Paz: Editorial Letras, 1963.
Donoso Torres, Vicente. *Filosofía de la educación boliviana*. Buenos Aires: Editorial Atlántida, 1946.
Donoso Torres, Vicente. *Lecciones de didáctica general*. Buenos Aires: Matera, 1964.
Landa, Quintin. *Anotaciones a La Ley Reglamentaria De Policia De Seguridad De La República De Bolivia*. La Paz: Tipografía Comercial de Ismael Argote, 1904.
Paredes, M. Rigoberto. "Altiplanicie, el habitante y la población." *Boletín de la Sociedad Geográfica de La Paz* 9, nos. 30–35 (1911): 130–5.
Salmón, Eloy. *La Paz en su IV centenario, 1548–1948*. Tomos 1–4. La Paz: Comité Pro Cuarto Centenario de la Fundación de la Paz, 1948.
Terán Gómez, Luis. "El Indio ante la realidad." *Boletín de la Sociedad Geográfica de La Paz* 52, no. 63 (1941): 80–90.

Secondary Sources

Abercrombie, Thomas Alan. *Pathways of Memory and Power: Ethnography and History Among an Andean People*. Madison: University of Wisconsin Press, 1998.
Alarcón A., J. Ricardo. *Bolivia en el primer centenario de su independencia*. New York: University Society, 1925.
Albó, Xavier. "From MNRista to Katarista to Katari." In *Resistance, Rebellion, and Consciousness in the Andean Peasant World, 18th to 20th Centuries*, edited by Steve J. Stern, 379–419. Madison: University of Wisconsin Press, 1987.
Albó, Xavier, and Josep M. Barnadas. *La cara india y campesina de nuestra historia*. La Paz: UNITAS, 1990.
Albro, Robert. "Confounding Cultural Citizenship and Constitutional Reform in Bolivia." *Latin American Perspectives* 37, no. 3 (2010): 71–90.
Alexander, Robert J., and Eldon M. Parker. *A History of Organized Labor in Bolivia*. Westport, CT: Praeger, 2005.
Antezana Ergueta, Luis. *Historia secreta del Movimiento Nacionalista Revolucionario*. 9 vols. La Paz: Librería Editorial "Juventud," 1984–2006.
Antezana Ergueta, Luis. *Historia secreta del Movimiento Nacionalista Revolucionario*. Tomo 2, *De la muerte de Busch al golpe revolucionario del 20 de diciembre de 1943*. La Paz: Librería Editorial "Juventud," 1985.
Antezana Ergueta, Luis. *Historia secreta del Movimiento Nacionalista Revolucionario*. Tomo 7, *La revolución del MNR del 9 de abril*. La Paz: Librería Editorial "Juventud," 1988.

Appelbaum, Nancy P., Anne S. Macpherson, and Karin Alejandra Rosemblatt. "Introduction: Racial Nations." In *Race and Nation in Modern Latin America*, edited by Nancy P. Appelbaum, Anne S. Macpherson, and Karin Alejandra Rosemblatt, 1–31. Chapel Hill: University of North Carolina Press, 2003.

Arnold, Denise Y., Rossana Barragán R., David Llanos, Carmen B. Loza, and Carmen Soliz. *¿Indígenas u obreros? la construcción política de identidades en el Altiplano boliviano*. La Paz, Bolivia: UNIR, 2009.

Arze, Silvia, and Rossana Barragán. *El centro urbano durante los siglos XIX y XX*. La Paz: Alcaldía Municipal de La Paz, 1988.

Arze, Silvia, and Rossana Barragán. *La Paz, Chuquiago: el escenario de la vida de la ciudad*. La Paz: Alcaldía Municipal de La Paz, Oficialía Mayor de Cultura, 1988.

Barcelli S., Agustín. *Medio siglo de luchas sindicales revolucionarias en Bolivia, 1905–1955*. N.p.: N.p., 1957.

Barragán, Rossana. "Entre polleras, ñañacas y lliqllas: los mestizos y cholas en la conformación de la tercera república." In *Tradición y Modernidad en los Andes*, edited by Henrique Urbano, 43–74. Cusco: Centro Bartolomé de las Casas, 1993.

Barragán, Rossana. *Espacio urbano y dinámica étnica: La Paz en el Siglo XIX*. La Paz: Hisbol, 1990.

Barragán, Rossana. *Indios, mujeres, y ciudadanos: legislación y ejercicio de la ciudadanía en Bolivia (siglo XIX)*. La Paz: Fundación Diálogo, 1999.

Barragán, Rossana. "Mas allá de lo mestizo, mas alla de lo aymara: organización y representaciones de clase y etnicidad en La Paz." *América Latina Hoy: Revista De Ciencias Sociales* 43 (2006): 107–30.

Barragán, Rossana. "The Census and the Making of a Social 'Order' in Nineteenth-Century Bolivia." In *Histories of Race and Racism: The Andes and Mesoamerica from Colonial Times to the Present*, edited by Laura Gotkowitz, 113–33. Durham, NC: Duke University Press, 2011.

Barragán, Rossana, and Dora Cajías, eds. *El siglo XIX: Bolivia y América Latina*. La Paz: Muela del Diablo Editores, 1997.

Barragán R., Rossana, and Cleverth Cárdenas Plaza. *Gran Poder: la morenada*. La Paz: Instituto de Estudios Bolivianos, 2009.

Berman, Marshall. *All That Is Solid Melts into Air: The Experience of Modernity*. New York: Simon and Schuster, 1982.

Bliss, Katherine Elaine. *Compromised Positions: Prostitution, Public Health, and Gender Politics in Revolutionary Mexico City*. University Park, PA: Pennsylvania State University Press, 2001.

Brienen, Martin. "Warisata y la renovación de la educación rural indigenal boliviana, 1931-1948." In *Campesinos y escolares: la construcción de la escuela en el campo latinoamericano, siglos XIX y XX*, edited by Alicia Civera, Juan Alfonseca G., and Carlos Escalante Fernández. Zinacantepec, Estado de México: Colegio Mexiquense, 2011.

Cajías de la Vega, Magdalena. "El Discurso Anarquista en el Discurso Minero del Pre-52." *Estudios Bolivianos 12: La Cultura del Pre-52* (2004): 15–79.

Capello, Ernesto. *City at the Center of the World: Space, History, and Modernity in Quito.* Pittsburgh: University of Pittsburgh Press, 2012.

Carter, William E., and Mauricio Mamani. *Irpa Chico: individuo y comunidad en la cultura aymara.* La Paz: Librería-Editorial "Juventud," 1983.

Castells, Manuel. *The City and the Grassroots: A Cross-Cultural Theory of Urban Social Movements.* Berkeley: University of California Press, 1983.

Caulfield, Sueann. "Interracial Courtship in the Rio de Janeiro Courts, 1918–1940." In *Race and Nation in Modern Latin America*, edited by Nancy P. Appelbaum, Anne S. Macpherson, and Karin Alejandra Rosemblatt, 163–87. Chapel Hill: University of North Carolina Press, 2003.

Chachaki, Waskar Ari. "Race and Subaltern Nationalism: AMP Activist-Intellectuals in Bolivia, 1921–1964." PhD diss., Georgetown University, 2004.

Chalhoub, Sidney. "The Politics of Disease Control: Yellow Fever and Race in Nineteenth-Century Rio de Janeiro." *Journal of Latin American Studies* 25, no. 3 (1993): 441–6.

Chambers, Sarah. *From Subjects to Citizens: Honor, Gender, and Politics in Arequipa, Peru, 1780–1854.* University Park: Pennsylvania State University Press, 1999.

Chambers, Sarah. "Little Middle Ground: The Instability of a Mestizo Identity in the Andes, Eighteenth and Nineteenth Centuries." In *Race and Nation in Modern Latin America*, edited by Nancy P. Appelbaum, Anne S. Macpherson, and Karin Alejandra Rosemblatt, 32–55. Chapel Hill: University of North Carolina Press, 2003.

Comité Pro Cuarto Centenario de la Fundación de La Paz and Eloy Salmón. *La Paz en su IV centenario, 1548–1948.* La Paz: Comité Pro Cuarto Centenario de la Fundación de la Paz, 1948.

Condarco Morales, Ramiro. *Zárate, el "temible" Willka: historia de la rebelión indígena de 1899 en la República de Bolivia.* La Paz: Talleres Graficos Bolivianos, 1965. World Cat.

Condori, Carlos Mamani. *Taraqu: 1866–1935: Masacre, guerra y "renovación" en la biografía de Eduardo L. Nina Qhispi.* La Paz: Ediciones Aruwiyiri, 1991.

Condori Chura, Leandro, and Esteban Ticona Alejo. *El escribano de los caciques apoderados = Kasikinakan purirarunakan qillqiripa.* La Paz: Hisbol, 1992.

Conniff, Michael L. *Populism in Latin America.* Tuscaloosa: University of Alabama Press, 1999.

Conniff, Michael L. *Urban Politics in Brazil: The Rise of Populism, 1925–1945.* Pittsburgh, PA: University of Pittsburgh Press, 1981.

Corbin, Alain. "Commercial Sexuality in Nineteenth-Century France: A System of Images and Regulations." *Representations* 14, no. 1 (1986): 209–19.

Costa Ardúz, Rolando. *La Paz: sus rostros en el tiempo.* Tomo 2. La Paz: Honorable Alcaldía de La Paz, 1993.

Costa Mattos, Romulo. "Shantytown Dwellers' Resistance in Brazil's First Republic (1890–1930): Fighting for the Right to Reside in the City of Rio de Janeiro." *International Labor and Working Class History* 83 (Spring 2013): 55–69.

Cuadros Bustos, Álvaro. *La Paz*. La Paz: Facultad de Arquitectura, Urbanismo y Artes, Universidad Mayor de San Andrés, 2002.

Dandler, Jorge, and Juan Torrico A. "From the National Indigenous Congress to the Ayopaya Rebellion: Bolivia, 1945–1947." In *Resistance, Rebellion, and Consciousness in the Andean Peasant World, 18th to 20th Centuries*, edited by Steve J. Stern, 334–78. Madison: University of Wisconsin Press, 1987.

De la Cadena, Marisol. "From Race to Class: Insurgent Intellectuals *de provincia* in Peru, 1910–1970." In *Shining and Other Paths: War and Society in Peru, 1980–1995*, edited by Steve Stern, 22–59. Durham, NC: Duke University Press, 1998.

De la Cadena, Marisol. *Indigenous Mestizos: The Politics of Race and Culture in Cuzco Peru, 1919–1991*. Durham, NC: Duke University Press, 2000.

Deledicque Melina, and Daniel Contartese. "Movimientos sociales en Bolivia: Las Juntas Vecinales de El Alto entre la institucionalidad y la rebellion." *Lavboratorio*, no. 23 (2010): 134–48.

Delgado González, Trifonio, and Guillermo Delgado. *100 años de lucha obrera en Bolivia*. La Paz: Ediciones ISLA, 1984.

De Mesa, José, Teresa Gisbert, and Carlos D. Mesa G. *Historia de Bolivia*. La Paz: Editorial Gisbert, 1998.

Díaz Machicao, Porfirio. *Toro, Busch, Quintanilla, 1936–1940*. La Paz: Editorial "Juventud," 1957.

Dibbits, Ineke. *Polleras libertarias: Federación Obrera Femenina, 1927–1964*. La Paz: Taller de Historia y Participación de la Mujer, 1986.

Dubois, Laurent. *Avenger of the New World: The Story of the Haitian Revolution*. Cambridge, MA: Belknap Press of Harvard University Press, 2004.

Dunkerley, James. *Bolivia: Revolution and the Power of History in the Present: Essays*. London: Institute for the Study of the Americas, 2007.

English, Adrian J. *The Green Hell: A Concise History of the Chaco War between Bolivia and Paraguay, 1932–35*. Spellmount Military Studies. New York: Spellmount Limited Publishers, 2008.

Farcau, Bruce W. *The Chaco War: Bolivia and Paraguay, 1932–1935*. Westport, CT: Greenwood Publishing Group, 1996.

Fischer, Brodwyn. "Quase Pretos De Tão Pobres? Race and Social Discrimination in Rio De Janeiro's Twentieth-Century Criminal Courts." *Latin American Research Review* 39, no. 1 (2004): 31–59.

French, John D. *The Brazilian Workers' ABC: Class Conflict and Alliances in Modern São Paulo*. Chapel Hill: University of North Carolina Press, 1992.

Garcia, Guadalupe. *Beyond the Walled City: Colonial Exclusion in Havana*. Berkeley: University of California Press, 2016.

Gildner, R. Matthew. "Andean Atlantis: Race, Science and the Nazi Occult in Bolivia." *The Appendix* 1, no. 2 (2013), http://theappendix.net/issues/2013/4/andean-atlantis-race-science-and-the-nazi-occult-in-bolivia.

Gill, Lesley. *Teetering on the Rim: Global Restructuring, Daily Life, and the Armed Retreat of the Bolivian State*. New York: Columbia University Press, 2000.

Goldstein, Daniel M. *The Spectacular City: Violence and Performance in Urban Bolivia*. Durham, NC: Duke University Press, 2005.

Gotkowitz, Laura. *A Revolution for Our Rights: Indigenous Struggles for Land and Justice in Bolivia, 1880–1952*. Durham, NC: Duke University Press, 2007.

Gotkowitz, Laura. "Commemorating the Heroínas: Gender and Civic Ritual in Early-Twentieth-Century Bolivia." In *Hidden Histories of Gender and the State in Latin America*, edited by Elizabeth Dore and Maxine Molyneux, 215–37. Durham, NC: Duke University Press, 2000.

Gotkowitz, Laura. "Introduction." In *Histories of Race and Racism: The Andes and Mesoamerica from Colonial Times to the Present*, edited by Laura Gotkowitz, 1–39. Durham. NC: Duke University Press, 2012.

Gotkowitz, Laura. "Trading Insults: Honor, Violence, and the Gendered Culture of Commerce in Cochabamba, Bolivia, 1870s–1950s." *Hispanic American Historical Review* 83, no. 1 (2003): 83–118.

Gould, Jeffrey. "'For an Organized Nicaragua': Somoza and the Labour Movement, 1944–1948." *Journal of Latin American Studies* 19, no. 2 (1987): 353–87.

Gould, Jeffrey. *To Die in This Way: Nicaraguan Indians and the Myth of Mestizaje, 1880–1965*. Durham, NC: Duke University Press, 1998.

Gould, Stephen Jay. *The Mismeasure of Man*. New York: Norton, 1981.

Grandin, Greg. *The Blood of Guatemala: A History of Race and Nation*. Durham, NC: Duke University Press, 2000.

Grieshaber, Erwin P. "Fluctuaciones en la definifición del indio: Comparación de los censos de 1900 y 1950." *Historia de Bolivia*, 5, nos. 1–2 (1985): 45–65.

Grieshaber, Erwin P. "Survival of Indian Communities in Nineteenth-Century Bolivia: A Regional Comparison." *Journal of Latin American Studies* 12, no. 2 (1980): 223–69.

Guss, David M. "The Gran Poder and the Reconquest of La Paz." *Journal of Latin American Anthropology* 11, no. 2 (2006): 294–328.

Gutiérrez, Ramón. *Pueblo de indios: Otro urbanismo en la región Andina*. Quito: Biblioteca Ayba-yala, 1993.

Harvey, David. *Paris: Capital of Modernity*. New York: Routledge, 2003.

Hines, Sarah. "La construccion historica de los usos y costumbres del agua en Cochabamba." In *Construcción de la Agenda Departamental del Agua de Cochabamba*, edited by Gobierno Autónomo Departamental de Cochabamba. Cochabamba: Gobierno Departamental, 2013.

Holloway, Thomas. *Policing Rio de Janeiro: Repression and Resistance in a 19th Century City*. Palo Alto, CA: Stanford University Press, 1993.

Holt, Thomas C. *The Problem of Race in the Twenty-First Century*. Cambridge, MA: Harvard University Press, 2000.

Irurozqui, Marta. *La armonía de las desigualdades: Élites y conflictos de poder en Bolivia, 1880–1920*. Cusco: Centro de Estudios Regionales Andinos: Bartolomé de Las Casas, 1994.

Irurozqui, Marta. *A Bala, Piedra y Palo: La construcción de la ciudadanía política en Bolivia, 1826–1952*. Seville: Diputación de Sevilla, 2000.

James, Danny. *Doña María's Story: Life History, Memory, and Political Identity.* Durham, NC: Duke University Press, 2000.

Kiddle, Amelia M., and María L. O. Muñoz. *Populism in Twentieth Century Mexico: The Presidencies of Lázaro Cárdenas and Luis Echeverría.* Tucson: University of Arizona Press, 2010.

Klein, Herbert S. *A Concise History of Bolivia.* Cambridge: Cambridge University Press, 2003.

Klein, Herbert S. *Parties and Political Change in Bolivia, 1880–1952.* London: Cambridge University Press, 1969.

Kloppenberg, James T. *Uncertain Victory: Social Democracy and Progressivism in European and American Thought, 1870–1920.* New York: Oxford University Press, 1986.

Knight, Alan. "Racism, Revolution, and Indigenismo: Mexico, 1910–1940." In *The Idea of Race in Latin America, 1870–1940,* edited by Richard Graham, 71–113. Austin: University of Texas Press, 1990.

Knudson, Jerry W. *Bolivia: Press and Revolution, 1932–1964.* Lanham, MD: University Press of America, 1986.

Kuenzli, E. Gabrielle. *Acting Inca: National Belonging in Early Twentieth-Century Bolivia.* Pittsburgh: Pittsburgh University Press, 2013.

Kuenzli, E. Gabrielle. "Acting Inca: The Parameters of National Belonging in Early Twentieth-Century Bolivia." *Hispanic American Historical Review* 90, no. 2 (2010): 247–81.

Langer, Erick D. "Andean Rituals of Revolt: The Chayanta Rebellion of 1927." *Ethnohistory* 37, no. 3 (1990): 227–53.

Langer, Erick D. *Economic Change and Rural Resistance in Southern Bolivia, 1880–1930.* Stanford, CA: Stanford University Press, 1989.

Larson, Brooke. "Capturing Indian Bodies, Hearths, and Minds: 'el hogar campesino' and Rural School Reform in Bolivia, 1920s–1940s." In *Proclaiming Revolution: Bolivia in Comparative Perspective,* edited by Merilee Serrill Grindle and Pilar Domingo, 32–59. London: Institute of Latin American Studies, 2003.

Larson, Brooke. *Cochabamba, 1550–1900: Colonialism and Agrarian Transformation in Bolivia.* Durham, NC: Duke University Press, 1998.

Larson, Brooke. "Forging the Unlettered Indian: The Pedagogy of Race in the Bolivian Andes." In *Histories of Race and Racism,* edited by Laura Gotkowitz, 134–56. Durham, NC: Duke University Press, 2011.

Larson, Brooke. "Redeemed Indians, Barbarized Cholos." In *Political Cultures in the Andes, 1750–1950,* edited by Nils Jacobsen and Cristóbal Aljovín de Losada, 230–52. Durham, NC: Duke University Press, 2005.

Larson, Brooke. *Trials of Nation Making: Liberalism, Race, and Ethnicity in the Andes, 1810–1910.* Cambridge: Cambridge University Press, 2004.

Lazar, Sian. *El Alto, Rebel City: Self and Citizenship in Andean Bolivia.* Durham, NC: Duke University Press, 2008.

Lear, John. *Workers, Neighbors, and Citizens: The Revolution in Mexico City*. Lincoln: University of Nebraska Press, 2001.
Libermann Z., Jacobo. *Bolivia: 10 años de revolución [1952–1962]*. N.p., 1962.
Lora, Guillermo. *Historia del movimiento obrero boliviano*. La Paz: Editorial "Los Amigos del Libro," 1967.
Mahoney, James. *The Legacies of Liberalism: Path Dependence and Political Regimes in Central America*. Baltimore, MD: Johns Hopkins University Press, 2001.
Malloy, James. *Bolivia: The Uncompleted Revolution*. Pittsburgh: University of Pittsburgh Press, 1970.
Mamani Condori, Carlos. *Taraqu, 1866–1935: Masacre, guerra y "renovación" en la biografía de Eduardo L. Nina Qhispi*. La Paz, Bolivia: Ediciones Aruwiyiri, 1991.
Mendieta, Pilar. *Entre la alianza y la confrontación: Pablo Zárate Willka y la rebelión indígena de 1899 en Bolivia*. Lima: Instituto Francés de Estudios Andinos, UMIFRE 17, CNRS-MAEE, 2010.
Mendieta Parada, Pilar. "De la Revolución del 52 a Evo Morales: El recorrido político del sindicalismo campesino en Bolivia." *Tinkazos* 18, no. 37 (2015): 35–47.
Mendieta Parada, Pilar. "Memorias de la Revolucion del 52." *Historia* 37 (August 2016): 11–42.
Mesa, G. C., and Jaime Sáenz. *Emilio Villanueva: Hacia Una Arquitectura Nacional, Con 111 Ilustraciones*. La Paz, Bolivia: Escuela Don Bosco, 1984.
Meyer, Michael C., William L. Sherman, and Susan M. Deeds. *The Course of Mexican History*. New York: Oxford University Press, 1999.
Möller, Edwin A. *El dios desnudo de mi conciencia revolucionaria: Autobiografía y revolución nacional*. La Paz: Plural Editores, 2001.
Montenegro, Carlos. *Frente al derecho del estado el oro de la Standard Oil*. La Paz: Editorial Trabajo, 1938.
Montenegro, Carlos. *Nacionalismo y coloniaje, su expresión histórica en la prensa de Bolivia*. La Paz: Ediciones Autonomía, 1943.
Murillo, Mario. *La bala no mata sino el destino: Una crónica de la insurrección popular de 1952 en Bolivia*. La Paz: Plural, 2012.
Nash, June C. *We Eat the Mines and the Mines Eat Us: Dependency and Exploitation in Bolivian Tin Mines*. New York: Columbia University Press, 1979.
Orlove, Benjamin S. "Down to Earth: Race and Substance in the Andes." *Bulletin of Latin American Research* 17, no. 2 (1998): 207–27.
Papp, Gregory J. "The Bolivian MNR: Aspects of Nationalism." MA thesis, University of Akron, 1973.
Perlman, Janice. *Favela: Four Decades of Living on the Edge in Rio de Janeiro*. Oxford: Oxford University Press, 2010.
Piccato, Pablo. *City of Suspects: Crime in Mexico City, 1900–1931*. Durham, NC: Duke University Press, 2001.
Piccato, Pablo. *The Tyranny of Opinion: Honor in the Construction of the Mexican Public Sphere*. Durham, NC: Duke University Press, 2010.

Platt, Tristan. *Estado Boliviano y Ayllu Andino: Tierra y Tributo en el Norte de Potosí*. Lima: Centro de Investigaciones Sociales de la Vicepresidencia mayo de 2016, 1982.

Platt, Tristan. "The Andean Experience of Bolivian Liberalism, 1825–1900: Roots of Rebellion in 19th-Century Chayanta (Potosí)." In *Resistance, Rebellion, and Consciousness in the Andean Peasant World, 18th to 20th Centuries*, edited by Steve J. Stern, 280–326. Madison: University of Wisconsin Press, 1987.

Quayum, Seemin. "Indian Ruins, National Origins: Tiwanaku and Indigenismo in La Paz, 1897–1933." In *Histories of Race and Racism*, edited by Laura Gotkowitz, 159–78. Durham, NC: Duke University Press, 2011.

Quayum, Seemin, María Luisa Soux, and Rossana Barragán. *De terratenientes a amas de casa: mujeres de la élite de La Paz en la primera mitad del siglo XX*. La Paz: Ministerio de Desarrollo Humano, Secretaría de Asuntos Étnicos, de Género y Generacionales, Subsecretaría de Asuntos de Género, 1997.

Quispe, Constantino Tancara. *La promesa de Warisata*. La Paz: Inst. Internacional de Integración del Convenio Andrés Bello, 2011.

Renique, Gerardo. "Race, Region, and Nation: Sonora's Anti-Chinese Racism and Mexico's Post-Revolutionary Nationalism, 1920s–1930s." In *Race and Nation in Modern Latin America*, edited by Nancy P. Appelbaum, Anne S. Macpherson, and Karin Alejandra Rosemblatt, 211–36. Chapel Hill: University of North Carolina Press, 2003.

Rivera Cusicanqui, Silvia. *Oppressed but Not Defeated: Peasant Struggles among the Aymara and Qhechwa in Bolivia, 1900–1980*. Geneva: United Nations Research Institute for Social Development, 1987.

Rodgers, Daniel T. *Atlantic Crossings: Social Politics in a Progressive Age*. Cambridge, MA: Belknap Press of Harvard University Press, 1998.

Roseberry, William. "Hegemony and the Language of Contention." In *Everyday Forms of State Formation: Revolution and the Negotiation of Rule in Modern Mexico*, edited by Gilbert M. Joseph and Daniel Nugent, 355–66. Durham, NC: Duke University Press, 1994.

Rosenberg, Charles E. *The Cholera Years: The United States in 1832, 1849, and 1866*. Chicago: University of Chicago Press, 1987.

Rosenberg, Charles E. *Framing Disease: Studies in Cultural History*. New Brunswick, NJ: Rutgers University Press, 1992.

Salmón, Eloy. *La Paz en su IV centenario, 1548–1948*. La Paz: Comité Pro IV Centenario de la Fundación de la Paz, 1948.

Sánchez Bustamante, Daniel. "Estudio Preliminar," in *Bolivia en el primer centenario de su independencia*, by J. Ricardo Alarcón A., I-xi–xii. New York: University Society, 1925.

Sanders, James. *Contentious Republicans: Popular Politics, Race, and Class in Nineteenth-Century Colombia*. Durham, NC: Duke University Press, 2004.

Sandoval, Godofredo, and Xavier Albó. *Ojje por encima de todo: historia de un centro de residentes ex-campesinos en La Paz*. La Paz: Centro de Investigación y Promoción del Campesinado, 1978.

Seligmann, Linda J. *Peruvian Street Lives: Culture, Power, and Economy Among Market Women of Cuzco*. Urbana: University of Illinois Press, 2004.

Serulnikov, Sergio. *Subverting Colonial Authority: Challenges to Spanish Rule in Eighteenth-Century Southern Andes*. Durham, NC: Duke University Press, 2003.

Scott, James. *Domination and the Arts of Resistance: Hidden Transcripts*. New Haven, CT: Yale University Press, 1990.

Shesko, Elizabeth. *Conscript Nation: Coercion and Consent in the Bolivian Barracks*. Pittsburgh: University of Pittsburgh Press, forthcoming.

Sierra, Luis M. "Colonial Specters: The Extramuro, History, Memory, and Urbanization in La Paz, Bolivia, 1900–1947." *Journal of Urban History* (Fall 2018): 1131–52.

Sierra, Luis M. "Union Activism in La Paz Before and After the Chaco War, 1920–1947." In *The Chaco War: Environment, Ethnicity, and Nationalism*, edited by Bridget María Chesterton, 43–66. London: Bloomsbury Press, 2016.

Silvia, Arze, and Rossana Barragán R. *La Paz, Chuquiago: El escenario de la vida de la ciudad*. La Paz: Alcaldía Municipal de La Paz, Oficialía Mayor de Cultura, 1988.

Skidmore, Thomas E., and Peter H. Smith. *Modern Latin America*, 5th ed. New York: Oxford University Press, 2001.

Stepan, Nancy Leys. *The Hour of Eugenics: Race, Gender, and Nation in Latin America*. Ithaca, NY: Cornell University Press, 1991.

Stepan, Nancy Leys. *Picturing Tropical Nature*. London: Reaktion Books, 2001.

Stephenson, Marcia. *Gender and Modernity in Andean Bolivia*. Austin: University of Texas Press, 1999.

Stern, Alexandra Minna. "From Mestizophilia to Biotypology: Racialization and Science in Mexico, 1920–1960." In *Race and Nation in Modern Latin America*, edited by Nancy P. Appelbaum, Anne S. Macpherson, and Karin Alejandra Rosemblatt, 187–210. Chapel Hill: University of North Carolina Press, 2003.

Taller de Historia Oral Andina. *Los constructores de la ciudad: Tradiciones de lucha y de trabajo del Sindicato Central de Constructores y Albañiles de La Paz, 1908–1980*. La Paz: THOA, 1986.

Tenemos pechos de bronce . . . pero no sabemos nada: Memoria de la Conferencia Internacional Revoluciones del siglo XX: Homenaje a los cincuenta años de la Revolución Boliviana. Bonn: Friedrich Ebert Stiftung-ILDIS, 2003.

Thomson, Sinclair. *We Alone Will Rule: Native Andean Politics in the Age of Insurgency*. Madison: University of Wisconsin Press, 2002.

Ticona Alejo, Esteban. *Bolivia en el inicio del "Pachakuti": la larga lucha anticolonial de los pueblos aymara y quechua*. Madrid: Akal, 2011.

Ticona Alejo, Esteban. *Saberes, conocimientos y prácticas anticoloniales del pueblo aymara-quechua en Bolivia*. La Paz: AGRUCO, UMSS-FCAyP/COSUDE, 2010.

Ticona Alejo, Esteban, and Xavier Albó. *Jesús de Machaca en el tiempo*. La Paz, Bolivia: Fundación Diálogo, 1998.

Vasconcelos. José. *La raza cósmica: Misión de la raza iberoamericana, Argentina y Brazil /Jose Vasconcelos*. México: Espasa-Calpe Mexicana, 1966.

Vasconcelos, José, and Didier T. Jaén. *The Cosmic Race: A Bilingual Edition*. Baltimore, MD: Johns Hopkins University Press, 1997.

Villagómez Paredes, Carlos, and Armando Silva. *La Paz imaginada*. Bogotá: Convenio Andrés Bello, 2007.

Wadsworth, Ana Cecilia, and Ineke Dibbits. *Agitadoras de buen gusto: Historia del Sindicato de Culinarias (1935–1958)*. La Paz: TAHIPAMU, 1989.

Walkowitz, Judith R. *City of Dreadful Delight: Narratives of Sexual Danger in Late-Victorian London*. Chicago: University of Chicago Press, 1992.

Weinstein, Barbara. "Racializing Regional Difference: Sao Paulo versus Brazil, 1932." In *Race and Nation in Modern Latin America*, edited by Nancy P. Appelbaum, Anne S. Macpherson, and Karin Alejandra Rosemblatt, 237–62. Chapel Hill: University of North Carolina Press, 2003.

Weismantel, Mary. *Cholas and Pishtacos: Stories of Race and Sex in the Andes*. Chicago: University of Chicago Press, 2001.

Wilkerson, Isabel. *The Warmth of Other Suns: The Epic Story of America's Great Migration*. New York: Vintage Press, 2011.

Wolfe, Joel. *Working Women, Working Men: São Paulo and the Rise of Brazil's Industrial Working Class, 1900–1955*. Durham, NC: Duke University Press, 1993.

Womack, John, *Zapata and the Mexican Revolution*. New York: Vintage Books, 1970.

Zook, David. *The Conduct of the Chaco War*. New York: Bookman Associates, 1960.

Zulawski, Ann. *Unequal Cures: Public Health and Political Change in Bolivia, 1900–1950*. Durham, NC: Duke University Press, 2007.

Index

Abercrombie, Thomas   191 n.44
Achachicala   5, 124
Alameda   27, 124
Alarcón, J.   176 n.56, 180 n.12
Albó, Xavier   162 n.32, 186 n.4, 203 n.12, 205 n.50
Albro, Robert   175 n.37
Alejandra Rosemblatt, Karin   170 n.61, 197 n.11, 213 n.2
Alto de San Francisco   5
Andean people   176 n.61
Antezana Ergueta, Luis   177 n.65, 183 n.53, 207 n.7, 208 nn.8, 10
Apasa, Julián   19
Appelbaum, Nancy P.   170 n.61, 197 n.11, 213 n.2
Arnold, Denise Y.   184 n.79
Arze, Jorge   144
Arze, Silvia   186 n.4, 187 n.5
Associacion de Mutiliados y Invalidos de la Guerra del Chaco (Mutilated and Invalid Veterans of the Chaco War)   138
ayllus   2, 4
  importance of   159 n.1, 166 n.31
  land tenure patterns and   159 n.2, 166 n.32
Aymara people   3, 8–9, 19, 20, 23–4, 29, 35–8, 40, 51, 66, 76, 103, 121, 154, 166 n.32
  cargo system and   89

Ballivián, Hugo   144, 145
Ballivián, Manuel   175 n.34
Barnadas, Josep M.   186 n.4
Barragán, Raquel   110–11
Barragán, Rossana   13, 113, 122, 159 n.2, 163 n.12, 166 n.32, 181 n.27, 184 n.79, 186 n.4, 187 n.5
Barrenchea, Adrián   146
"barrio," significance of   186 n.4
Barrios, Graciela   64–5

Barzolas group   148, 211 n.79
Berman, Marshall   189 n.26
biopolitics   15–16, 24, 164 n.15
biopower   16
Blacutt, General   145
Bliss, Katherine Elaine   170 n.61
Boletín de la Sociedad Geográfica de La Paz   42, 52
Bolivia. *See also individual entries*
  economy, in first half of twentieth century   9–10
Bolivian history   1, 4, 152–3
Boyle, Danny   186 n.3
Brazil   31, 100
Brienen, Martin   172 n.6
Busch, Germán   73, 77, 81, 129–30, 134

Cacique Apoderado movement (1920–50)   9, 34, 40, 113, 166 n.32, 192 n.53
caciques, elected   192 n.59
Cajías, Dora   159 n.2, 166 n.32
Cajías de la Vega, Magdalena   183 n.56
Capello, Ernesto   14–15, 213 n.4
Cárdenas Plaza, Cleverth   186 n.4
cargo system   89, 191 n.44
Castells, David   189 n.26
Castro, José   106
Caulfield, Sue Ann   101
Céspedes, Augusto   69
Chachaki, Waskar Ari   164 n.15, 178 n.72
Chaco War   2, 7, 10, 17, 39, 60, 80, 183 n.52. *See also* urban La Paz, before and after Chaco War
  effect, on racial discourse   45–9
  politics and racial discourse before   40–5
  and postwar alignments   68–70, 127–9
  racial and class discourses after   49–55
  racial discourse and activism after   82–3

union activism before 62–8
worker activism after 70–3
Chalhoub, Sidney 170 n.61
Challapampa 5, 6, 20, 28, 124, 187 n.5
Challapata 90
Chambers, Sarah 14, 85, 212 n.2, 213 n.4
Chayanta rebellion (1927) 9, 40, 44, 174 n.23
Chijini 28
  association 92–3
Chinahuanca, Andrés 97, 103, 105, 114
cholajes 66
cholo (mixed race) identity 12–13, 25, 39, 76, 107, 108; See also *indígenas*; mestizos
  and mestizos compared 43–4
  significance of 122–3, 153
Choque, Roberto 119
Choquehuanca family case 97–8, 103, 105–8, 114
Choqueyapu River 5–6, 16, 18, 83
Christmas Bonus law 48, 135
chronotype, significance of 15
city council, significance of 26, 29–31, 206 n.53
city government, significance of 190 n.35, 192 n.52, 193 n.68
city spaces and modernity 14–15
Club Select 28
Cochabama 101
coco leaf and alcohol, effect on Indian race 50
Comité Pro Cuarto Centenario de la Fundación de La Paz 185 n.83, 186 n.4, 187 n.5, 188 n.10
Concordancia 47–8, 74, 86, 120
Condarco Morales, Ramiro 23
Condori Chura, Leandro 119–20, 166 n.32, 203 n.14
Cornejo, Muñoz 72, 81
corregidors, significance of 36
Costa Mattos, Romulo 85, 189 n.27
court records 97–8, 103–8, 114
craft-based unions 80–1, 90
Crespo, Luis S. 175 n.34
Cuadros Bustos, Álvaro 186 n.4, 187 n.5, 194 n.72

de Chusi, Carmen 155
de la Cadena, Marisol 14, 86, 176 n.46, 179 n.106, 213 n.4
de Mesa, José 194 n.72, 208 n.15
Díaz, Porfirio 163 n.12
Dibbits, Ineke 182 n.45, 183 n.47, 184 nn.72, 79, 193 n.68, 195 n.3, 206 n.53
Donoso Torres, Vicente 38, 51–6, 153, 154, 174 n.18
dress, significance of 162 n.8

Ecuador 15
1899 civil war effects 23–5, 40, 82
El Alto neighborhood association 147, 148, 157
El Día de los Reyes Magos 126
El Diario (newspaper) 70
"El Factor Humano en la Geografía Nacional" (The Human Factor in National Geography) (Donoso Torres) 51
El Figaro (newspaper) 11
"El Indio ante la realidad" (The Indian in Reality) (Terán) 49
Eloy, Salmón 185 n.83, 186 n.4, 187 n.5, 188 n.10
Endara, Felipe 97
English, Adrian J. 183 n.52
En Marcha (newspaper) 141, 142, 208 n.16
extramuro 11, 205 n.40
  city council and *indígenas* in public space 29–31
  1899 civil war effects and 23–5
  geography and human settlement and 18–19
  imaginary walls and 15–16
  infrastructure and public health transformation and 25–8
  Katari rebellions and 19–20
  Latin American context of 14–15
  racial dynamics and 17
  significance of 11–13, 162 n.2, 163–4 n.14
Ex-Vinculación Laws (1874) 3, 166 n.32

Falange Socialista Boliviano (FSB) 140, 144, 210–11 n.61
Farcau, Bruce W. 183 n.52
Federación de Juntas Vecinales (Federation of Neighborhood Associations) (FEDJUVE) 81, 95, 138, 139, 149, 191 n.37
  significance of 86–7, 187–8 n.10

Federación Obrera de La Paz (La Paz Workers' Federation) (FOL)   7, 12, 13, 59–61, 71, 73, 75, 76, 126, 129
Federación Obrera de La Paz (Workers' Labor Federation)   90
Federación Obrera del Trabajo (The Workers' Labor Federation) (FOT)   59–61, 68, 127
Federación Obrera Femenina (FOF)   7, 59, 63, 65, 66, 73–6, 126, 129, 157
Federación Obrera Sindical   138
Federación Sindical de Trabajadores Mineros de Bolivia (Sindicalist Federation of Mine Workers) (FSTMB)   49, 135, 149
Figueres Ferrer, Jose   163 n.12
Fischer, Brodwyn   100, 189 n.26, 202 n.82
Forasteros   4
Foucault, Michel   15–16
14th of September Neighborhood Association   87

Garcia, Guadalupe   15
Garita de Lima   5, 6, 20, 124, 167 n.37
garitas   167 n.37
Gisbert, Teresa   194 n.72, 208 n.15
Gotkowitz, Laura   91, 101, 105, 122, 167 n.32, 169 n.60, 178 n.72, 180 n.107, 192 n.59, 197 nn.9, 11, 199 n.25, 203 n.10, 212 n.1
Gould, Stephen Jay   178 n.85
Grandin, Greg   213 n.4
Gran Poder   25, 124
Grieshaber, Erwin P.   167 n.32
Guaraní people   52
Guardia, Tomas   163 n.12
Guatemala   82, 213 n.4
Guelier, Lydia   149
Guillen Olmos, Nestor   136
Guss, David M.   120, 186 n.4, 187 n.5
Gutiérrez, Ramón   161 n.22, 205 n.41
Gutierrez Granier, Juan Luis   211 n.77
Gutiérrez Guerra, José   8, 62
Guzman Galarza, Mario   143, 146

Harvey, David   189 n.26
Havana   15
Hertzog, Enrique   136, 208 n.17

Holloway, Thomas   26, 169 n.60
honor
 class and gender and   101–3
 significance of   98–9, 101
 Chinahuanca case   105
 Monje case   103–5
hygiene and modernity, significance of   193 n.71

imaginary walls, significance of   15–16, 30
Incas   37
indígenas   4, 17, 24, 28, 153. *See also cholo* (mixed race) identity; mestizos
 cholos and   122
 corregidors and   36
 and mestizos compared   42
 in public spaces   29–31
 racial thinking on   38–43, 50–1
 significance of   19, 34–5, 167 n.32
 Torres on   51–5
indigenous communal lands, dispossession of   121
indigenous neighborhoods   3, 5, 7, 20, 25, 27, 30, 31, 57, 64, 66, 151. *See also individual neighborhoods*
 discourse and practice in   100–1
 housing in   195 n.4
 as mixed-use localities   110
 negotiated modernity and (*see* negotiated modernity)
 significance of   79, 186 n.4
 urban spaces and   112–13
indigenous neighborhoods and revolution   156–7
indigenous people   1–2. *See also individual entries*
 in colonial era   2–4
indigenous rebellions, in early twentieth century   8–9
indio, significance of   19
Infantes, Petronila   63, 65
Irpa-Chico community   97, 103
Iturralde, Abel   40–1, 174 n.24

Jesús de Machaca rebellion (1921)   8, 40, 44, 161 n.32, 171 n.82, 174 n.23, 176 n.54, 180 n.3, 205 n.50
Juárez, Benito   163 n.12

Katari rebellions 19–20
Klein, Herbert 117, 159 n.1, 162 n.32, 166 n.31, 175 n.33, 176 n.53, 177 n.65, 182 n.42, 183 n.52, 185 n.95, 193 n.68, 196 n.8, 205 n.50, 208 n.10
Ksejwa people 52
Kuenzli, E. Gabrielle 23, 24, 37, 44, 168 n.45, 169 n.54, 173 nn.16–17, 174 nn.18–19, 197 n.9, 199 n.25

labor and race, in 1920s and 1930s 59
 Chaco War
  and postwar realignments and 68–70
  worker activism in La Paz after 70–3
 unions and 59–62
  activism, before Chaco War 62–8
labor activism, in 1940s 73–5
La Calle (newspaper) 47
La Paz 21–2, 151–2, 167 n.34. *See also individual entries*
 ayllus and 2
 Catholic lay brotherhoods of 88–90
 Chaco War and 17–18
 city council 29–31
 1899 civil war effects on 23–5
 indigenous neighborhoods and 79–80
 discourse and practice 100–1
 influential mayors of 206 n.54
 infrastructure and public health transformation of 25–8
 Larson on 159 n.4
 modernity and 189 n.26
 social relations, race, and reputation in 114–16
 Superior District Court 198 n.21
 worker activism after Chaco War in 70–3
La Paz Geographic Society 42, 175 n.34
La Reforma (newspaper) 41, 62
Larson, Brooke 23, 159 nn.1–2, 4, 166 nn.31–2, 167 n.34, 172 n.6, 176 nn.48, 61, 179 n.103, 196 n.7, 199 n.25
lay brotherhoods 88–90, 151, 191 nn.44, 49

lay religious organizations 80–1
Lear, John 169 n.61
leftist parties and military socialist rule 47
Leguía, Augusto B. 161 n.29, 205 n.47
Liberal Party 8, 23, 140
Llanos, David 184 n.79
Lora, Guillermo 174 n.31
Los Andes Neighborhood Association 91, 191 n.49
Low, Setha 26, 169 n.60
Loza, Carmen B. 184 n.79
Loza, Pastor 97, 107
Luna, Domingo 106, 111–12, 201 n.71
Luna, Félix 111–12

Machicao, Díaz 188 n.10
MacMaster, Neil 197 n.11
Macpherson, Anne S. 170 n.61, 197 n.11, 213 n.2
Malloy, James 211 n.57
Manuel Elio, Tomas 140
Méndez, Armando 103, 104
Mendieta, Pilar 23, 117, 203 n.11, 207 n.7
Mendoza, Felipe 107
Mendoza, Octavio 107
Mendoza, Vicente 180 n.12
Mesa, Carlos D. 194 n.72, 207 n.7, 208 n.15
mestizos 5, 6, 13, 39; *See also cholo* (mixed race) identity; *indígenas*
 and *cholos* compared 43–4
 coco plant and 50
 and *indígenas* compared 42
 significance of 122, 152–3
 racial thinking on 43
 whites and 122
Mexico 14, 31, 82, 86
 public transportation and urban identities link in 169 n.61
Mexico city 26
migration, significance of 165 n.29
military socialist rule (1936–9) 46–7, 70, 161 n.30, 188 n.10, 194 n.72, 205 n.48
 end of 47
 leftist parties and 47
Millán, Donato 144, 210 n.57
Milluni miners 147–8

Miraflores 6, 27, 124
Miranda, Exaltación 65
Möller, Edwin A. 208 n.10
Monje, Carlos 100, 103–5, 109
Monje, Sabelia 103, 105, 199 n.36
Monje Gutierrez, Tomas 136
Montenegro, Carlos 69, 177 n.65, 185 n.95, 207 n.61
Montes, Ismael 8
Moreno, Antonio 109
Movimiento Nacionalista Revolucionario (MNR) 10, 48–9, 74, 130–4, 139, 177 n.64, 194 n.72, 207–8 n.7, 208 nn.8–9, 210 nn.41, 55, 211 nn.77–8
    comandos zonales (zonal commands) 149
    militants of 131–2, 156, 211 n.63
    1951 elections and 141–2
    unexpected victory and 143–9
    and Villarroel regime 132–3, 135–6
municipal government expansion 5–8
Murillo, Mario 150, 202 n.7, 207–8 n.7, 211 n.63
Murillo Bocángel, Max 72

Nacionalismo y Coloniaje (Montenegro) 177 n.65
Nash, June C. 191 n.44
negotiated modernity (1900–52) 79–82
    Catholic lay brotherhoods and 88–90
    indigenous citizens and 90–3
    new infrastructure and 84–6
    power and 86–8
    racial discourse and activism after Chaco War and 82–3
    significance of 93–6
neighborhood activism, significance of 194 n.72
neighborhood associations and urbanization 155–6; *See also individual neighborhood associations*
neighbourhood associations, significance of 87–8, 190–1 n.37
    and lay brotherhoods 89
1917 rebellion 8, 174 n.23
Nuevo Potosí neighborhood association 87–90, 95, 136–7

Obrajes 124
Originarios 4
Orlove, Benjamin S. 213 n.4

Paceño elites 23–4, 29, 44, 122, 154
Paco Cariaga, Adolfo 47
Palza, Humberto 137
Pando, Manuel Jose 8
Paraguay 68, 80, 83
Paredes, M. Rigoberto 38, 39, 42–4, 51, 56, 122, 173 nn.13, 16–17, 176 n.48
Partido de la Unión Republicana Socialista (Socialist Republican Union Party) (PURS) 133, 137, 140
Partido Obrero Revolucionario (POR) 177 n.64
Partido Republicano Genuino (Genuine Republican Party) 136
Patiño, Simon I. 9, 176 n.53
Patón, Tomasita 64, 65, 182 n.34
Paz Estenssoro, Víctor 69, 118, 128, 134, 140, 141, 148, 177 n.65, 183 n.53
Peñaranda, Enrique 74, 134, 136
Peru 14, 27, 86, 213 n.4
Piccato, Pablo 26, 98, 102, 169 nn.60–1
Platt, Tristan 36, 159 n.1, 166 n.31, 166 n.32, 196 n.7
Plaza Alonso de Mendoza 5, 18, 124
Plaza de Armas. *See* Plaza Murillo
Plaza Murillo 5, 13, 18, 27, 124, 161 n.21, 205 n.40
pollera 181 n.27
Ponce Sanjinés, Carlos 199 n.25
Pongueaje, significance of 182 n.36
"popular classes," significance of 123
Posnansky, Arturo 51, 55, 153, 199 n.25
prefecture, significance of 189 n.25, 192 n.55
prohibition, significance of 164 n.15
prostitution 27–8, 71
Pura Pura 5, 124

Quayum, Seemin 178 n.85
Quechua language and people 37, 51, 66, 76, 121, 153
Quintanilla, Carlos 73–4
Quispe, Santiago 155

Index

race and class, significance of   106–10
racial democracy, myth of   100, 197 n.11
racial thinking, of government officials and intellectuals   33
  before Chaco War   40–5
  Chaco War
    effect   45–9
    racial and class discourses   49–55
  indígenas and   34–6, 38–9
Radio Illimani   145
Razón de Patria (RADEPA)   48
Renique, Gerardo   213 n.2
Rentería, Gregorio   109
republican democracy   49
Rio de Janeiro   26
Rioja, Bilbao   142
Ríos, Alfredo   110–11, 200 n.52
Rivera Cusicanqui, Silvia   119
Rodríguez   88
Rodríguez, José   106
Román, Justo   80
Roseberry, William   171 n.2
Rosenberg, Charles   193 n.71
rural and urban connections   113–14

Saavedra, Juan Bautista   6, 8, 9, 12, 13, 33, 41–2, 45, 51, 56, 68, 76–7, 118, 125–6, 128, 148, 154, 175 n.33, 177 n.62, 181 n.16
  labour activism and   7, 59–63, 161–2 n.32
  and Leguía compared   161 n.29, 205 n.47
  nickname of   163 n.12
Salamanca, Daniel   60, 68, 127, 136
Salazar, Félix   88
Sanchez Bustamante, Daniel   34–6, 38, 39, 42, 56, 174 n.18
Sanders, James   196 n.9
San Francisco   5, 18, 20, 124
San Jorge   27, 124
San Jose   26
San Pedro   5, 18, 25, 124
San Sebastián   5, 18, 124
Santa Barbara   5, 18, 124
Scott, James   197 n.9
Seleme, Antonio   144, 145, 146, 210 n.57
Seligmann, Linda J.   181 n.27, 213 n.4
Serulnikov, Sergio   159 n.1, 166 n.31

Shesko, Elizabeth   214 n.14
Siles Reyes, Hernando   8, 126, 177 n.65
Siles Zuazo, Hernán   69, 128, 132, 134, 146
Sindicato Central de Constructores y Albañiles de Bolivia (Central Union of Construction Workers and Bricklayers of Bolivia)   67
Sindicato de Constructores y Albaniles (construction workers' union)   59, 76
Sindicato de Culinarias (cooks's union)   8, 48, 59, 63–7, 70–3, 76
  significance of   65
Sindicato de Graficos   59, 61
Sindicato de Telegrafistas ('Telegraphers' Union)   68
Skidmore, Thomas E.   161 n.29, 205 n.47
Smith, Peter H.   161 n.29, 205 n.47
Solíz, Carmen   184 n.79
Somoza, Anastasio   163 n.12
Sopocachi   5, 20, 27, 41, 124, 191 n.45
Soruco, Ximena   13
Stepan, Nancy Leys   169 n.61
Stern, Alexandra Minna   179 n.85
Stoler, Ann   17, 170 n.79
Sucre   3, 23
suffrage, significance of   117–18, 173 n.13, 182 n.42, 212 n.1

Taller de Historia Oral Andina   162 n.8, 183 nn.46–7, 187 n.5, 188 n.10, 191 n.44, 193 n.68, 195 n.3
Tamayo, José   41, 51, 174 n.31
tambos   5, 18, 20, 124, 167 n.37, 194 n.72
  meaning and significance of   161 n.23, 165–6 n.30, 205 n.39
Tancara Quispe, Constantino   172 n.6
Tejada Sorzano, José Luis   68
Terán Gómez, Luis   38, 39, 49–51, 56, 153–4, 174 n.18, 178 n.77
Thomson, Sinclair   159 n.1, 166 n.31
Ticona Alejo, Esteban   119, 162 n.32, 166 n.32, 203 n.14, 205 n.50
Tiwanaku   37
Toro government (1936–7)   69

Toro Ruilova, David 81
Torres Ortiz, Humberto 144–5
trams, prohibition in 70–1
Trujillo, Rafael 163 n.12
Túpac Katari Rebellion (1780–1) 11, 19
Tyranny of Opinion, The (Piccato) 98

Ultima Hora (newspaper) 137, 140
Uncía miners' strike 176 n.53, 180 n.3, 205 n.50
Union of Free Seamstresses 139
Únzaga de la Vega, Óscar 144–5
urban crime 169 n.60
urban growth and planning 5–8
urban La Paz, before and after Chaco War 117–23
  labor and indigenous identities in 126–7
  postwar realignments and 127–9
  urban growth, planning, and municipal expansion and 123–6
urban revolution 131–4
  1951 elections and 141–2
  1946–51 134–40
  unexpected victory and 143–9

urban spaces 110–13
  conflicts over 113
  indigenous neighborhoods and 112–13
  Luna case and 111–12
Urriolagoitía, Mamerto 133, 136, 137, 139–41, 208 n.17

vecino 92
Villa Potosí neighborhood association 80, 86, 157
Villarroel, Gualberto 91, 118, 120, 125, 134, 143, 208 n.16
  regime of 6, 48–9, 132–6, 177 n.65, 192 n.59
Villa Victoria neighborhood 132, 141, 146–7, 156–7

Wadsworth, Ana Cecilia 182 n.45, 183 n.47, 193 n.68
Weinstein, Barbara 213 n.2
Weismantel, Mary 26, 169 n.60, 181 n.27, 213 n.4

Zook, David 183 n.52

www.ingramcontent.com/pod-product-compliance
Lightning Source LLC
Chambersburg PA
CBHW072148290426
44111CB00012B/2009